D040431S

# GREEK

Many people who would welcome an opportunity to get on nodding terms with Greek are repelled by the austerity of the traditional Greek Course. They want to be able to read, not to write, Greek. The long apprenticeship of translating sentences from English into Greek is for them a tedious irrelevance that stands between them and their limited objective. Many, it is to be feared, turn away sorrowfully from the prospect, and are the poorer in consequence.

It is primarily for this class that the authors of this book have endeavoured to cater. They believe that it is possible to introduce simple pieces of actual Greek from the very beginning. They provide no translation from English into Greek. **They expect no previous knowledge of Latin or any other inflected language.**

TEACH YOURSELF BOOKS

οὐ γάρ τι νῦν γε κἀχθές, ἀλλ' ἀεί ποτε ζῇ ταῦτα.

Soph. Ant. 456

'For these things live not today or yesterday,
but for all time.'

# GREEK

**F. Kinchin Smith, M.A.**
and
**T. W. Melluish, M.A.**
Sometime Scholar of Christ's College, Cambridge
Formerly Senior Classical Master of Bec School

TEACH YOURSELF BOOKS
Hodder and Stoughton

*First printed 1947*
*Second edition 1968*
*Sixth impression 1977*
*Seventh impression 1978*

*Copyright © 1968 edition*
*Hodder and Stoughton Ltd.*

All rights reserved. No part of this publication may be reproduced or transmitted in any form or by any means, electronic or mechanical, including photocopy, recording, or any information storage and retrieval system, without permission in writing from the publisher.

This volume is published in the U.S.A. by David McKay Company Inc., 750 Third Avenue, New York, N.Y. 10017.

ISBN 0 340 05793 9

*Printed in Great Britain*
*for Hodder and Stoughton Paperbacks, a division of Hodder*
*and Stoughton Ltd., Mill Road, Dunton Green, Sevenoaks, Kent*
*(Editorial Office: 47 Bedford Square, London WC1 3DP)*
*by Richard Clay (The Chaucer Press), Ltd., Bungay, Suffolk*

# CONTENTS

# GREEK PASSAGES

# PREFACE

MANY people who would welcome an opportunity to get on nodding terms with Greek are repelled by the austerity of the traditional Greek Course. They want to be able to read, not to write, Greek. The long apprenticeship of translating sentences from English into Greek is for them a tedious irrelevance that stands between them and their limited objective. Many, it is to be feared, turn away sorrowfully from the prospect, and are the poorer in consequence.

It is primarily for this class that the authors of this book have endeavoured to cater. They believe that it is possible to introduce simple pieces of actual Greek from the very beginning. They provide no translation from English into Greek. They expect no previous knowledge of Latin or any other inflected language. On the other hand, no attempt has been made to include the whole of the grammar; the Dual, for instance, is omitted; the syntax is but sketchily outlined. It is not, indeed, a book for the scholar or the specialist.

One of the most familiar experiences of the teacher of Greek is the delight and surprise of pupils upon discovering that they have actually been using Greek words in the English language without being aware of it. M. Jourdain's pleasure on learning that he had been talking prose all his life without knowing it is only faintly comparable. The authors have tried to make capital out of this attraction by stressing from the outset the close connection between Greek and English. In fact, for the first few chapters Greek is taught through English, and a systematic attempt is made to build up a vocabulary in this way.

The original intention in writing this book was to admit no made-up Greek. Unfortunately it proved impossible to adhere strictly to this resolution. To give practice in the verb, " synthetic " Greek was employed in the chapters on the Middle and Passive. With the greatest reluctance it was then decided to give further practice in the fresh points of Grammar made by inserting exercises, which should have the extra function of preparing the reader for each piece of translation. It has not been possible to include extracts from all the great writers such as Homer, Æschylus, and Thucydides, but less-known writers such as Strabo, Menander, Plutarch, and Euclid have been drawn upon, and easy passages included from Euripides and the New Testament. Simple lines from the tragedians are given with the object of facilitating the approach to Greek Drama. Occasionally the text has been slightly adapted or simplified. Here and there a phrase from modern Greek has been included where it resembles the ancient usage. Greek is a living language, and has changed less in two thousand years than any other spoken tongue.

The translations in the Key are, for the most part, literal, it being assumed that this is what the reader wants rather than an elegant or polished rendering.

Accents have been omitted. If Ancient Greek is pronounced as Modern Greek there is a case for their retention. Otherwise there is no case for them whatever. They were not written originally in Greek. Greek is always intelligible without them. They were introduced by an Alexandrian grammarian to guide foreigners in a pronunciation which to us now must be largely a matter of conjecture. If Plato and Euripides did not need them, why should we?

The price which must be paid for variety of reading matter is a large vocabulary. An *ad hoc* vocabulary of new words has been added to most chapters, and there is a general vocabulary at the end of the book. The difficulty of Greek to most beginners is not the script (which is a fascination if thoroughly mastered at the beginning by practice in reading and writing) or the syntax (which is simpler than that of Latin and more like English), but the large variety of the verb forms and the number of irregular verbs. The commonest of these have been listed in Chapter XXV, and the student is advised to read them over and over again, until he can recognise any part of them in a passage of Greek.

Finally, it is hoped that for his interest and enlightenment the reader will study the notes given on the texts. They contain a good deal of information more or less relevant, and are meant to interest the student of literature at large no less than one whose interest is directed in particular to the social life and history of the Greeks. And if, as the result of this book, here and there a casual reader may be tempted to struggle on yet further towards the treasure he has glimpsed from afar, the authors of this volume will feel that their labours have not been wholly in vain. "Greek is a door that opens straight to Paradise."

F. K. S.<br>T. W. M.

## PREFACE TO SECOND EDITION

Mr. Francis Kinchin Smith died on October 16th 1958, but his bright spirit, I am sure, lives on in these pages.

Experience has shown that the omission of English meanings to the Greek words of the Vocabulary proves a hindrance to the rapid reading of the book. I have therefore decided, though fully aware of the weaknesses of an "Ad hoc" vocabulary of this kind, to insert the English meanings, in order to help the reader as much as possible.

T. W. M.

# HOW TO USE THIS BOOK

1. I suggest that you make a resolution at the start (and stick to it!) that you will not use the Key at the back until you have done all in your power to manage without. If you constantly have one eye on the Greek in front and the other on the English at the back, you will no more make progress than if you tried to learn to swim always keeping one foot on the bottom of the bath. Making the Greek fit the English merely retards progress.

2. Make sure you have thoroughly mastered the grammatical explanation. Then attempt the exercise, where there is one, placing a piece of paper over the Key underneath, and jotting down on it your attempt. If you come across a word you don't know, look for it in the vocabulary at the end of the next piece of connected Greek. If it is not there, you have had it before; turn to the general vocabulary at the end of the book, which will indicate the meaning and where it first occurs. Then look it up. Never be slack about looking things up. Do not remove the paper which covers the Key until you have made a full attempt on that piece of paper.

3. When you have mastered the grammar, learnt what you have been told to learn, and done the preliminary exercise, you will be in a fitter state to tackle the piece of actual Greek. Read it through two or three times before beginning the translation. You will find it comes easier that way. Use the notes. They will give you much assistance. Again we insist, when you are

given a cross reference, look it up. When you think you understand the Greek, write down the translation on a piece of paper. Then compare it with the Key. Have it in writing. Don't look at the Key and say to yourself, " Well, that's roughly the idea that I had in my mind." Lay not that flattering unction to your soul.

4. If any piece of Greek seizes your fancy, learn it by heart. It's good to have Greek inside you. Recite it constantly to yourself, letting your mind linger on its meaning and getting its full flavour. Repeat it to your friends, wife, children, mother, or long-suffering landlady. You will be surprised how extraordinarily fond of Greek you will grow in the process.

5. Don't bite off more than you can chew. Work slowly through the book section by section, never passing on to new work till you have thoroughly mastered the old. Constantly revise.

6. This book does not require you to write much Greek. It is obvious, however, that the alphabet must be learnt, and the best way to do this is to practise writing a number of Greek words. This has the additional advantage that it enables you to remember them.

7. Try to acquire a vocabulary as you go along. The most important words have been underlined for you. Whenever you come across a word that is new to you in your reading—let us say " allergic " or " pædiatrician " —try to think of it in terms of its Greek components. It will pay you to look it up in an English etymological dictionary. You will find thus that English will become for you a language richer and lovelier far than it was before.

# INTRODUCTION

ISOLATIONISM we hope is dead and buried for ever. No one believes now that it is possible or proper to withdraw from the world of his fellow human-beings, confining his interest to his country-men, his habits of thought and his own language. Suppose that this view is denied. We will return with another question. Does it pay to be an Isolationist in time? Is it possible, in other words, to believe that the achievements of the age in which we happen to live alone merit our attention? Is it right to allow greatness to the twentieth century only? Unless this insular view is taken, one must concede that humanity has had its great moments before today, and that these are as well worth our study as we hope our own will be worth posterity's.

The Greeks.—The truth is that, boast as we may of our technicolour talkies or our atomic bombs, many centuries ago there lived in the Mediterranean a people whose achievements were no less remarkable. They were the Ancient Greeks. History tells us that half way through the thirteenth century B.C. a tall fair-haired race came down from the North to settle in the Greek peninsula and on the coasts of Asia Minor. They had much to learn from the inhabitants they met, much too, perhaps, to give. Their coming caused a ferment in Greece, and an age followed of expansion, adventure and colonisation, in token of the restless activity which always characterised the Greeks. By the eighth or ninth century there had already appeared one who seems to mark the culmination of a brilliant, if forgotten, epoch. The two poems of Homer, the Iliad and the Odyssey, long epics telling of the fortunes of the Greeks before Troy, and of the adventures of Odysseus on his way home from Troy, have deservedly won for their reputed author the title of " the father of poetry ". Not only have these poems provided for the delight of succeeding ages a rich store-house of fireside yarns and bed-time stories, but they are acknowledged by all to be literary masterpieces.

**Greek Ancient and Modern.**—Many are under the impression Greek is a dead language. But it is spoken today by millions round the shores of the Eastern Mediterranean. Every week there is printed in London a newspaper in Greek which Plato would have had no difficulty in reading. Notices in trains in Greece, such as " Don't lean out of the window " or " Don't spit " are written in good classical Greek. An ancient and a modern Greek greeting each other with a " Good day " (kalê [h]êméra) would use exactly the same words, although the ancient might be a little surprised at the modern's pronunciation. Of course new words have been added to the language, and many grammatical forms have been changed, but the language has changed less in 2000 years than any other spoken tongue. Modern Greek is nearer to the Greek of Homer than modern English is to Chaucer. The alphabet and the script are the same.

**Greek Words in the English Language.**—Moreover every Englishman uses every day, possibly without knowing it, many words in " broken Greek "—e.g. telephone, cinema, theatre, gyroscope, atomic, and hundreds of others. We are going more and more to Greek for new words. " At no other time in our history have there been so many words of Greek origin on the lips of the English-speaking peoples," says Mr. Bodmer in the *Loom of Language*. Greek is by no means " dead " in English.

**Pronunciation.**—The biggest change wrought by the years has been in the pronunciation of Greek. The modern Greek pronounces according to the accents on his words, and there has been some change in the value of the vowels. A guide to the modern Greek pronunciation is provided in Chapter II. At one time schoolboys were taught to pronounce Greek exactly as if it were English, and to this day many retain the English pronunciation they learnt in their schools. Since the beginning of this century, however, a committee of experts has given guidance in the pronunciation of Greek, which, as far as is known, will enable those who use it to pronounce Greek at least approximately as it was spoken by the Greeks of Classical times. This is called the Revised Pronunciation, and it is given here. At the same time, it is admitted that much of it is uncertain, and if you should decide to pronounce Greek as if it were English, you will not find your enjoyment greatly hampered.

**Accents.**—If you have seen Greek written elsewhere, you will be surprised at this book, because Greek is here written without accents. This has been done deliberately. The writing of accents on Greek is a conservative tradition from which we might with advantage break away. The ancient Greeks themselves never wrote them. They are said to be the invention of a grammarian named Aristophanes of Byzantium (260 B.C.) who wanted to guide his readers in the reading of Homer. Accents do not appear in manuscripts before the seventh century A.D. The Greek language, however, is quite intelligible without accents. Sappho and Plato did not need them. We may well be rid of an unnecessary burden.

# CHAPTER I

## THE ALPHABET

| Letter. | English. | Greek small. | Capital. |
|---|---|---|---|
| Alpha | a | α | Α |
| Beta | b | β | Β |
| Gamma | g | γ | Γ |
| Delta | d | δ | Δ |
| Epsilon | e (short) | ε | Ε |
| Zeta | z | ζ | Ζ |
| Eta | e (long) | η | Η |
| Theta | th | θ | Θ |
| Iota | i | ι | Ι |
| Kappa | k | κ | Κ |
| La(m)bda | l | λ | Λ |
| Mu | m | μ | Μ |
| Nu | n | ν | Ν |
| Xi | x | ξ | Ξ |
| Omikron | o (short) | ο | Ο |
| Pi | p | π | Π |
| Rho | rh | ρ | Ρ |
| Sigma | s | σ or ς | Σ |
| Tau | t | τ | Τ |
| Upsilon | u | υ | Υ |
| Phi | ph | φ | Φ |
| Chi | ch | χ | Χ |
| Psi | ps | ψ | Ψ |
| Omega | o (long) | ω | ω or Ω |

**Names of the Letters.**—Here is a jingle to help you remember the names of the Greek letters, and the order in which they come :—

> " This is Greek, and how they spelt her—
> Alpha, Beta, Gamma, Delta,
>         Epsilon, Zeta,
>         Eta, Theta,
>     Then Iota, Kappa too,
> Followed up by Lambda, Mu,
>         Nu, Xi,
>         Omikron, Pi,
> After that, Rho, Sigma, Tau,
> Upsilon, Phi, and still three more,
> Chi, Psi, and Omega's twenty-four."

**How to Write Greek.**—Draw a double line across the paper, and practise writing the letters thus :—

It is best to begin making the letter at the point indicated by the asterisk. Nearly all the letters can be made without lifting the pen from the paper, and should be so made. Do not attempt to join one letter to another. Keep the letters close together, however, with good spaces between the words. Greek small letters are really a development of hastily written Greek capitals, which was the only form of writing the Greeks themselves knew before the seventh century A.D. You will notice that the letters β δ ʒ θ λ ξ φ and ψ protrude above the top line, and β γ ʒ η μ ρ φ χ and ψ below. Greek is usually written with a very slight slope. Be careful not to give too large a tail to ʒ and ξ and ς; distinguish between the rounded and pointed bottoms of υ and ν; and don't give omikron a peaked cap, or he will look like sigma.

**Capitals.**—Don't worry too much about the capitals at first. You will find that you can pick them up as you go along. You need only use capital letters to begin proper names with, as in English, but it is not necessary to begin a sentence with a capital. Many of them are identical, of course, with the English forms, but beware of H P X and Y. What sounds do they represent in Greek? How would you write in Greek the English letters P and X?

**Breathings.**—As a matter of fact in the very earliest times H represented the aitch sound. But you must remember that the Greek language travelled both East and West. The Ionians to the East had no use for aspirates, and transferred the symbol H to another sound, the long E (as in père). The Greeks of Italy, however, liked to distinguish between an aspirated and an unaspirated vowel, took the old symbol ⊩ and chopped it in half, using ⊢ in front of a vowel which was preceded by the aitch sound, and ⊣ before a vowel with no aitch sound. It was not long before these signs were being written thus— ' and ' before the vowel. In the standardised script they are written like commas ' and ' over the vowel, or just in front if they are used with capital letters. Thus the Greek for a horse, hippos, is written ἵππος, and Hector is written Ἕκτωρ. This sign is called a ' rough breathing '. If a word begins with a vowel, it must have either a ' rough breathing ' or a ' smooth breathing '. A smooth breathing is the ' sign placed over a vowel not preceded by the aitch sound. Thus ' alpha ' is written ἀλφα, and Agamemnon Ἀγαμεμνων. The Greek ρ at the beginning of a word always has a rough breathing—e.g. ῥητορικη (rhetoric). That is why so many English words begin with rh-.

Vowels.—Greek not only has the same vowels as English (α ε ι ο υ), but two of the vowels have separate letters for the short and long sounds, viz. ε (short e) and η (long e), also ο (short o) and ω (long o). The letter ι, never dotted in Greek (so sensible !), when it follows a long vowel at the end of a word is written in miniature underneath the vowel, and is called ' *Iota subscript* '. In capitals it must be written on the line—e.g. to Daphne, Δαφνη or ΔΑΦΝΗΙ. Iota subscript also occurs in the middle of one or two words—e.g. ᾠον, an egg; Ὠιδειον, the Odeon.

The letter s is written as ς when it is the last letter of a word, but in all other positions it is written as σ. E.g. stasis—a revolt—is written in Greek στασις.

*Notes on the Alphabet.*

α β, A B    Now you know why the alphabet is so called.

| | | |
|---|---|---|
| γ | Γ | Gammadion is another name for a swastika, formed by four Γs. There was an ancient letter in Greek called Digamma, Ϝ, formed by placing one gamma on another. It had the sound of W, but dropped out of Greek, although it frequently shows up again in Latin words beginning with v: e.g. Ϝοινος, wine; Latin, vinum. |
| δ | Δ | Its Hebrew counterpart, Daleth, meant the 'tent-door'. Upside-down it is the shape of the island at the mouth of the Nile, the Delta. |
| ε | E | ἐψιλον—'simple' e, so called to distinguish it from a diphthong which had the same sound in later Greek. |
| ζ | Z | English zed. |
| η | H | Don't confuse with the English 'n'—it's easily done!—nor its capital H with the English aspirate. The counterpart of H in Russian is И, 'ee'. |
| θ | Θ | An ominous letter—the initial letter of θανατος (death). Scratched on a potsherd, it was the juror's vote for the death-penalty. |
| ι | I | So insignificant was the iota subscript that in English the word is 'jot' or 'particle'. The above four letters ζηθι mean "Live!" in Greek. |
| κ | K | Always hard in Greek. |
| λ | Λ | The Chinese are prone to lambdacism! |

| | | |
|---|---|---|
| μ | M | Written in earliest times thus—Μ. |
| ν | N | Don't confuse with the English ' v ', and don't write carelessly, or it will be confused with ' υ '. |
| ξ | Ξ | This difficult letter needs practice. |
| ο | Ο | o-mikron means little (short) ' o '. |
| π | Π | An old friend of geometry students ! |
| ρ | Ρ | Don't confuse it with its predecessor. |
| σς | Σ | Another common form of the capital was C, which survives in Russian. ς only at the end of the word. |
| τ | Τ | St. Anthony's cross was a tau-cross. |
| υ | Υ | u-psilon. ' Simple ' u, to distinguish it from a similar sound in late Greek, represented by a diphthong (see Epsilon). Υ is called the Pythagorean letter, as it was used by Pythagoras to teach the divergent paths of Good and Evil. |
| φ | Φ | Phi Beta Kappa—an American College Society—from Φιλοσοφια Βιου Κυβερνητης—Philosophy (is) of Life the Governour. |
| χ | Χ | Do not confuse with the English ' x '. Chiasmus is a parallelism which has become crossed like a chi (χ)—e.g. Do not live to eat, but eat to live. |
| ψ | Ψ | Survives in English in words such as psalm, psychology, etc. |
| ω | Ω | o-mega. Big ' o '. The ω shape was formed by running two o's together, thus oo. |

The first two letters of the name of Christ (ΧΡΙΣΤΟΣ) are sometimes seen in churches as a monogram, ☧; sometimes also the first three letters of the name Jesus, 'ΙΗΣ (ους) or IHS.

The Christians frequently used the sign of a fish as a mark of their faith. The Greek for a fish is 'ΙΧΘΥΣ, said to be the initial letters of 'Ιησους Χριστος Θεου Υιος Σωτηρ, Jesus Christ, Son of God (and) Saviour.

An illiterate rustic in Euripides' play " Theseus " tries to describe a word of six capital letters that he has seen in lines that might be translated like this—

" Oi baint no scholard in my chriss-cross-row,
The shapes Oi'll tell thee, an' thee'll know for sure.
A ring, marked out, as 'twere, wi' pin and string,
Slap in 'er middle wur a mark to see.
The second it wur first a brace o' stroaks,
Kept wonn from t'other by a bar midmoast.
The third were curly as a twist o' hair.
The fourth wur straight an' upright as a poast,
Three traverse beams a-jointed to it athwart.
The fifth to tell aroight be moighty hard,
A pair o' stroaks that start from East and West
Run plumb together to a single foot.
The last, the selfsame letter as the third."

What word did the rustic see?
A short invitation to lunch—η β π !

# CHAPTER II

## PRONUNCIATION

HERE is a guide to help you with the pronunciation of Greek. The pronunciation is the Revised Pronunciation, as recommended some years ago by a Committee of the Classical Association. For your interest the modern Greek pronunciation is added.

### VOWELS

| *Ancient Greek.* | *Modern Greek.* |
|---|---|
| α (i) Long as in father. | α As in father, but shorter. |
| (ii) Short as in aha. | |
| ε As in fret. | ε As in fret. |
| ι (i) Long as in feed. | ι As in feed. |
| (ii) Short as in pit. | |
| ο As in not. | ο As in not. |
| υ (i) Long as in French rue. | υ As in feed. |
| (ii) Short as in French du pain. | |
| η As in French père. | η As in feed. |
| ω As in home. | ω As in fortune. |

### DIPHTHONGS

*Ancient Greek.*      *Modern Greek.*

| Ancient Greek | Modern Greek | | |
|---|---|---|---|
| αι As in Isaiah. | αι As in fret. | | |
| οι As in boil. | οι As in feed. | | |
| υι As in French lui. | υι As in feed. | | |
| | | Before vowels and γβδζλμνρ | Before κπτχφθσξψ |
| αυ As in gown. | αυ = av. | αυ = av. | αυ = af. |
| ευ As in few. | ευ = ev. | ευ = ev. | ευ = ef. |
| ηυ As in few. | ηυ = iv. | | ηυ = if, sometimes iv. |
| ου As in moon. | ου As in put. | | |
| ει As in grey. | ει As in feed. | | |

28

It will be noticed that there are six ways of representing the sound ' ee ' in Modern Greek. There are no real diphthongs in Modern Greek, and no distinction between long and short vowels.

## CONSONANTS

| *Ancient Greek.* | *Modern Greek.* |
|---|---|
| β   As in *b*ad. | β   As v in *v*ase. The English ' b ' sound is represented by μπ. Thus ' bar ' is spelt in Modern Greek μπαρ. |
| γ   As in *g*et.<br>When γ precedes another γ it is pronounced as ' ng ' in ' a*ng*er ', before κ, as ' ngk ' in Chu*ngk*ing, before χ, as ' nkh ' in mo*nkh*ood ', before ξ, as ' nx ' in ' ly*nx* '. | γ   As in *g*et.<br>Also γ and γι sometimes represent the ' y ' sound, as in English ' *y*es '. γγ is pronounced as ' ng ' in ' a*ng*er '. |
| δ   As in *d*oes. | δ   As ' th ' in fa*th*er. The English ' d ' sound is represented by ντ. A Greek official may write the name Dodd thus—Ντοντντ! |
| ζ   As ' zd ' in Ma*zd*a. | ζ   As in *z*eal. |
| θ   As ' th ' in *th*in. | θ   As in *th*in. |
| κ   As in *k*ing. | κ   As in *k*ing. |
| λ   As in *l*yre. | λ   As in *l*yre. |
| μ   As in *m*use. | μ   As in *m*use. |
| ν   As in *n*ow. | ν   As in *n*ow. |
| ξ   As in wa*x*. | ξ   As in wa*x*. |
| π   As in *p*ush. | π   As in *p*ush. |
| ρ   As in *r*ich (trilled). | ρ   As in *r*ich (trilled). |
| ῥ   As in *rh*ombus. | |
| σς   As in mou*s*e.<br>Before β γ δ or μ as English ' s ' in ha*s* been, ha*s* gone, ha*s* *m*ade. | σς   As in mou*s*e.<br>Before β γ δ μ or ν pronounced as English ' z '. |

| *Ancient Greek.* | *Modern Greek.* |
|---|---|
| τ  As in *t*ap. | τ  As in *t*ap. |
| φ  As in *f*ish. | φ  As in *f*ish. |
| χ  As in lo*ch*. | χ  As in lo*ch*; also soft as in the German ' *ich* ', ' *recht* '. |
| ψ  As in la*ps*e. | ψ  As in la*ps*e. |

*Note.*—In giving the Revised Pronunciation, consideration has been given to the convenience of the student as well as to strict accuracy. It is probable, for instance, that θ and φ were pronounced by the ancient Greeks themselves as the ' th ' in ' po*th*ook ' and the ' ph ' in ' ha*ph*azard '. In view of the difficulty of English readers in pronouncing an aspirated consonant, it has been thought wiser to retain the modern Greek pronunciation of those letters.

**Pronunciation Exercise.**—Read the Greek of the Lord's Prayer, keeping the English pronunciation covered up : then test your pronunciation by reference to the next line.

ê = è as in p*è*re; ī = i as in m*i*ne; ō = o as in h*o*me; ā = a as in f*a*ther.

## THE LORD'S PRAYER

Πατερ ἡμων ὁ ἐν τοις οὐρανοις, ἀγιασθητω το
Pater hêmōn ho en tois ooranois, hagiasthêtō to
ὀνομα σου. Ἐλθετω ἡ βασιλεια σου. γενηθητω
onoma soo. Elthetō hê basilaya soo. genêthêtō
το θελημα σου, ὡς ἐν οὐρανῳ και ἐπι γης· τον
to thelêma soo, hōs en ooranō kī epi gês; ton
ἀρτον ἡμων τον ἐπιουσιον δος ἡμιν σημερον.
arton hêmōn ton epioosion dos hêmeen sêmeron;
και ἀφες ἡμιν τα ὀφειληματα ἡμων ὡς και
kī aphes hêmeen ta ophaylêmata hêmōn hōs kī

ἡμεῖς ἀφήκαμεν τοῖς ὀφειλέταις ἡμῶν. καὶ μη
hêmace aphêkamen tois ophayletice hêmōn.   Ki mê
εἰσενεγκῃς ἡμᾶς εἰς πειρασμον, ἀλλα ῥυσαι ἡμας
ace-enengkês hêmās ace payrazmon, alla rhoosī hêmās
ἀπο του πονηρου.   ὁτι σου ἐστιν ἡ βασιλεια
apo too punêroo.   Hoti soo estin hê basilaya
καὶ ἡ δυναμις καὶ ἡ δοξα εἰς τους αἰωνας.
kī hê dewnamis kī hê doxa ace toos   īōnas.
ἀμην.
amên.

---

**Exercise 2.**—Pronounce the following words—cover up the key until you have made your attempt.

| | | |
|---|---|---|
| 1. υἱος. | 2. ναυτου. | 3. φαλαγξ. |
| 4. σπογγος. | 5. βρογχια. | 6. ᾿Αμαζων. |
| 7. ἀσβεστος. | 8. ηὑρηκα. | 9. χασμα. |
| 10. εὐπεψια. | 11. χαρακτηρ. | 12. ἐμισγον. |

### KEY

| | | |
|---|---|---|
| 1. Hweeos. | 2. Now-too. | 3. Phalanx. |
| 4. Spon-gos. | 5. Bronchia. | 6. Amazdōne. |
| 7. Azbestos. | 8. Heurêka. | 9. Chasma. |
| 10. Eupepsia. | 11. Charactêr. | 12. Emizgon. |

# CHAPTER III

## READING PRACTICE

### Exercise 1

THIS story contains every letter of the alphabet in words that are identical with English words. Read it, transliterating the Greek letters. Then correct your solution from the key at end of book.

## ΚΑΤΑΣΤΡΟΦΗ

Ἑκτωρ and Δαφνη were exploring the μητρο- πολις. They dined at the Κριτηριον on ἀμβροσια,

---

μητροπολις  from μητηρ (mother) and πολις (city).

κριτηριον  See κρισις. 'A means of judging, standard, test.'

ἀμβροσια  a heavenly food, the food of the immortals. ἀμ- or ἀ at the beginning of a word negatives the rest of the word (cf. ' un- ' in Engl.), βροτος (a mortal).

32

drank a delicious νεκταρ and listened to the ὀρχηστρα.
After that their ἰδεα was to go to a κινημα to see a
δραμα. But before they got there things reached a
horrid κλιμαξ for poor Δαφνη, who was overcome
with κωμα accompanied by strange convulsions of
the θωραξ. She collapsed in the arms of the faithful
'Εκτωρ, who exclaiming " φευ, φευ," called a physician,
whose διαγνωσις, after a careful ἀναλυσις of the
symptoms, was that the γενεσις of her trouble was
not her ψυχη but δυσπεψια contracted from a long

---

| | |
|---|---|
| ὀρχηστρα | originally the circular dance-floor in front of the stage, where the chorus danced. |
| ἰδεα | ' form ' a favourite word of Plato. He is famous for his ' theory of ideas '. |
| κινημα | ' a thing moved ' (hence a ' moving picture ' in mod. Gk.). |
| δραμα | ' a thing done or acted '. The termination -μα regularly has this sense at end of a Gk. root. δρα—the root of the verb δραν, ' to do '. |
| κλιμαξ | originally ' a ladder ', later ' a gradual ascent to a climax '. |
| κωμα | ' deep sleep, slumber '—a word as old as Homer. |
| φευ | Phew, but in Gk. the exclamation for grief or anger. φευ = ' oh ! ' ' ah ! '. |
| διαγνωσις | δια—preposition meaning ' through '. γνωσις— ' the process of investigating ', ' knowing '. So δια-γνωσις, ' distinguishing ' or ' looking right through ' something. An *agnostic* is ' one who does not know '. The termination -σις denotes the ' active ' process of a verb. |
| ἀναλυσις | ' taking to pieces '. ἀνα, prep. ' up ', ' from bottom to top '. λυσις, ' a setting free ', ' loosing ', ' unravelling '. |
| γενεσις | ' origin, source, manner of birth '. |
| ψυχη | a very common Gk. word for which Engl. has no equivalent—neither exactly ' breath ', |

sojourn in the tropic ζωνη. Daphne's ἀσβεστος digestion had not been proof against the νεκταρ. She reached and passed the κρισις three days later, although the affair nearly ended in a καταστροφη. Fate, however, was determined to punish her, in spite of the fact that ἀμβροσια was ἀναθεμα to her afterwards; for it was soon found that she was suffering

---

'life', 'spirit', nor 'soul', yet something of each. In Homer it is 'the life or spirit of man which survives death', almost 'ghost'. In Gk. philosophy 'the vital principle, the animating spirit (e.g. of the Universe)'. In Gk. art frequently represented as a butterfly. Cf. the lovely story of Cupid (or rather Eros) and Psyche (ΨΥΧΗ) in the *Golden Ass* of Apuleius.

δυσπεψια    'indigestion'. δυσ-πεπτος, adj. 'hard to digest'. The prefix δυσ- common in Gk. has the notion of 'hard, bad, unlucky, etc.'. Cf. our *un-* or *mis-* (e.g. in unrest, mischance, etc.).

ζωνη    In Gk. a 'belt or girdle'. So 'zone' in Eng. 'a girdle of the earth, or the part which the girdle encloses'.

ἀσβεστος    'inextinguishable', and so 'incombustible

κρισις    originally the process of separating, distinguishing. Its translation 'judgment' in the N.T. disguises the true meaning of the word, which contains no idea of condemnation, but means 'separating' (e.g. sheep from goats). So 'crisis', frequently wrongly used in English, should be kept for 'turning-points that necessitate a parting of the ways'.

καταστροφη    κατα (down) στροφη (turning). 'Overturning, sudden end'.

ἀναθεμα    an interesting word. Originally 'anything offered up or dedicated'. In the N.T. 'an accursed thing' because pagan votive offerings were regarded as such.

from ἀφασια brought on by the νεκταρ, which left
its στιγμα upon her for the rest of her life. The
ἠχω of her hollow groans used to scare the passers-
by, who wondered what strange χαρακτηρ dwelt
there. At last νεμεσις overtook her, and she faded
away, the sad σκηνη reaching the ἀκμη of παθος.

---

| | |
|---|---|
| ἀφασια | ' speechlessness '. α (not) φασις (the process of speaking, speech). |
| νεκταρ | Homer's word for the ' drink of the gods ', as ἀμβροσια was their food. |
| στιγμα | ' a thing pricked, tattooed ', so ' a tattoo mark ', ' a brand '. From root στιγ—' to brand '. Cf. St. Francis and his stigmata. |
| ἠχω | the Greeks personified Echo. ' Lost Echo sits amid the voiceless mountains ', Shelley, *Adonais*. |
| χαρακτηρ | ' a mark engraved, impress, stamp '. So ' a distinctive mark ', ' the peculiar nature of someone '. |
| νεμεσις | ' righteous indignation of the gods ', ' divine vengeance '—one of the many words for which we have no exact equivalent. Others are ὑβρις, ἠθος, ἀρετη, σωφροσυνη. |
| σκηνη | originally the hut or dressing-room at the back of the Gk. stage, which was painted to represent a ' scene ' or ' scenery '. |
| ἀκμη | ' highest or culminating point ' of anything. |
| παθος | ' experience ', gen. calamitous experience, so ' suffering '. |

## Exercise 2

Here are some more actual Greek words that are
the same in English, to give you practice in reading.
Look up any that you don't know in an *English*
dictionary. It is good to transliterate them into
English, and then back again into Greek without
looking at the Greek words.

| κωλον | κανων | *For practice in capitals.* |
| μιασμα | θερμος | |
| ἀντιθεσις | στολη | ῾ΕΛΛΑΣ |
| βαθος | πνευμονια | ΠΗΝΕΛΟΠΗ |
| φαλαγξ | ἀσθμα | ΔΩΡΟΘΕΑ |
| ἱβις | φθισις | ΖΩΗ |
| ἐμφασις | χαος | ᾿ΑΓΑΘΑ |
| αὐτοματον | ἀποθεωσις | ΧΛΟΗ |
| δογμα | διπλωμα | ΛΗΘΗ |
| ἠθος | φαντασια | ΚΥΚΛΩΨ |
| ὑβρις | συγκοπη | ΦΟΙΝΙΞ |
| κοσμος | δελτα | ΣΕΙΡΗΝ |
| ὀνυξ | κυδος | ᾿ΑΚΡΟΠΟΛΙΣ |
| ὑποθεσις | | |

The following table of equivalents should be carefully studied :—

| *Greek.* | *English.* | | *Example.* |
|---|---|---|---|
| υ | y | e.g. Ψυχη | = Psyche. |
| αι | ae | Αἰγινα | = Ægina. |
| ει | i | Εἰρηνη | = Irene. |
| οι | oe or sometimes e | ⎧ Φοιβη<br>⎨ but<br>⎩ οἰκονομια | = Phœbe<br><br>= economy. |
| ου | u | Οἰδιπους | = Œdipus. |
| γγ | ng | ἀγγελος | = Angelus. |
| γξ | nx | Σφιγξ | = Sphinx. |
| γκ | nc | ᾿Αγκυρα | = Ancyra. |

### Exercise 3

The following story contains more words which were originally Greek, and which we have introduced into our language. Try to read them, and where you can't, write the letters in English and they will become clear.

## Daphne's Mishap

Early one morning, taking her ἀτλας,[1] Δαφνη wandered down to the βασις[2] of the κρατηρ[3] to write the συνοψις[4] of her θεσις[5] on the Ὑδρα[6] of the Παρθενων. The ἰρις and ἀνεμωνη[7] and ἀστηρ[8] were in bloom, and she thought of all the ἡρωες[9] who had trod this ζωνη before. With this ἰδεα in her νους,[10] she heard from over the water a χορος[11] as if from the μαρτυρες.[12] Suddenly to her great διλημμα[13] near the ὁριζων[14] what should she see but a πυθων, a πανθηρ, a λυγξ and a βισων making their ἐξοδος[15] from Ἁιδης![16] In her screams she burst her λαρυγξ and was taken with acute παραλυσις[17]

---

1. Called after the Titan who held up the sky.
2. Originally a ' stepping ' or ' step ', then ' what you step on ', a ' pedestal ' or ' base '.
3. Originally a ' mixing-bowl ', or large ' cup '.
4. Lit. ' a seeing together ' or ' general view '. Cf. the synoptic Gospels.
5. Lit. a ' placing ' or ' arranging '.
6. ' Watersnake ', der. from ὑδωρ, ' water ' (why is *hydrogen* so named ?).
7. Lit. ' wind-flower ' (ἀνεμος, ' wind '). Olympia is carpeted with them (red and blue) in April.
8. Lit. ' star '.
9. Nom. plur. of ἡρως (3rd decl.).
10. ' Mind '.
11. Originally ' dance ', then ' those who made up the dance '.
12. Nom. plur. of μαρτυς, ' a witness '. In Eng. there is of course no ' e '. Very common word in the N.T.
13. Lit. ' double proposition '.
14. Participle from ὁριζειν, to ' bound '.
15. ὁδος ' way ', ἐξ ' out ' (prep.). At the exit of the Underground Station in Athens today is a notice ΕΞΟΔΟΣ.
16. Eng. has dropped the ' i ' in this word.
17. Lit. ' a loosening by the side of ', so ' a disabling of the nerves in the limbs of one side '.

of the σπλην. Hearing her cries, Φοιβη hastened to offer her a τηλεφωνη,[18] but found she had succumbed already to the βακτηρια [19] of χολερα, leaving only an ίσοσκελες [20] σκελετον behind.

---

18. Lit. τηλε ' from afar ' (adv.), φωνη ' voice '. A mod. Gk. compound from two classical Gk. words.
19. Lit. ' little sticks ', as microbes appear to be when seen through a microscope. Latin ' bacilli '.
20. ίσος, ' equal '; σκελος, ' leg '.

## CHAPTER IV

## INFLECTIONS: FIRST AND SECOND DECLENSION NOUNS AND ADJECTIVES

1. ἀγαθη κορη λευσσει κακον ἀνθρωπον.
   (A) good girl  sees (a) bad  man.

2. ὦ ἀγαθη κορη, φυλασσου!
   O  good  girl, be careful!

3. ὁ κακος ἀνθρωπος ἁρπαζει την ἀγαθην κορην.
   The bad  man  seizes the  good  girl.

4. " ὦ κακε ἀνθρωπε," λεγει ἡ κορη τῳ κακῳ
   " O bad  man,"  says the girl to the bad
   ἀνθρωπῳ, " ἀπιθι ".
   man,  " go away ! "

5. ὁ ἀνθρωπος κλεπτει τον της ἀγαθης κορης
   The  man  steals  the {of the good  girl / good  girl's}
   ἀσκον
   bag

6. και λεγει τῃ ἀγαθῃ κορῃ κακον λογον.
   And says to the good  girl (a) bad  word.

7. ἡ ἀγαθη κορη τυπτει το του κακου ἀνθρωπου
   The good  girl smacks the {of the bad  man / bad  man's}
   προσωπον.
   face.

Let us follow the fortunes of the good girl in this human drama. You will observe that she undergoes some surprising transformations. In the first sentence she is just ἀγαθη κορη. In the second she is much the same, except that we try to attract her attention by prefacing with the word ὧ (O). In the third sentence she has become, however, την ἀγαθην κορην, although the English still seems to regard her as the same good girl. Omit for a moment the fourth. In the fifth sentence she has become της ἀγαθης κορης. Well, but hasn't ' girl ' become ' girl's '? True, but ' good ', we notice, has changed in the Greek as well. In the sixth the good girl has broken out into a rash of iotas subscript, as τῃ ἀγαθῃ κορῃ.

What is the explanation of all this?

You cannot have failed to notice that in each of these sentences, although she is the same girl, she plays a different part.

For instance, in sentence 1 she does the seeing. She is the *doer* of the action implied in the verb. The word or words representing the *doer* is called the *subject*.

In sentence 2 she is the person addressed.

In sentence 3 she is the person immediately affected by the action of the *doer*. A person or thing suffering the action of the *doer* is said to be the *object*.

In sentence 5 she is simply the owner of the bag.

In sentence 6 she is the person indirectly affected by the doer's action. The doer is ' the man '. What he does is ' says '. The thing immediately suffering his action is ' a bad word ' (it gets said). The good girl is indirectly affected by his saying the bad word, because he says it *to* her. She is therefore called the *indirect object*.

In English we have two ways (or even three) of showing the part played by a word in a sentence. We usually find the subject or object of a verb by the order of the words; the subject usually precedes, the object usually succeeds the verb. The way to get at this is to ask Who? or What? in front of the verb to get the subject, and Whom? or What? after the verb. Try it. " My mother bids me bind my hair." Who bids me bind my hair? Subject. Bids whom or what bind my hair? Object. If we deviate from the natural order of the words, as we often do, we have to rely on the sense of the passage to tell us which is the subject, and which the object. It may be obvious (" Hell ! " said the Countess), less obvious (" Hands that the rod of empire might have swayed "), or not obvious at all (" And all the air a sudden stillness holds ").

Secondly, prepositions like ' to ' or ' of ' may denote the indirect object or the owner, respectively. " The ploughman . . . leaves the world *to* darkness and *to* me." " The bosom *of* his Father and his God."

Thirdly, the actual form of the word may, in one or two words, change in accordance with the part played by the word : e.g., subject, ' girl '—possessor, ' girl's '; subject, ' he '—object, ' him '—possessor, ' his '.

Inflections.—It is on this third method that Greek relies. Greek indicates the part that a word plays in the sentence by having a fixed part of the word (called the stem) into which a number of different tailpieces can be slotted as the word is required to do one job or another. These endings are called case-endings. The cases are five.

Cases.—NOMINATIVE to represent the SUBJECT.
VOCATIVE to represent the PERSON ADDRESSED.
ACCUSATIVE to represent the OBJECT.
GENITIVE to represent the POSSESSOR.*
DATIVE to represent the INDIRECT OBJECT.

There is a different set of endings for the plural.

The Importance of Endings.—Remember that it is not the order of the words, as in English, that decides the meaning of the sentence in Greek. If sentence 3 ran : την ἀγαθην κορην ἁρπαζει ὁ κακος ἀνθρωπος (as it well might), the meaning would be almost the same. It follows that the exact form of the word-ending is of paramount importance. Small boys who have learnt the difference between the doer and the sufferer of an action soon become sensitive as to their endings.

Prepositions are sometimes used in Greek in addition to case-endings of nouns, but they only serve to define with a little more exactness the case already shown by the ending. There are a good many other meanings of the five cases besides those given. You will meet them later.

Adjectival Agreement.—You will have already noticed that ἀγαθη changes in the same way as

* Note the curious order of Sentence 7. Frequently in Greek a genitive comes in between the article and the noun on which it depends.

κορη. κορη is a noun, but ἀγαθη (good) an
adjective describing the noun. An adjective always
adopts a similar case-ending to the noun which it
describes. It is then said to *agree* with the noun.
Although at first the noun endings and the adjective
endings are similar in sound, it will not always be
so—but where an adjective qualifies a noun it will
always be in the same case, number, and gender.
Thus, when ' girl ' becomes ' girl's ' κορη becomes
κορης, and when ' good girl ' becomes ' good girl's '
ἀγαθη κορη becomes ἀγαθης κορης.

**Number.**—What do we mean by number? Number is the quality of being one (singular) or more
(plural). In English we add ' s ' on to the noun to
show the plural number—e.g. boy, boys; or it may
be -en, e.g. ox, oxen. Greek has various plural
endings which you will learn later.

**Gender.**—Let us turn to the villain of the bag-
snatching episode. You will observe that he undergoes even more transformations than his fair victim.
See if you can identify the cases of the κακος
ἀνθρωπος from what you already know of their
functions.

In sentence 1 he is the object of her gaze. Case?
In sentence 3 he does the seizing. Case?
In sentence 4 he is first addressed by her. Case?
In sentence 4 she says " Go away ! " *to him*.
Case?
In sentence 7 he owns a smacked face. Case?

One thing you cannot fail to have noticed : that the
man possesses an entirely different set of tail-pieces

from the girl. Why is this? The answer is to be found in the difference between the man and the girl. The man possesses *masculine* endings (-ος -ε -ον -ου -ῳ), the girl *feminine* (-η -η -ην -ης -η). There is a further category that is neither masculine nor feminine, which is called *neuter*. Its endings (-ον -ον -ον -ου -ῳ), differ only in the nominative and vocative singular, and nominative, vocative and accusative plural. All nouns come into one or another of these three classes. Sometimes the meaning, as in man and girl, will enable you to at once determine what gender the noun is. But more often you will not know whether the word is masculine, feminine, or neuter until you have seen the actual Greek word. What, for instance, is the difference between a man's face and a bag? (We are speaking grammatically.) Yet Greek has it that the man's face is *neuter* (το προσωπον), and the girl's bag is masculine (ὁ ἀσκος). It is mainly the form of the word itself which will enable you to determine whether the word is masculine, feminine, or neuter.

**1st and 2nd Declension.**—It is time now to tabulate the endings met so far. As it happens, the feminine, masculine, and neuter endings of the adjective κακος (bad) exactly correspond with the feminine nouns of the 1st declension and the masculine and neuter nouns of the 2nd declension. If, therefore, you learn the word across (κακος, κακη, κακον), you will have an adjective at your fingertips, and if you also learn it downwards (κακος, κακε, κακον . . . κακη, κακη, κακην), you will have three nouns.

### Κακος—Bad

| Sing. | Mas. | Fem. | Neuter. |
|---|---|---|---|
| Nom. | κακ-ος. | κακ-η. | κακ-ον. |
| Voc. | κακ-ε. | κακ-η. | κακ-ον. |
| Acc. | κακ-ον. | κακ-ην. | κακ-ον. |
| Gen. | κακ-ου. | κακ-ης. | κακ-ου. |
| Dat. | κακ-ῳ. | κακ-ῃ. | κακ-ῳ. |

| Plur. | | | |
|---|---|---|---|
| Nom. | κακ-οι. | κακ-αι. | κακ-α. |
| Voc. | κακ-οι. | κακ-αι. | κακ-α. |
| Acc. | κακ-ους. | κακ-ας. | κακ-α. |
| Gen. | κακ-ων. | κακ-ων. | κακ-ων. |
| Dat. | κακ-οις. | κακ-αις. | κακ-οις. |

*Note.*—(1) It is always true of the neuter that the nominative, vocative, and accusative are always the same, whether in the singular or the plural.

(2) The dative case always has an iota. It is subscript in the singular of the 1st and 2nd declension.

(3) The plural of the adjective, if used alone, or with the article, often means that the word ' men ' has to be supplied for the masculine, ' women ' for the feminine, and ' things ' for the neuter, e.g. κακα, evil *things*—i.e. troubles, evils. οι κακοι, the wicked; bad *men*.

# CHAPTER V

## SECOND DECLENSION (continued)

THE Greeks to-day still use cases. In the Underground in Athens you can read the notice ΚΙΝΔΥΝΟΣ ΘΑΝΑΤΟΥ near the electrified rail. It means ' danger of death '. In the railway carriages you will see ΜΗ ΠΤΥΕΤΕ—i.e. ' do not spit ', and :—

θεσεις καθημενων 16,

θεσεις ὀρθιων 40,

i.e. ' sitters' places 16, standing-room for 40 '.

In the following story are a number of 2nd declension Greek nouns and some adjectives in various cases. Look carefully at the ends of the words, referring, if necessary, to the declension of κακος for the case and its meaning. Use the notes and an English dictionary to translate the story. Most of the words have derivatives in English.

### Stephan's Secret Weapon

(N.B.—*The words italicised should, of course, be in Greek.*)

Στεφανος ἦν (was) νεος ἰατρος ὁς (who) *lived* μονος

---

English derivatives, which will help you to discover the meaning of the Gk. words. Where there is no derivative, the meaning is given.

| *Greek.* | | *Derivative.* |
|---|---|---|
| νεος | a. | neo-Gk., neophyte, neo-Platonist. |
| ἰατρος | s. | a psychiatrist is a mind-*doctor*. |
| μονος | a. | monologue, monogamy, monoplane. |
| | s. = substantive. | a. = adjective. |

ἐν (in) παλαιῳ οἰκῳ ἐν μεσῃ τῃ νησῳ. Γεωργος ὁ
ἀδελφος ἠν τυραννος και *sat* ἐπι (on) Ὀλυμπικου
θρονου, ἀλλα παντες (all) οἱ ἀριστοι του δημου *thought*
Στεφανον ἰσον θεῳ και ἀξιον χλωρου στεφανου. εἰχε
(he had) κρυπτον (secret) ὁπλον, φαρμακον κρυπτον
(hidden) παρα (against) τον νομον ἐν ποταμῳ. ἐπει

| Greek. | | Derivative. |
|---|---|---|
| παλαιος | a. | palæography, palæolithic (λιθος, stone). |
| οἰκος | s. | economy (management of the *house*), |
| μεσος | a. | Mesopotamia (ποταμος, river). Note that in Greek the order is ' middle the island '. |
| νησος | fem. s. | Dodecanese (12 ——). Polynesia (many ——). Peloponnese (—— of Pelops). |
| Γεωργος | s. | George (γη—land, ἐργον—work. So ' farmer '). |
| ἀδελφος | s. | Adelphi (called after the Adam *brothers*), Philadelphia, Christadelphians. |
| τυραννος | s. | tyrannical. |
| θρονος | s. | means ' throne '. |
| ἀλλα | conj. | means ' but '. |
| ἀριστος | a. | aristocratic, aristocracy (government by the *best*). |
| δημος | s. | democracy. |
| ἀξιος | a. | worthy (takes gen.). |
| στεφανος | s. | means ' *a crown* '. Green olive crowns were the prizes at the Olympic games. |
| χλωρος | a. | chlorine (so called from its yellow-*green* colour). |
| κρυπτος | a. | cryptic, crypt. |
| ὁπλον | s. | panoply, hoplite. |
| φαρμακον | s. | pharmacist (because he sells *drugs* or *poison*). |
| νομος | s. | Deuteronomy (second ——). |

s. = substantive.　　　a. = adjective.

(when) ὁ ἀδελφος ἦν ἐν μακρῳ ὑπνῳ Στεφανος *said*
τῃ καθαρᾳ και καλη Δαφνη ὁτι (that) *he would give
her* ὁλον ᾠον εἰ (if) *she would be his* ἀγγελος και *run*
ὁμοια τῳ ἀνεμῳ και *get* τον θησαυρον ὁς ἦν κρυπτος
ὑπο (under) λευκῳ λιθῳ. Δαφνη *began* ἐργον *at once,*
ἀλλα *what should she see but* πολεμιον ταυρον *having*
προσωπον ὁμοιον μισανθρωπῳ στρατηγῳ. ἀλλα το
εἰδωλον του κακου ζῳου *frightened* την ἀγαθην
νυμφην *so much that she could not utter* λογον, ἀλλα

| Greek. | | Derivative. |
|---|---|---|
| μακρος | a. | macrometer, macrocosm. |
| ὑπνος | s. | hypnotic (because causing *sleep*). |
| καθαρος | a. | Katharine, cathartic. (For this ending of dat. fem. v. next chapter.) |
| καλος | a. | kaleidoscope (*beautiful*—patterns—see). |
| ὁλος | a. | holocaust (because the *whole* is burnt). catholic (over (κατα) the *whole*). |
| ᾠον | s. | oval, ovum (originally written ὠϜον v. ch. 1 under γ, notes on Alphabet). |
| ἀγγελος | s. | an angel is a *messenger* of God. |
| ὁμοιος | a. | homœopathic (because such drugs excite symptoms *like* the disease). |
| θησαυρος | s. | a thesaurus is a *treasury* of knowledge. So= treasure. |
| λευκος | a. | leucocyte (*white* corpuscle of blood.) |
| λιθος | s. | lithograph. |
| ἐργον | s. | erg (unit of *work*), energy (something that works in you). |
| πολεμιος | a. | polemical. |
| ταυρος | s. | Minotaur, Taurus. |
| μισανθρωπος | a. | misanthropic (μισος = hate). |
| στρατηγος | s. | strategic, strategy. So one who *leads* a στρατος (army). |
| εἰδωλον | s. | idol, originally 'representation, likeness, image'. |
| ζῳον | s. | what is kept in the Zoo ? |
| νυμφη | s. | nymph. |

s. = substantive.          a. = adjective.

*held up her* βιβλιον εὐαγγελικων ὑμνων μετεωρον ὁ (which) το ζῳον *swallowed thinking* ὁτι ἐστι δωρον σιτου.

## A Limerick

An author with fancy αἰσθητικ(ος)
Once developed ambitions κοσμητικ(ος).
After agonies χρονικ(ος)
And results ἐμβρυονικ(ος)
His exit was truly παθητικ(ος).

In the following exercise the missing words are English words derived from Greek words listed below. Can you discover them ?  E.g. the first is ' plutocrat', derived from πλουτος (wealth) and κρατειν (to have power over), and the third is an animal derived from two Greek words.  Some letters are given as a help.

The missing English words are each derived from two Greek words, except those marked with a ', which are derived from one.  The dots represent the number of letters contained in the English words.  Read the Greek words below the exercise and their meanings several times before attempting to fill in the missing words.

| Greek. | | Derivative. |
|---|---|---|
| βιβλιον | s. | Bible, bibliography, bibliomania. |
| εὐαγγελικος | a. | for εὐ see eulogy, euthanasia, eurhythmics. Why is εὐαγγελιον the Gk. for gospel ? |
| ὑμνος | s. | hymnal. |
| μετεωρος | a. | a meteor is a star that shoots *in mid air*. |
| δωρον | s. | Dorothy, Theodore—a *gift* from God. |
| σιτος | s. | parasite (one who is at hand to pick up the *food*). |

s. = substantive.   a. = adjective.

## Hector's Misadventure

Ἕκτωρ was a pl....... who grew prize
ch............. He kept a pet h....p......
and owned the H......... θεατρον. As if this
wasn't enough for one man, he studied o....d..
th..l..., and what with walking among the
r............ brandishing a s'......, declaiming
t'...... e'....... before the m........., and
calling upon the h...a.... to e.orc... his
βακτηρια, it was all too much for the poor creature,
and he became an a'...... and interested in
p...g.... But after that it became worse, for he
used to ride a c'.... round the c...t..., studying
a'......... and b..1... aloud and declaring that
he was a m'....... m'.......t. Then he tried
c'........ and s'......., contracted o'.........
and ch'..... h....ph.... and turned a d'........l
h....t.... colour.

| | | | |
|---|---|---|---|
| ἀνθος | } flower. | δρομος | racecourse. |
| ἀνθεμον | | ἐξ | out of. |
| ἀριθμος | { number. | ἐπιταφιος | lit. on a tomb. |
| ἀριθμητικος | to do with numbers. | ἡλιος | sun. |
| ἀρχη | beginning, first place or power. | θεος | god |
| | | ἱερος | sacred. |
| ἀθεος | non-believer in God. | ἱππος | horse. |
| | | κενος | empty. |
| βιος | life. | κοσμος | { order, adornment. |
| γαμος | marriage. | κοσμητικα | things that adorn |
| δενδρον | tree. | | |
| διαβολος | devil, lit. slanderer. | κρατειν | to have power over. |
| δοξα | opinion. | κυκλος | circle, wheel. |

| | | | |
|---|---|---|---|
| λογος | word, reason. | στρατηγος | a general. |
| μεθοδος | scientific enquiry. | ταφος | tomb. |
| μικρος | small. | τοπος | place. |
| μυστικος | a mystic. | τοπικος | to do with a place, local. |
| ὀρθος | right, straight. | τροπος | turning. |
| ὅρκος | oath. | ὑδωρ | water. |
| ὀφθαλμος | eye. | φοβος | fear. |
| πλουτος | wealth. | φωνη | voice. |
| πολυ | much. | χρυσος | gold. |
| ποταμος | river. | χρονος | time. |
| ῥοδον | rose. | χρονικος | to do with time. |
| σκηπτρον | sceptre. | | |

# CHAPTER VI

## THE DEFINITE ARTICLE

GREEK has a word for 'the', but not for 'a', unless there is special need to express 'a' as meaning 'a particular or certain (person or thing)', when τις is used following the noun (see c. 24). This is one of the many examples where the Greek language avoids ambiguity and makes for definiteness. ὁ, ἡ, το, called the *definite article*, is declined like κακος in all cases except the nominative and accusative singular and the nominative plural. It is well worth learning its declension by heart. Learn it across.

### DEFINITE ARTICLE—'THE'

| Sing. | Mas. | Fem. | Neuter. |
|-------|------|------|---------|
| Nom. | ὁ | ἡ | το |
| Acc. | τον | την | το |
| Gen. | του | της | του |
| Dat. | τῳ | τῃ | τῳ |
| Plur. | | | |
| Nom. | οἱ | αἱ | τα |
| Acc. | τους | τας | τα |
| Gen. | των | των | των |
| Dat. | τοις | ταις | τοις |

As a general rule use the definite article in Greek whenever you have the definite article in English. Note, however, the following :—

1. *Abstract Nouns.* Abstract nouns (those like wisdom, faith, courage, honour, etc.) usually have the definite article, e.g. wisdom—ἡ σοφια, courage—ἡ ἀρετη.

2. *Whole Classes.* When a plural noun denotes all members of a class, use the definite article, e.g. Horses are noble animals; i.e. all horses; translate οἱ ἱπποι.

3. *Proper Names.* The definite article is often used with proper names, e.g. Greece—ἡ Ἑλλας, Hector—ὁ Ἑκτωρ.

## A FLOWER SONG

Here are two lines of an ancient Flower Song, which Greek children used to sing—like our ' Nuts in May ' :—

(Leader) που μοι τα ῥοδα;    που μοι τα ἰα;
      where for me the roses ?    violets ?
  = where are my roses . . . .
     που μοι τα καλα σελινα;
      beautiful parsley ?

(Chorus) ταδε τα ῥοδα, ταδε τα ἰα, ταδε τα καλα
     (i.e. here) these are the roses, etc., σελινα.

Parsley was admired by the Greeks because of its feathery leaves, and used to make the victors' crowns at the Isthmian games. A town in Sicily was called after this word.

## Greek Punctuation.

Comma (,) and full-stop (.) are the same as in English.

The sign (;) is used as a question mark.

A point above a line (·) is used for the semi-colon or colon.

## ORIGINAL GREEK

You should now be able to translate some original Greek. ἐστι (is) is understood in 1, 2, 3, 5 and 7.

1. μεγα βιβλιον, μεγα κακον.—Callimachus.

2. ὁ ἀνεξεταστος (unexamined) βιος οὐ βιωτος (livable) ἀνθρωπῳ.—Plato.

3. ἀνθρωπος πολιτικον ζῳον.—Aristotle.

4. ὁ φιλος ἐστιν ἀλλος (another) αὐτος (self).

5. ἀθλιος (wretched) ὁ βιος των ἀθεων.

6. χρονος παιδευει (educates) τους σοφους.

7. ὁ ὑπνος ἰατρος νοσου.

8. ἐν ἀρχῃ ἦν (was) ὁ λογος, και ὁ λογος ἦν προς τον Θεον, και Θεος ἦν ὁ λογος.—S. John I. 1.

9. ἐγω εἰμι (am) το Ἀλφα και το Ὠμεγα, ἀρχη και τελος, ὁ πρωτος και ὁ ἐσχατος.

---

1. μεγα, ' big ' (megaphone). It is neuter of μεγας, a 2nd declension adj.
βιβλιον, ' book ' (hence bible).
2. Said by Socrates at his trial.
βιος. What does ' biology ' mean ?
οὐ = ' not ' (οὐκ before a vowel, οὐχ before an aspirate).
4. φιλος. What does ' philanthropist ' mean ? Here ὁ φιλος is the generic use of the definite article, and = ' friends '. Gk. says ' the friend,' when we say ' friends ' (generally) '.
5. ἀθεος, ' not godly ', so ' godless ' (atheist).
6. σοφος, adj. ' wise ' (philosophy).
7. νοσος (f.) ' disease '. In Gk. the article goes with the subject (not with the complement as in Eng.). See next section.
8. ἀρχη, subs. ' beginning '.
προς, prep., ' towards, near, relating to '.
9. τελος, 3rd decl. neuter subs. = ' end.'
πρωτος, ' first ' (prototype).
ἐσχατος, ' last ' (eschatology).

### Three Lines from Greek Plays

Read these aloud, and you will notice a similarity
of rhythm. They are in the *iambic* metre, the usual
metre of dialogue in Greek drama.

1. κακον φερουσι καρπον οἱ κακοι φιλοι.—Menander.
2. παντων ἰατρος των ἀναγκαιων κακων
   χρονος ἐστιν.—Menander.
3. τα βαρβαρων γαρ δουλα παντα πλην ἑνος.
   Euripides.

### THE VERB 'TO BE'

ἐστι (he, she, it) is.    εἰσι (they) are.
ἠν      ,,      was.    ἠσαν  ,,  were.

The verb 'to be' is unlike most verbs, inasmuch as
it does not express action. Its chief use in statements
is to tell us, in conjunction with other words, something about the state, condition, or character of the
person or thing indicated in the subject : e.g. The
man *is* bad ; Stephan *was* a doctor. The words
*bad* and *a doctor* therefore do not stand for a person
or thing affected by an action ; they are *not* objects

---

1. φερουσι, ' they bring ', or ' bear '.
   καρπον, acc. of καρπος, subs., ' fruit '.
2. παντων, gen. plur. of adj., πας, ' all '.
   ἀναγκαιος, adj., ' necessary '.
3. τα βαρβαρων, lit. ' the things of barbarians '.
   γαρ conj. = for (usually placed second word in a
   sentence—never first).
   δουλος, adj., ' enslaved ', as a noun, ' a slave '.
   παντα, neut. plur. of πας (' all ').
   πλην ἑνος, ' except one man ', πλην, prep., ' except
   (takes gen.).
   ἑνος, gen. of εἱς, ' one ',

(see c. 4); and consequently their equivalents in Greek are *not* put in the accusative case. They merely *complete* the meaning of *is* and *was*; they constitute what is called the *complement*; and in Greek statements their equivalents are put in the same case as the word to which they refer in the subject—namely, the nominative.

1. The complement, whether noun or adjective, cannot be in the accusative case after the verb ' to be '. ' To be ' takes the same case after it as before it.

> e.g. ὁ ἀνθρωπος ἐστι κακος.
> The man (nom.) is bad (nom.).
> ὁ Στεφανος ἠν ἰατρος.
> Stephan was a doctor.

2. The complement never has a definite article, even though there is one in the corresponding English.

> e.g. ὁ Γεωργος ἠν ἀδελφος του Στεφανου.
> George was *the* brother of Stephan.

# CHAPTER VII
## THE FIRST DECLENSION

You have learnt κακος, κακη, κακον, and in doing so you have learnt not only an adjective, but also the case endings of a masculine noun of the 2nd declension (κακος); a feminine noun of the 1st declension (κακη); and a neuter noun of the 2nd declension (κακον).

(Although the nouns ending in -ος in the 2nd declension are mostly masculine, there are a few ending in -ος, declined in exactly the same way, which are feminine—e.g. νησος (island), ὁδος (way), νοσος (disease).)

**The First Declension.**

1. *Nouns declined like* κακη are many; here are some examples; τεχνη (art), λυπη (grief), ὀργη (anger), γη (earth), ψυχη (soul), σιγη (silence), μελετη (practice).

τεχνη is declined thus :—

|       | *Sing.* | *Plur.* |
|-------|---------|---------|
| N.V.  | τεχνη   | τεχναι  |
| A.    | τεχνην  | τεχνας  |
| G.    | τεχνης  | τεχνων  |
| D.    | τεχνῃ   | τεχναις |

2. *Nouns ending in* α. There is also, however, a large number of 1st declension nouns that end in α. These fall into two classes :—

(i) -α *after* ρ *or a vowel*. If the final α follows the

letter ρ or a vowel, the word is declined like τεχνη, except that η is everywhere replaced by α. Examples of this kind are πετρα (a rock). (Do you remember St. Peter—" On this rock I will build my Church "?) and φιλια (friendship). Only the singular is given below; the plural of *all* 1st declension nouns is always the same.

| N.V. | πετρα | N.V. | φιλια |
|------|-------|------|-------|
| A. | πετραν | A. | φιλιαν |
| G. | πετρας | G. | φιλιας |
| D. | πετρα | D. | φιλια |

Further nouns of this kind are :—

| Noun. | Meaning. | Derivative. |
|-------|----------|-------------|
| χωρα | country | — |
| θυρα | door | — |
| ὡρα | hour | hour |
| ἡμερα | day | ephemeral |
| σκια | shadow | skiagraphy |
| ἑσπερα | evening | Hesperus |
| αἰτια | cause | — |

---

Adjectives with ρ or a vowel preceding the ending are similarly declined—e.g. μικρος (small).

| | Mas. | Fem. | Neuter. |
|------|------|------|---------|
| N. | μικρος | μικρα | μικρον |
| V. | μικρε | μικρα | μικρον |
| A. | μικρον | μικραν | μικρον |
| G. | μικρου | μικρας | μικρου |
| D. | μικρω | μικρα | μικρω |

Other adjectives of this kind are :—

| Adjective. | Meaning. | Derivative. |
|---|---|---|
| ὅμοιος | like | homœopathic (suffering the like) |
| ἀξιος | worthy | — |
| φιλιος | friendly | philanthropic (loving mankind) |
| νεος | young | neolithic (new stone) |
| παλαιος | ancient | palæolithic (old stone) |
| δευτερος | second | Deuteronomy (second law) |
| ἱερος | sacred | hieroglyph (sacred carving) |
| ἑτερος | other | heterodox (other opinion) |
| καθαρος | pure | Catharine |

(ii) *Nouns ending in* α *after a consonant* (*not* ρ). All nouns of this declension in which the final α is not preceded by a vowel or ρ, but by a consonant, decline in the nominative, vocative, and accusative like πετρα, but in the genitive and dative like τεχνη, e.g. θαλασσα (sea).

N.V. θαλασσα
A. θαλασσαν
G. θαλασσης
D. θαλασση

Other examples are :—

| Noun. | Meaning. | Derivative. |
|---|---|---|
| γλωσσα | tongue | glossary |
| δοξα | opinion | orthodox |
| μουσα | muse | music |

3. *Masculine nouns of the first declension*. The
1st declension should really have been a purely
feminine affair, and would have been but for the
unwarranted intrusion of a few male characters,
ending in -ης, and a few in -ας. These males are
a mixed lot, and may remind you of the English
jingle :—

" Tinker, tailor, soldier, sailor."

Here are a few examples :—

| | | | |
|---|---|---|---|
| ὑποκριτης, | ἀθλητης, | στρατιωτης, | ναυτης, |
| actor, | athlete, | soldier, | sailor, |
| ποιητης, | προφητης, | λῃστης, | κλεπτης, |
| poet, | prophet, | pirate, | thief, |
| κριτης, | δεσποτης, | πολιτης, | |
| judge, | master, | citizen, | |
| ταμιας, | νεανιας, | Νικιας. | |
| steward, | young man, | Nicias. | |

The singular of the two kinds is thus declined;
the plural, of course, is like all other 1st declension
nouns.

|    |          |         |
|----|----------|---------|
| N. | πολιτης  | νεανιας |
| V. | πολιτα   | νεανια  |
| A. | πολιτην  | νεανιαν |
| G. | πολιτου  | νεανιου |
| D. | πολιτῃ   | νεανιᾳ  |

Notice three things :—

(1) To show that they were masculine, these
    nouns had to import from the 2nd declen-
    sion the genitive in -ου.
(2) The vocative is rather odd.

(3) In νεανιας the α, following a vowel, replaces η all the way through.

ὑποκριτης has an interesting history. It originally meant 'the answerer', and was the title of the person '*who replied*' to the song and dance of the Chorus in the beginnings of Greek drama. Later it came to mean 'actor', and later still, 'one who pretends to be what he isn't', 'a hypocrite'.

Now you should be able to translate the following sentences from actual Greek writers:

### From Greek Literature

1. ἡ γλωσσα πολλων ἐστιν αἰτια κακων.
2. ὁ βιος βραχυς, ἡ τεχνη μακρα.—Hippocrates.
3. λυπης ἰατρος ἐστιν ὁ χρηστος φιλος.—Menander.
4. πολλ' ἐχει σιγη καλα.

---

*Sentence* 1.  ν is added to ἐστι for euphony, i.e. to sound better.  The Greeks dislike a short open -ι at the end of a word when followed by another word beginning with a vowel.  The same is true, you will find later, of -ε in the verb 3rd person singular.

*Sentence* 2.  βραχυς, a 3rd declension adjective.  See 'brachycephalic'.  The Latin 'Ars longa, vita brevis' is well-known.

*Sentence* 3.  χρηστος, good, useful.  What is 'chrestomathy'?  When the Romans first heard the name of Christ they did not understand its meaning (the Anointed One); they thought the name must be Chrestus, i.e. the Useful, a name that might well be given to slaves.

*Sentence* 4.  Poetry and late Gk. frequently omit the article with abstract nouns.  πολλ' for πολλα.  When a vowel at the end of one word is followed by a vowel at the beginning of the next, in certain cases it is dropped, and an apostrophe is substituted.  The vowel is then said to be 'elided'.  Elision of α and ε is frequent, especially in poetry.

5. ὁ θεος ἀγαπη ἐστιν, και ὁ μενων (he that remains) ἐν τῃ ἀγαπῃ μενει ἐν τῳ θεῳ, και ὁ θεος ἐν αὐτῳ (him).

6. θησαυρος ἐστι των κακων κακη γυνη.

7. εὐδαιμονια ἐστιν ἐνεργεια της ψυχης κατ' ἀρετην ἐν τῳ τελειῳ βιῳ.—Aristotle's Ethics.

8. ἰσον ἐστιν ὀργῃ και θαλασσα και γυνη.

## Proper Names

Many English proper names are derived from Greek words of the 1st and 2nd declensions, e.g. :—

| Name. | From. | Meaning. |
|---|---|---|
| Margaret | μαργαριτης | a pearl |
| Eunice | εὐ (well) νικη (victory) | |
| Dorothy | δωρον (gift) θεου (of God) | |
| Phœbe | Φοιβη (bright) | the moon |
| Christopher | Χριστος (Christ) φερω (I carry) | |

Can you discover the meanings of :—

Agatha, Zoe, Daphne, Cora, Irene, Iris, Penelope, Philip, and Timothy—by looking in an English dictionary?

---

*Sentence* 5. ἀγαπη. See the word 'Agape' in the dictionary, which is used of a 'love-feast' of the Early Christians, at which contributions for the poor were collected, and also of 'Love', as in I Corinthians xiii.

*Sentence* 6. For the word γυνη see 'gynæcology', 'misogyny'.

*Sentence* 7. εὐδαιμονια, the state of having a good spirit (demon) in you, and so 'happiness'. κατ' ἀρετην, 'according to right functioning'. There is no exact equal of ἀρετη in English. 'Fitness for purpose' comes nearest to its meaning. The ἀρετη of a soldier is 'bravery'. The ἀρετη of a knife is 'sharpness'. τελειος, complete.

*Sentence* 8. The neuter ending of adjective may surprise you, but the adjective is here being used almost as a noun, i.e. an equal thing'. ὀργη = in anger.

## The Story of the Archbishop

Fill in the missing English words, as in the Exercise in Chapter V.

### 'Ο 'ΑΡΧΙΕΠΙΣΚΟΠΟΣ

*To illustrate first declension nouns.*

(Some of the Greek words below would be in other cases if the whole was in Greek.)

It was the fault του ἀρχιεπισκοπου. If he hadn't started running a c....., οἱ παιδες would never have developed a μανια for γεωμετρια.[1] ἡ Δαφνη was listening to a διατριβη ἥν ὁ Φιλιππος ὁ ποιητης was delivering at a late ὡρα περι ἱστοριας, in the course of which he said that ὁ ἀρχιεπισκοπος ἐστιν ὁμοιοτερος (comp.) μηχανη ἡ (than) ἀνθρωπῳ ἐκκλησιαστικῳ.

Of course Γεωργος ὁ τυραννος, ὁς ἦν νυν (now) μαλλον (more) δεσποτης than ever, and becoming something of a k.....m....c, added his remarks περι της τραγῳδιας.[2] He said that ὁ ἀρχιεπι-

---

1. γεωμετρια. Lit. : ' earth measuring ' (γη = earth, μετρειν = to measure). At the entrance to Plato's Academy was written ιιρ, μηδεις ἀγεωμετρητος εἰσιτω, ' let none who cannot do geometry enter '.

2. τραγῳδια, κωμῳδια. The derivation of both these words is uncertain. τραγος means ' a goat '. If τραγῳδια originally meant ' goat-song ', it may be because at early *tragedies* a goat was the prize, or because the actors dressed in goat skins.

κωμος means ' revel '.
κωμη ,, ' village '.
Aristotle prefers the ' village-song ' theory.

σκοπος had c.....c trouble through bringing n......l expressions into his sermons in the c.......l. There had been an awful σκηνη one Sunday, when, forgetting his usual p... of manner, he had produced a λυρα and discoursed on it in a very t........³ way; and even then, he made no ἀπολογια for his lapse. He then quarrelled with the ποιητης, ὁς ἠν somewhat of an a......, and had written quite a ἀγαθην ὠδην περι διαιτης which really wasn't in his s..... at all. This κωμωδια ἠν too much for Δαφνη, ἡ being e.......l, και o......x had an ἰδεα και married a c....c φιλοσοφιας and finally took to h...... and t.......y.⁴

| | | | |
|---|---|---|---|
| ἀθλητης | athlete. | ἐπισκοπος | *one who watches* (σκοπος) *over* (ἐπι), so *overseer* (Eng. deriv. 'bishop'). |
| διαιτα | way of life. | | |
| δεσποτης | a despot. | | |
| δοξα | opinion. | | |
| καθεδρα | seat. | διατριβη | a wearing away (of time). |
| καρδια | heart. | | |
| κλεπτης | a thief. | ἐκκλησια | assembly (of citizens at Athens). The Christians took over the word for 'church'. |
| κλινη | bed. | | |
| κλινικος | to do with beds. | | |
| κριτης | decider, judge. | | |
| κριτικος | able to discern. | | |
| ἡμερα | day. | | |
| ἐφημερος | living but a day. | | |

---

3. τεχνη. 'Craftsmanship', the skill or 'art' of making anything from a pot to a poem. Art with a capital ' A ' has no equivalent in Greek.

4. τηλεφωνια. A modern Greek word, derived from the ancient τηλε = far off. φωνη = voice. So ' a voice from afar '.

ἱστορια — learning by enquiry ('history' to the Gks. means 'finding out' things).

μανια — madness.

ναυτης — a sailor.
ναυτικος — to do with a sailor.

μαλλον — rather, here = 'more of a'.

ὀρθος — straight, correct.

περι — preposition 'about' (takes gen).

πομπη — mission, escort, pomp.

σοφια — wisdom.

σφαιρα — a ball, globe.

τεχνη — craftsmanship, skill, art.

τηλε — adv. far off.

ὑγιεια — health.

φωνη — voice.

ᾠδη — ode.

## CHAPTER VIII

## THE VERB—PRESENT AND FUTURE

JUST as nouns and adjectives in Greek alter their endings to express cases (although in English we do not now do this to any great extent, but put ' of ', ' by ', ' to ', etc., in front of a word), so the Greeks alter the ends of the words that express actions (called *verbs*) when they denote *who* does anything, or *when* anyone does it. Sometimes we do this in English—e.g. we say " I dance ", " you dance ", " they dance ", but we do not say " he dance ". Nevertheless, there is not much difference in the endings in English, and ' dance ' would remain exactly the same whether ' I ', ' you ', ' we ', or ' they ' preceded it. This is not so in Greek. Each person, 1st, 2nd, or 3rd, singular and plural, in the present and future, at any rate, has an entirely distinct ending. These endings speak so much for themselves that it is not necessary to have a pronoun in front of them, as in English. In English, the meaning of the word ' dance ' would probably be incomplete until ' I ' or ' you ' had been put in front. In Greek, χορευω means ' I dance ' because of the termination -ω. It would be possible to say ἐγω χορευω, but it is not necessary to use the pronouns, and, in fact, they are not used unless a special emphasis is intended, as if we were to say, " It is *I* who am dancing." Look carefully at the endings of the following six words, which make up what is

called the *present* tense of the verb in -ω. Learn it
thoroughly.

Termination of—

Sing.

| | | | |
|---|---|---|---|
| 1st person | -ω | χορευω | I dance. |
| 2nd person | -εις | χορευεις | you dance (referring to a single person; we used to say " thou dancest ".) |
| 3rd person | -ει | χορευει | he (or she) dances. |

Plur.

| | | | |
|---|---|---|---|
| 1st person | -ομεν | χορευομεν | we dance. |
| 2nd person | -ετε | χορευετε | you dance (two more people). |
| 3rd person | -ουσι(ν) | χορευουσι(ν) | they dance. |

*N.B.*—ν is added for euphony (εὐ, well; φωνη, voice;
pleasant sound) if the following word begins with a vowel—
e.g. χορευουσιν ἀβρως, they dance delicately.

The present tense in Greek describes action going
on at the time of the speaker, and in English is
equivalent to ' I dance ', ' I do dance ', or ' I am
dancing '.

You should now be able to read an actual Greek
poem, or at any rate the first five lines of it. It is
an ancient drinking song, and we do not know who
wrote it. Look for the verb in the first two lines.

'Η γη μελαινα [1] πινει, [2]
πινει δε [3] δενδρε' [4] αὐτην. [5]

---

1. μελαινα, ' black '. It is the nominative feminine
singular of an irregular adj., μελας, μελαινα, μελαν. Why
are the Melanesian Islands in the S. Pacific so called ?

2. πινω means ' I drink '. So what does ' πινει ' mean ?

3. δε means ' and ' or ' but ', whichever is appropriate.
It must be second word in the sentence. If a vowel follows

πινει θαλασσα κρουνους, [6]
ὁ δ' ἡλιος θαλασσαν,
τον δ' ἡλιον σεληνη.[7]
τι [8] μοι μαχεσθ,' [9] ἑταιροι,
καὐτῳ [10] θελοντι πινειν ; [11]

If you would like to learn this poem by heart, you will find that the metre will help you. It is interesting to compare this song with Shelley's poem, " The fountains mingle with the river," and to notice his characteristically less bibulous ending.

---

it, as in lines 4 and 5, it loses its final vowel, and an apostrophe is put instead. This is called ' elision '. See lines 2 and 6.

4. Loses an α by elision. In Attic Gk. the plural of δενδρον would be δενδρα. δενδρεα is an Ionic and older form.

5. αὐτος can be used in two ways. It can mean -self in all cases, ' myself ', ' himself ', etc., in accordance with the pronoun expressed or implied with which it is used (see line 6), or in the accusative, genitive, and dative, it can mean ' him, her, it, them, etc.'. Our word ' it ' in English suggests a neuter gender, but in Gk. ' it ' must be in the gender of the noun to which it refers; here ' earth ', feminine.

6. κρουνος, ' spring '.

7. What drinks (i.e. takes the light from) the sun ?

8. " Why with me do you fight, comrades, when I too wish to drink ? " (Lit. with me myself also wishing to drink).

9. This is the 2nd person pl. of the Middle verb (see c. 14) μαχομαι in the present, ' you fight '.

10. καὐτῳ is what is called crasis (κρασις, ' mixing '). The vowel of και is mixed with the first syllable of αὐτῳ. When this happens, the smooth breathing is retained, although the word now starts with a kappa.

11. Notice the ending -ειν, which is the form of the present infinitive.

## NEUTER PLURAL SUBJECT AND SINGULAR VERB

One thing should have puzzled you if you translated the drinking song properly. δενδρεα is plural, ' trees ', but πινει is singular. Why not πινουσι? This is due to a very curious rule in Greek. If the subject is neuter plural, the verb is singular. This seems a very puzzling habit, hard to explain, easy to forget. The explanation may be something like this. Neuter plurals usually stand for things, and things in the plural are likely to be thought of as quantity or mass, likc the Gadarene swine, and not as individuals. If the neuter plural subject does refer to people, the verb sometimes is plural.

κακου γαρ ἀνδρος δωρ' ὀνησιν οὐκ ἐχει.

For the gifts (δωρα) of a bad man do not bring (singular) blessing.

## FUTURE TENSE

You have now had the whole of the *present* tense. If you can recognise the six personal endings of this tense, you should have no difficulty in recognising any of the *future* tense, as the terminations are the same, with merely the insertion of the letter σ between the stem (e.g. χορευ-) and the termination (-ω -εις -ει, etc.). Thus χορευσεις; means ' Will you dance ? ' ( ; is the Greek form of a question mark) and χορευσομεν = ' We will dance '.

If the stem of the verb ends in a short vowel, as in ποιε-ω, ' I do ' or ' make ', τιμα-ω, ' I honour ', λυ-ω, ' I loose ', it is replaced by the corresponding longer vowel in the future, η being considered a longer form of both α and ε, e.g. ποιη-σω τιμη-σω, λυ-σω.

If the stem ends in a consonant, the effect of adding σ will necessarily change the consonant :—

π, πτ, β, φ + σ = ψ, e.g. κλεπτω, fut. κλεψω, ' steal '.

κ, γ, χ, + σ = ξ, e.g. πραττω, fut. πραξω, ' do ' (stem πραγ-).

θ or ζ + σ = σ, e.g. πειθω, fut. πεισω, ' persuade'.

Here is the Septuagint Version of the 20th chapter of Exodus, containing the Ten Commandments. You are probably familiar with the English already. So much the better. It will enable you to see the parts of some of the tenses you have already learned in action. You will also get a foretaste of some you have not yet learned. In particular, notice the 2nd person of the future indicative in verbs with vowel stems and consonantal stems.

*Note.*—The Septuagint is the name given to a translation from Hebrew into Greek of the Old Testament and the Apocrypha. The translation of the first five books at least was made, according to tradition, for Ptolemy Philadelphus in the third century B.C. by seventy Jews on the island of Pharos. Hence came the name, Septuaginta, being Latin for 70 ; it is often referred to as LXX. There are other traditions, one being that the work was completed in seventy days, another that each translator was kept in solitary confinement while the work was in progress, but that upon emerging the translators all produced versions that were

word for word identical ! One or two very unimportant
changes have been made here for the sake of clarity.

## Exodus XX. 2.

2. ˙ Εγω εἰμι Κυριος ¹ ὁ Θεος σου, ὁστις ² ἐξηγαγον
(led) σε⁴ ἐκ γης Αἰγυπτου, ἐξ οἰκου δουλειας.

3. Οὐκ ἐσονται ³ σοι ⁴ θεοι ἑτεροι πλην ἐμου ⁵.

4. Οὐ ποιησεις σεαυτῳ ⁶ εἰδωλον, οὐδε ⁷ παντος ⁸
ὁμοιωμα, ⁹ ὁσα ¹⁰ ἐν τῳ οὐρανῳ ¹¹ ἀνω, ¹² και ὁσα
ἐν τῃ γῃ κατω, και ὁσα ἐν τοις ὑδασιν (waters)
ὑποκατω της γης.

5. Οὐ προσκυνησεις ¹³ αὐτοις, οὐδε λατρευσεις ¹⁴
αὐτοις· ἐγω γαρ εἰμι Κυριος ὁ Θεος σου, Θεος

---

1. Κυριος. Catholics will recognise the vocative of this
word in the Kyrie Eleison. The ‘ Κυριακη οἰκια ’, ‘ the
Lord’s House ’, survives more obviously in the Scot.
‘ kirk ’ than in the Eng. ‘ church ’. K. before modern
Gk. names is an abbreviation for Κυριος, equivalent to
‘ Mr.’. 2. ὁστις, an emphatic form of ὁς, see lesson 5.
3. ἐσονται, 3rd person plural of the future of εἰμι. 4. σοι,
dative of συ, which goes N. συ, Acc. σε, Gen. σου, D. σοι.
This dative indicates possession—e.g. οἰκια ἐστι σοι, lit.
‘ a house is to you ’, which is another way of saying, “ You
have a house ”. 5. ἐμου, gen. of ἐγω, which goes thus,
N. ἐγω, A. (ἐ)με, G. (ἐ)μου, D. (ἐ)μοι. πλην (6) is always
followed by gen. 6. σε + αὐτον became one word, with the
gen. σεαυτου, dat. σεαυτῳ. 7. οὐ + δε = οὐδε. 8. παντος
here means ‘ of anything ’. Lit. ‘ of everything ’. The
former meaning occurs several times in this passage, but it
is late Gk., and would not be allowed in Classical Gk., which
in a case like this regularly uses a double negative, and says
‘ of nothing ’, οὐδενος. 9. ὁμοιωμα, the noun from ὁμοιος
(c. 5). 10. ὁσα, n. pl. ‘ as many things as ’. Supply ἐστι
(are). Why not εἰσι ? 11. What planet was named the
old god who symbolised ‘ Heaven ’, οὐρανος ? 12. ἀνω, κατω,
adverbs from the prepositions ἀνα, κατα (up, down), meaning
‘ above, below ’. The form ὑποκατω, ‘ underneath ’, is rare.
13. προσκυνεω, ‘ bow down ’, ‘ make obeisance ’. 14.
λατρευω, ‘ worship ’. Idolatry has become corrupted through
the French. It should have been Idololatry = εἰδωλον +
λατρευω.

ζηλωτης,[15] ἀποδιδους (referring) ἁμαρτιας[16]
πατερων[17] ἐπι τεκνα,[18] ἑως (until) τριτης και
τεταρτης γενεας[20] τοις μισουσι[21] (for those hating)
με.

6. Και ποιων ἐλεος[22] εἰς χιλιαδας[23] τοις ἀγαπωσι[24]
με και τοις φυλασσουσι[25] τα προσταγματα[26] μου.

7. Οὐ ληψει[32] (2nd pers. sing. fut. middle
λαμβανω—take : see c. 14) το ὀνομα Κυριου του Θεου
σου ἐπι ματαιω[27] οὐ γαρ καθαριει[28] Κυριος ὁ Θεος
σου τον λαμβανοντα[21] το ὀνομα αὐτου ἐπι ματαιω.

---

15. ζηλωτης, 'jealous', is derived from ζηλος, 'rivalry',
'zealous'. 16. ἁμαρτια, 'a miss', 'error', 'sin'. 17.
πατερων, gen. pl. of πατηρ. See first word of your
Pronunciation Exercise. 18. τεκνον, 'child'. Caesar did
*not* say, " Et tu, Brute " when he was murdered. He spoke
in Gk., as many cultured Romans often did, and said to
Brutus, " και συ, τεκνον " (" You too, son ! "). 20. For
τριτος, τεταρτος, see Numerals. γενεα, 'generation'; cf
genealogy, a study of the family. 21. The article and the
participle, ὁ μισων, means 'The man hating', i.e. 'He who
hates', or, in the plural, 'Those who hate'. This construction is very common in Gk. It occurs twice in the
next verse. For the meaning cf. miso-gynist, μισω-γυνη,
'woman-hater'. 22. This is the noun (mercy), which is to
be seen in the verb Eleison of the Kyrie Eleison. It is close
to the Gk. word ἐλεημοσυνη, which became shortened in
Eng. to 'alms' (a *singular* word). 23. χιλιαδες, 'thousands'. 24. 'Αγαπωσι. You have seen the noun before
(c. 7). The verb has an α in the stem, and in the dat. pl.
of the participle might have been ἀγαπα-ουσι, like μισουσι
and φυλασσουσι, but the vowels run together to form -ω.
25. φυλασσουσι, 'guard'. The imperative middle 'guard
yourself ! ' was used in the second sentence of c. 4. 26.
προσταγματα, 'commands'. 27. ματαιος, 'vain', useless'.
ἐπι ματαιω, 'for a vain (purpose)'. 28. καθαριει, 'will
make καθαρος' (c. 5), 'unstained with guilt'. This verb
is future, although it has no 'σ'. Though other verbs
whose stem ends in ζ have σ in the future, all verbs ending
in -ιζω have the following endings in the future : -ιω, -ιεις,
-ιει, -ιουμεν, -ιειτε, -ιουσι.

8. Μνησθητι (remember) την ἡμεραν των σαββατων, [29] ἁγιαζειν [30] αὐτην.

9. Ἐξ [31] ἡμερας ἐργασει [32] (middle) και ποιησεις παντα τα ἐργα σου

10. Τῃ δε ἡμερᾳ τῃ ἑβδομῃ [33], σαββατα Κυριῳ τῳ Θεῳ σου· οὐ ποιησεις ἐν αὐτῃ παν [8] ἐργον, συ και ὁ υἱος σου, και ἡ θυγατηρ [34] σου, ὁ παις [35] σου, και ἡ παιδισκη σου, ὁ βους [36] σου και το ὑποζυγιον [37] σου, και παν κτηνος [38] σου, και ὁ προσηλυτης [39] ὁ παροικων [21] ἐν σοι

11. Ἐν γαρ ἐξ [31] ἡμεραις ἐποιησε (made) Κυριος τον οὐρανον και την γην και την θαλασσαν και παντα τα ἐν αὐτοις, και κατεπαυσε (paused, rested *) τῃ ἡμερᾳ τῃ ἑβδομῃ· δια τουτο [40] εὐλογησε [41] Κυριος την ἡμεραν την ἑβδομην και ἡγιασεν (made holy) αὐτην.

---

29. Σαββατα. The word is usually plural in Gk. In Hebrew it means ' rest '. 30. ἁγιος, ' holy '. Look up Hagiology. ἁγιαζω, ' to make holy'; notice the Infinitive ending in -ειν. 31. ἐξ. See Numerals. Extent of time *over* which something happens is shown by the accusative case in Gk. 32. ἐργασει. Do one's ἐργα. Be careful of this 2nd pers. fut. mid.—it looks like 3rd sing. fut. active (see c. 14). 33. See Numerals— how often does the French journal ' Hebdomadaire ' appear? 34. θυγατηρ. Ger. tochter, Scot. dochter, Eng. daughter. 35. παις, means a servant in the house, as well as a ' boy '. We sometimes refer to natives as ' boys '. The next noun is its feminine counterpart. 36. βους. The digamma reappears in the Lat. bos, bovis. Cf. Eng. ' bovine '. 37. ὑποζυγιον ὑπο, ' under ', and ζυγον, ' yoke ' = a beast of burden. 38. κτηνος, neuter, ' possession ', nearly always of cattle. 39. προσηλυτης, lit. one who comes to you. Look up ' proselyte '. He has his house alongside in your land. 40. δια τουτο, lit. ' on account of this ', i.e. therefore. 41. εὐλογησε, eulogy is a ' speaking well of someone '—' blessed '.

* This Intransitive meaning to an Active form is late Gk.; in Classical Gk. it would more likely be Middle (see c. 14).

12. Τιμα⁴² (imperative) τον πατερα σου και την
μητερα σου ἱνα (in order that) εὐ σοι γενηται
(subjunctive, see c. 28 : it may become, or be) και
ἱνα μακροχρονιος⁴³ γενῃ (2nd pers. γενηται) ἐπι της
γης της ἀγαθης ἡν Κυριος ὁ Θεος σου διδωσι (gives)
σοι.

13. Οὐ μοιχευσεις.⁴⁴

14. Οὐ κλεψεις.

15. Οὐ φονευσεις.⁴⁵

16. Οὐ ψευδομαρτυρησεις⁴⁶ κατα⁴⁷ του⁴⁸ πλησιον
σου μαρτυριαν⁴⁶ ψευδη (acc. fem.).

17. Οὐκ ἐπιθυμησεις⁴⁹ την γυναικα του πλησιον
σου, οὐκ ἐπιθυμησεις την οἰκιαν του πλησιον σου,
οὐτε τον ἀγρον⁵⁰ αὐτου, οὐτε τον παιδα αὐτου, οὐτε
την παιδισκην αὐτου, οὐτε τον βουν αὐτου, οὐτε το
ὑποζυγιον αὐτου, οὐτε παν κτηνος αὐτου, οὐτε ὁσα
τῳ πλησιον σου ἐστιν.

### Exercise

Translate into English :—

1. οἱ βαρβαροι λατρευουσι τῳ εἰδωλῳ. 2. ὁ
Ἀγαμεμνων οὐ θελει φονευειν το τεκνον. 3. τα

---

42. The imperative is used when one gives a command
—'honour'. 43. You have had both μακρος and χρονος
before. This adjective is a combination of both. 44.
μοιχευσεις, 'commit adultery'. 45. φονευσεις, 'shed blood'
—i.e. 'do murder'. 46. ψευδομαρτυρησεις. See Eng. words
beginning pseudo-. You have had μαρτυς (c. 3). What does
this mean? (For ψευδη, see c. 12.) 47. κατα, 'against'.
The prepositions have many meanings, and need very careful learning (see c. 22). 48. ὁ πλησιον, lit. 'the one near'
—i.e. neighbour. πλησιον is an adverb, and therefore does
not change its ending. 49. ἐπιθυμησεις. Θυμος, 'heart',
'soul'—ἐπι, 'on', 'to set one's heart on', 'covet'. 50
ἀγρος, Lat. ager—cf. 'agriculture—tilling of the field'.

ὑποзυγια πινει τον κρουνον. 4. τι οὐ χορευετε, ὦ ἑταιροι ; 5. φυλασσομεν τα δενδρα ἐν τοις ἀγροις. 6. οὐ κλεψεις το βιβλιον μου. 7. οὐ προσκυνησομεν τῷ ἡλιῳ, ὦ βαρβαροι. 8. ἀβρως χορευσουσιν αἱ γυναικες περι το δενδρον. 9. ὁ πατηρ οὐ τιμησει τα τεκνα, τα δε τεκνα μισησει τον πατερα. 10. οὐ πραξω το ἐργον τῃ ἑβδομῃ ἡμερᾳ. 11. τις πεισει τον ποιητην κλεπτειν το του ἑταιρου ἀγαθον ὀνομα ; 12. παντες (all) ποιησετε το του στρατηγου ἐργον. 13. ὁ στρατηγος πινει τον των στρατιωτων οἰνον. 14. φονευουσιν οἱ ἀνθρωποι τα ὑποзυγια. 15. πεισομεν την παιδισκην ποιειν το ἐργον. 16. ἀγαθα ἐστι τα του Κυριου ἐργα. 17. τῃ ἑβδομῃ ἡμερᾳ, ὦ βαρβαροι, κλεψει ὁ Κυριος την σεληνην. 18. αὐτος λυσω το ὑποзυγιον. 19. θελομεν χορευειν παντες ἐν κυκλῳ. 20. τυπτει τα τεκνα την κορην.

## KEY

1. The barbarians serve the idol. 2. Agamemnon does not wish to slay the child. 3. The beasts of burden are drinking the stream. 4. Why do you not dance, comrades ? 5. We guard the trees in the fields. 6. You shall not steal my book. 7. We shall not bow down to the sun, barbarians. 8. The women will dance delicately round the tree. 9. The father will not honour the children, and the children will hate the father. 10. I shall not do the task on the seventh day. 11. Who will persuade the poet to steal the good name of the (i.e. his) comrade ? 12. You will all do the general's task. 13. The general is drinking the soldiers' wine. 14. The men are slaying the beasts. 15. We shall persuade the maid to do the task. 16. Good are the works of the Lord. 17. On the seventh day, barbarians, the Lord will steal the moon. 18. I myself shall loose the beast. 19. We all wish to dance in a ring. 20. The children are striking the girl.

# CHAPTER IX

## THIRD DECLENSION. CONSONANT STEM

THE 3rd declension is a portmanteau one, and includes all nouns not belonging to the 1st and 2nd. It is consequently a large one, and far commoner in Greek than either of the first two. One standard Greek Grammar (Abbott and Mansfield) gives no fewer than forty-five different forms, another (Rutherford) sixty, and if you wanted to write Greek correctly or get full marks on a senseless grammar paper, you would have to know all these, including the declension of the Greek words for ' mustard ', ' fore-arm ', and ' liver ' ! But if you want to *read* Greek, all that matters is that you recognise a 3rd declension word when you see it in all the cases, and be able to find the word in a dictionary if you do not know its meaning. The first of these two things is comparatively simple, since as far as the termination of the cases goes, the many apparent forms can be reduced *to two main types* :—

 1. So-called Consonantal stems (this chapter will deal only with these).
 2. Vowel or Diphthong stems.

But because the 3rd declension has so many variations for the termination of the nominative singular, and dictionaries list words by the nominative singular and not by the stem, therefore a nodding acquaintance at least must be made with the commonest of the forms, in the nominative, if you want to acquire any facility in reading Greek.

## I. THE CONSONANTAL STEMS

These can be reduced to five masculine and feminine types and one neuter, though each type in all cases, except the nominative singular, ends in the same letter (or letters), thus :—

| Masc. or Fem. Nouns. | Neuter. | Masc. or Fem. | Neuter. |
|---|---|---|---|
| *Sing.* | | *Plur.* | |
| Nom.     many forms | -μα | Nom. stem. + ες | -ματα |
| | | Acc.  „  + ας | -ματα |
| Acc. stem + α | -μα | Gen.  „  + ων | -ματων |
| Gen.  „  + ος | -ματος | Dat.  „  + σι(ν) | -μασι(ν) |
| Dat.  „  + ι | -ματι | | |

How to Find the Stem.—The stem is that part of the word to which the case-endings are added. It cannot always be found from the nominative singular, but it can by dropping the -ος of the genitive. E.g. ἐλπις, ' hope '—genitive ἐλπιδος. ∴ stem ἐλπιδ-; χρημα, ' thing ' —genitive χρηματος. ∴ χρηματ-.

How to Find the Nominative

*Singular Nominative.* The numerous forms are best learnt by practice, but it is sometimes formed by adding ' ς ' to the stem after dropping the consonant—e.g. ἐλπις—and sometimes by adding ' ς ' and making the necessary euphonic changes—

e.g. *stem* γυπ- : *nom.* γυψ (for γυπς), ' vulture '.

„    φλεβ- :    „    φλεψ (for φλεβς), ' vein '
                                    (phlebitis).

„    νυκτ- :    „    νυξ (for νυκτς), ' night '.

Masculine and feminine stems in ν, ρ and ς lengthen the final vowel of the stem if it is short, but keep it if it is long.

e.g. *stem* δαιμον- : *nom.* δαιμων—' divinity ' (demon),
    *gen.* δαιμονος.

    *stem* λιμεν- : *nom.* λιμην—' harbour ', *gen.* λιμενος.

but *stem* λειμων- : *nom.* λειμων—' meadow ', *gen.*
    λειμωνος.

    *stem* θηρ- : *nom.* θηρ—' beast ', *gen.* θηρος.

*Dative Plural.   N.B.*—When -σι is added to the stem, euphonic change must frequently be made thus :—

    ἐλπις : ἐλπισι(ν) instead of ἐλπιδ-σι(ν).
    γυψ : γυψι(ν).
    νυξ : νυξι(ν).

We can now take examples of the five commonest *Consonantal (M. & F.) types.*

1. *Stem in* -ντ.

            λεων, ' lion ' (leonine).

|  | Sing. | Plur. |
|---|---|---|
| N. | λεων | λεοντες |
| A. | λεοντα | λεοντας |
| G. | λεοντος | λεοντων |
| D. | λεοντι | λεουσι (note this carefully— euphonic change for λεοντ-σι). |

*Similarly,*

| Nom. | Stem. | Gen. sing. | Dat. plur. | Eng. | Eng. Deriv. |
|------|-------|------------|------------|------|-------------|
| γερων | γεροντ- | γεροντος | γερουσι | old man | gerontocratic |
| δρακων | δρακοντ- | δρακοντος | δρακουσι | snake | dragon |
| ἐλεφας | ἐλεφαντ- | ἐλεφαντος | ἐλεφασι | elephant | elephantine |
| γιγας | γιγαντ- | γιγαντος | γιγασι | giant | gigantic |

N.B.—In the following examples practise declining aloud the words, and try to discover for yourself the English derivative. In each of the five types, nouns that you have already met are placed first. Incidentally in Chapter III, out of fifty-one words thirty-eight are 3rd declension—which all goes to show how common this declension is !

### 2. Stems in Gutturals (-γ, -κ, -χ).

| Nom. | Stem. | Gen. sing. | Dat. plur. | Eng. | Deriv. |
|------|-------|------------|------------|------|--------|
| γ ⎰ φλοξ | φλογ- | φλογος | φλοξι | flame | phlox |
| φαλαγξ | φαλαγγ- | φαλαγγος | φαλαγξι | phalanx | — |
| λαρυγξ | λαρυγγ- | λαρυγγος | λαρυγξι | larynx | — |
| συριγξ | συριγγ- | συριγγος | συριγξι | pipe | syringe |
| πτερυξ | πτερυγ- | πτερυγος | πτερυξι | wing | pterodactyl |
| αἰξ | αἰγ- | αἰγος | αἰξι | goat | — |
| κ ⎰ κλιμαξ | κλιμακ- | κλιμακος | κλιμαξι | ladder | climax |
| ἀνθραξ | ἀνθρακ- | ἀνθρακος | ἀνθραξι | ashes | anthracite |
| σαρξ | σαρκ- | σαρκος | σαρξι | flesh | sarcophagus |
| φυλαξ | φυλακ- | φυλακος | φυλαξι | guard | prophylactic |
| χ ὀνυξ | ὀνυχ- | ὀνυχος | ὀνυξι | nail | onyx |

### 3. Stems in Dentals (-δ, -τ, -θ). N.B.—A few nouns ending in -ις make the accusative singular in -ιν.

| Nom. | Stem. | Acc. sing. | Gen. sing. | Dat. plur. | Eng. | Deriv. |
|------|-------|------------|------------|------------|------|--------|
| ἐρις | ἐριδ- | ἐριν | ἐριδος | — | strife | — |
| χαρις | χαριτ- | χαριν | χαριτος | χαρισι | grace or favour | — |
| ὀρνις | ὀρνιθ- | ὀρνιν | ὀρνιθος | ὀρνισι | bird | ornithology |

BUT

| Nom. | Stem. | Acc. sing. | Gen. sing. | Dat. plur. | Eng. | Deriv. |
|---|---|---|---|---|---|---|
| ἐλπις | ἐλπιδ- | ἐλπιδα | ἐλπιδος | ἐλπισι | hope | — |
| ἀσπις | ἀσπιδ- | ἀσπιδα | ἀσπιδος | ἀσπισι | shield | aspidistra |
| παις | παιδ- | παιδα | παιδος | παισι | child or boy | peda-gogue |
| Ἑλλας | Ἑλλαδ- | Ἑλλαδα | Ἑλλαδος | — | Greece | Helladic |
| λαμπας | λαμπαδ- | λαμπαδα | λαμπαδος | λαμπασι | torch | lamp |
| ἐρως | ἐρωτ- | ἐρωτα | ἐρωτος | ἐρωσι | love | erotic |
| γελως | γελωτ- | γελωτα | γελωτος | — | laughter | |
| πους | ποδ- | ποδα | ποδος | ποσι | foot | octopus, chiropodist |

4. *Stems ending in* ρ. Most lengthen the final vowel to form the nom. A few are irregular in the cases underlined, though the longer forms (πατερος, ἀνερος * etc.) are sometimes found in poetry.

| Nom. | Acc. | Gen. | Dat. sing. | Dat. plur. | Eng. | Deriv. |
|---|---|---|---|---|---|---|
| ἀηρ | ἀερα | ἀερος | ἀερι | — | air | aerial aeroplane |
| αἰθηρ | αἰθερα | αἰθερος | αἰθερι | — | upper air | ether, ethereal |
| <u>χειρ</u> | χειρα (poet.) | χειρος | χειρι | χερσι | hand | chiro-podist |
| | χερα | χερος | χερι | | | |
| πατηρ | πατερα | <u>πατρος</u> * | πατρι | πατρασι | father | patriarch |
| μητηρ | μητερα | <u>μητρος</u> | <u>μητρι</u> | <u>μητρασι</u> | mother | metro-polis |
| θυγατηρ | θυγατερα | <u>θυγατρος</u> | θυγατρι | θυγατρασι | daughter | |
| γαστηρ | γαστερα | <u>γαστρος</u> | γαστρι | — | stomach | gastritis |

*but* ἀνηρ omits ε throughout, and inserts δ, thus :—

| | | | | | | |
|---|---|---|---|---|---|---|
| — | ἀνδρα | <u>ἀνδρος</u> * | ἀνδρι | ἀνδρασι | man | philander |
| ἀστηρ | ἀστερα | <u>ἀστερος</u> | ἀστερι | <u>ἀστρασι</u> | star | aster |
| ἠρ,ἐαρ(n.) | ἠρ | ἠρος | ἠρι | — | spring | — |
| θηρ | θηρα | θηρος | θηρι | θηρσι | beast | — |
| κρατηρ | κρατηρα | κρατηρος | κρατηρι | κρατηρσι | bowl | crater |
| πυρ (n.) | πυρ | πυρος | πυρι | — | fire | pyrex, pyro-technics |
| ῥητωρ | ῥητορα | ῥητορος | ῥητορι | ῥητορσι | speaker | rhetoric |

Translate :—

1. οἱ μεν ἄνθρωποι ἐχουσι χειρας και ποδας, οἱ δε θηρες μονον ποδας.

2. τοις μεν ὀρνισιν εἰσι πτερυγες, τῳ δε λεοντι οὐ.

3. αἱ λαμπαδες λαμπουσιν ἐν ταις των ʿΕλληνων χερσιν.

4. οἱ ἀνδρες ἐλευθερουσι τας γυναικας και τους παιδας ἐκ των του πυρος φλογων.

5. τα του γεροντος ὀμματα ἐλαμπε πολλῃ ἐλπιδι.

6. δυο (two) ἄνθρωποι παρεκυψαν (looked out) ἐκ δεσμωτηριου (prison) ὁ μεν εἰς πηλον ἐβλεψε (looked), ὁ δε ἀστερας.

### KEY

1. Men have hands and feet, but wild beasts only feet.
2. Birds have wings (lit. to birds there are wings), but the lion has not.
3. The torches shine in the hands of the Greeks.
4. The men free the women and children from the flames of the fire.
5. The old man's eyes were shining with much hope.
6. Two men looked out from a prison; one saw mud, the other stars.

### Passages from Greek Literature

1. οὐ παντος ἀνδρος εἰς Κορινθον ἐσθ᾽ ὁ πλους.

2. ʿΕλληνες ἀει παιδες, γερων δε ʿΕλλην οὐκ ἐστιν.  Plato.

3. δις παιδες οἱ γεροντες.

4. ἐλεφαντα ἐκ μυιας ποιει.

---

1. Proverb. ʿ Non cuivis homini contingit adire Corinthum ʾ—ʿ We can't all go to New York.ʾ ἐστι with gen. often means, ʿ it is the characteristic, duty, fate, etc., of ʾ—as if that ʿ belongs to him ʾ.
2. Said by an Egyptian priest to Solon. Keats understood this quality of the Greeks—ʿ for ever panting and for ever young ʾ.
3. Sc. εἰσι. How can you tell which word is the subject?
4. Proverb. Cf. our ʿ he makes a mountain out of a molehill ʾ.

5. ἀλλ' εἰσι μητρι παιδες ἀγκυραι βιου.—Soph.
6. ἀνδρων ἐπιφανων πασα γη ταφος.—Thuc.
7. και γαρ χερος χειρ και ποδος πους ἐνδεης.
8.                              ὠ παιδες ῾Ελληνων ἰτε,
ἐλευθερουτε πατριδ', ἐλευθερουτε δε
παιδας, γυναικας, θεων τε πατρῳων ἑδρας,
θηκας δε προγονων· νυν ὑπερ παντων ἀγων.
Æsch.
9. ὠ βαρβαρ' ἐξευροντες ῾Ελληνες κακα.—Eur.

*Epigrams*

*On a Boy of Twelve*

10. Δωδεκετη τον παιδα πατηρ ἀπεθηκε Φιλιππος
ἐνθαδε την πολλην ἐλπιδα, Νικοτελην.
Callimachus.

---

6. From the famous Funeral Oration of Pericles. These
words are inscribed over the War Memorial in front of the
Palace in Athens. Sc. ἐστι, as frequently.
8. The war-cry of the Gk. sailors at the battle of Salamis
(from the play celebrating the victory—the ' Persians ' of
Æschylus). νυν ὑπερ παντων ἀγων, ' the fight now is for
your all '. Metaxas, the Prime Minister of Greece, quoted
these words in his proclamation to the Gk. people in Oct.,
1940, when Italy invaded Greece, and Greece refused to
give in. γυναικας, C. 7, c. 13.
9. ἐξευροντες, aor. part. from ἐξευρισκω—find out, devise.
A line from ' The Trojan Women ', by Euripides.
10–12. Three ' Epigrams ', the first by Callimachus (an
epitaph on a boy of twelve), the next two by Plato. They
come from a collection of over 6000 short elegiac poems,
known as the *Palatine Anthology*, because it was discovered
in the Palatine Library at Heidelberg by a young scholar of
nineteen in 1606. Over 300 writers are included, ranging
from about 700 B.C. to A.D. 900. The collection consists of
epitaphs, dedications, love-poems, reflections on life and
death and other subjects—thus giving us a glimpse into the
Gk. mind through seventeen centuries. The word ' epigram '
is misleading. In Gk., ἐπιγραμμα means only a ' thing
written—on (something) ', and has none of the straining

## Star-gazing

11. Ἀστέρας εἰσαθρεῖς, Ἀστὴρ ἐμός· εἴθε γενοίμην
οὐρανος, ὡς πολλοῖς ὄμμασιν εἰς σε βλέπω.

Plato.

## Aster

12. Ἀστὴρ πρὶν μὲν ἔλαμπες ἐνὶ ζῳοισιν Ἐῴος
νῦν δὲ θανὼν λαμπεις Ἐσπερος ἐν φθιμένοις.

Plato.

---

after cleverness, sting-in-the-tail aim of Eng. epigrams.
These three little gems are good examples of the directness
and simple charm of the Gk. which is so difficult to reproduce
in Eng. When you have puzzled them out, you might like
to compare the well-known renderings by Shelley of the two
from Plato with a more literal translation.

11. " Sweet child, thou star of love and beauty bright,
    Alone thou lookest on the midnight skies;
Oh, that my spirit were yon heaven of light,
    To gaze upon thee with a thousand eyes."
    —SHELLEY.

This is at least twice as long as the Gk., which contains, for
instance, nothing of ' love and beauty bright '. S. misses
the play upon the words in Gk., ἀστέρας, ἀστηρ, and his last
two lines have less simplicity and restraint. Ἀστηρ is a
boy's name, as well as meaning ' a star '. ' Stella ' is perhaps
the nearest Eng. equivalent. Try to make your own translation. Criticise the following attempt :—

" Gazing at stars, my Stella ? Might I be
The sky with many eyes to gaze on thee."—F. K. S.

12. " Thou wert the morning star among the living,
    Ere thy fair light had fled;
Now having died thou art as Hesperus giving
    New splendour to the dead."—SHELLEY.

S. misses ἔλαμπες, λαμπεις, ' fair light ', ' new splendour ', not
in the Gk. Try to improve on—

" Aster, once our Morning Star,
    What light on men you shed;
Now having died, an Evening Star
    You shine among the dead."—F. K. S.

## VOCABULARY

πλους, voyage.

Ἑλλην, a Greek (v. c. 10).

ἀει, adv. always.

δις, twice.

μυια, -ας, fly.

ἐκ, prep. with gen., out of (written ἐξ before vowel).

ἀγκυρα, -ας, anchor.

ἐπιφανης, adj. appearing manifest, conspicuous (epiphany), famous.

ἐνδεης, adj. (with gen.) lacking, in need (of).

ἰτε, go (ye), imper. of εἰμι (ibo).

ἐλευθερουτε, free (ye).

πατρις, -ιδος, country.

πατρῳος, paternal, ancestral.

ἑδρα, -ας, seat, so (of the gods) temples.

θηκη, -ης, chest, tomb.

προγονος, -ου, ancestor (born before).

νυν, adv., now.

ὑπερ, prep. with gen. ' on behalf of '.

ἀγων, contest, c. 10.

δωδεκετης, twelve years old (why the Dodecanese ?).

ἐνθαδε, adv., here.

ἀπεθηκε, laid by (v. c. 16).

πολλην, acc. fem. sing. of πολυς, much. Here = great.

εἰσαθρεω, I gaze on.

ἐμος, my.

εἰθε γενοιμην, would I were ! (εἰθε, a particle expressing a wish.)

ὡς, conj. that (expressing purpose).

ὀμμα, eye.

βλεπω, I see, look.

πριν, adv. formerly.

μεν, particle pointing the way to a following δε, ' On the one hand ' but better omitted in Eng.

ἐλαμπες, you were shining. Impf. tense (v. c. 11).

λαμπω, I shine (lamp).

ἐνι, poet. for ἐν.

Ἐῳος, adj. of Dawn.

ἀποθνησκω (see c. 15).

θανων, having died. } (both irregular verbs).

φθιμενοις, the dead.

# CHAPTER X

## THIRD DECLENSION NOUNS (continued)

5. *Stems in Nasal ν.* There is a large number of nouns ending in ν (mostly -ην or -ων) which are not declined like λεων (see previous chapter), but thus:—

| | Sing. | Plur. | | Sing. | Plur. |
|---|---|---|---|---|---|
| N. | λιμην (harbour) | λιμενες | | μην (month, deriv. moon) | μηνες |
| A. | λιμενα | λιμενας | | μηνα | μηνας |
| G. | λιμενος | λιμενων | | μηνος | μηνων |
| D. | λιμενι | λιμεσι | | μηνι | μησι |

*Like* λιμην *are declined—*

| | Meaning. | Deriv. |
|---|---|---|
| ποιμην, | shepherd | (Philo-poemen) |
| φρην, | mind | (phreno-logy) |

*Like* μην*—*

| | Meaning. | Deriv. |
|---|---|---|
| Ἑλλην, | a Greek | (Hellenic) |
| Σειρην, | a Siren | (siren) |

| | Sing. | Plur. | | Sing. | Plur. |
|---|---|---|---|---|---|
| N. | λειμων (meadow) | λειμωνες | | ἀηδων (nightingale) | ἀηδονες |
| A. | λειμωνα | λειμωνας | | ἀηδονα | ἀηδονας |
| G. | λειμωνος | λειμωνων | | ἀηδονος | ἀηδονων |
| D. | λειμωνι | λειμωσι | | ἀηδονι | ἀηδοσι |

*Like* λειμων *are declined—*

| | Meaning. | Deriv. |
|---|---|---|
| ἀγων, | contest struggle | (agony) |
| χειμων, | winter, storm | |
| χιτων, | tunic | (chiton) |
| πυλων, | gateway | (pylon) |

*Like* ἀηδων*—*

| | Meaning. | Deriv. |
|---|---|---|
| τεκτων, | crafts-man | (architect) |
| χθων, | earth | (chthonian) |
| ἡγεμων, | general | (hegemony) |
| δαιμων, | divinity | (demon) |
| εἰκων, | image | (iconoclast) |
| χιων, | snow | |

Can you now translate this lovely fragment of Sappho?

ἦρος ἄγγελος ἱμεροφωνος ἀηδων

ἱμερος, 'yearning'. ἱμεροφωνος adj. 'of lovely voice'—the voice of desire.

6. *Neuter nouns with termination in* -μα. There are hundreds of these—we had twelve in the early chapters. How many of them can you remember, and what does the ending -μα usually denote? (See c. 3.) They all have stem -ματ- and decline like (το) χρημα, '*thing*' (in plur. often 'money ').

|  | Sing. | Plur. |
|---|---|---|
| N.V.A. | χρημα | χρηματα |
| G. | χρηματος | χρηματων |
| D. | χρηματι | χρημασι |

*Note* that the final consonant of stem drops out before the termination -σι of the dative plural.

Here are some common examples with English derivatives. Cover up all but the first column, and try to discover their meanings. The first four you have had already.

|  | Meaning. | Deriv. | Notes. |
|---|---|---|---|
| δραμα | — | — | |
| κυμα | — | kymograph | |
| στιγμα | — | — | |
| δογμα | — | — | |
| πραγμα | deed, matter, affair | pragmatic | ἀνεστραφη γαρ παντα νυν τα πραγματα.—Palladas. " All the world is now upside down." |
| γραμμα | writing | grammar, telegram | |
| σχημα | figure | scheme, show | |
| μαθημα | lesson, learning | mathematics | τα μαθηματα, 'mathematics '. |

|  | *Meaning.* | *Deriv.* | *Notes.* |
|---|---|---|---|
| παθημα | suffering | sympathy | Gk. proverb—παθηματα μαθηματα—experientia docet. |
| σωμα | body | chromosome | |
| χρωμα | colour | panchro-matic | |
| σημα | sign, tomb | semantics | το σωμα σημα, 'the body is a tomb', because it imprisons the spirit. |
| ὀνομα | name | anonymous onomato-pœia | |
| αἰνιγμα | riddle | enigma | |
| χασμα | a yawning hollow | chasm | |
| ῥευμα | stream, flow | rheum | |
| στομα | mouth | stomata | |
| αἱμα | blood | hæmorrhage | and many medical terms. |
| πνευμα | breath | pneumatic | |
| δερμα | skin | dermatitis | |
| σπερμα | seed | sperm | |
| τερμα | boundary | term | |

7. *Neuter nouns with terminations in* -ος. Also a very common type, but must be carefully distinguished from 2nd declension *masculine* nouns ending in -ος. You have had the following six already. What do they mean? τελος, παθος, χαος, βαθος, φεγγος, θερος, and ἠθος. They all decline like μερος, 'share' or 'part'.

*Sing.*

N.V.A. μερος
    G. μερους (contract-ed from μερε-ος).
    D. μερει (contract-ed from ε-ι).

*Plur.*

N.V.A. μερη (contracted from μερε-α)
    G. μερων (contract-ed from μερε-ων).
    D. μερεσι.

Learn this carefully by heart, and notice the dative plural.  Similarly are declined :—

|  |  | Gen. sing. | N. & A. plur. | Eng. |
|---|---|---|---|---|
| (το) | ἔτος | ἔτους | ἔτη | year. |
|  | κερδος | κερδους | κερδη | gain. |
|  | κλεος |  | κλεα (irreg.) | glory. |
|  | λεχος | λεχους | λεχη | bed. |
|  | μενος | μενους |  | might, strength. |
|  | τειχος | τειχους | τειχη | city wall. |
|  | σκευος |  | σκευη | implement (pl. gear). |

And many other words with English derivatives, e.g.:—

|  |  | Engl. | Deriv. |  |
|---|---|---|---|---|
| (το) | ἄλγος | grief, pain | neuralgia |  |
|  | ἄνθος | flower | { anthology<br>{ polyanthus |  |
|  | ἔθνος | nation, race | ethnology |  |
|  | γενος | family | genealogy |  |
|  | ἔπος | word | epic | τα ἔπη = epic poetry. |
|  | μελος | song | melic | τα μελη = lyric poetry. |
|  | ἔθος | custom |  | 'ethics' is derived from ἠθος = moral character.  Latin. mores. |
|  | πληθος | crowd, multitude | plethora |  |
|  | εἰδος | form | kaleidoscope |  |
|  | βαρος | weight | barometer |  |
|  | ἀχος | pain | ache |  |
|  | ἀκος | cure | panacea | cures all. |
|  | μισος | hate | misogyny |  |
|  | παθος | suffering | sympathy |  |
|  | ψευδος | falsehood | pseudonym |  |
|  | ὀρος | mountain | an Oread |  |
|  | κρατος | might, rule | democracy. |  |
|  | καλλος | beauty | } callisthenics |  |
|  | σθενος | strength |  |  |

Translate :—

1. παντων χρηματων ἀνθρωπος μετρον ἐστιν.

2. ἡ Σφιγξ εἰχε[1] προσωπον μεν γυναικος,[2] στηθος δε και οὐραν λεοντος,[3] και πτερυγας[4] ὀρνιθος.[5]

## 3. HOW TO CATCH A CROCODILE

### (adapted from Herodotus)

Ἐν τῳ Νειλῳ κροκοδειλοι πολλοι εἰσιν· οἱ γαρ Αἰγυπτιοι οὐκ ἀποκτεινουσιν αὐτους, ἱερους νομιζοντες. του δε κροκοδειλου ἡ φυσις[6] ἐστι τοιαδε.[7] τους του χειμωνος μηνας[8] ἐσθιει οὐδεν· τικτει δε ᾠα ἐν τῃ γῃ, και ἐκλεπει, και το πολυ της ἡμερας[9] διατριβει ἐν τῃ γῃ, την δε νυκτα[10] πασαν ἐν τῳ ποταμῳ· θερμοτερον[11] γαρ ἐστι το ὑδωρ[12] του τε αἰθερος[13] και της δροσου.

ἐχει δε ὁ κροκοδειλος ὀφθαλμους ὑος, μεγαλους[14] δε ὀδοντας κατα λογον[15] του σωματος.[16] γλωσσαν δε μονον θηρων οὐκ ἐχει, οὐδε κινει την κατω γναθον.[17] ἐχει δε και ὀνυχας[18] καρτερους και δερμα[19] παχυ. τυφλον δε ἐν τῳ ὑδατι, ἐν δε τῳ ἀερι[20] ὀξυ βλεπει. και οἱ μεν ἀλλοι ὀρνιθες και θηρες φευγουσιν αὐτον, ὁ δε τροχιλος εἰρηναιος αὐτῳ ἐστι· ὁ γαρ κροκοδειλος

---

(Numbers refer to chapter and section.)

1. Impf. of ἐχω, ' I have '.  2. v. 12. 5.  3. v. 9. 1.
4. v. 9. 2.  5. v. 9. 3.  6. v. 13. 1.  7. Of such a kind
(referring to what follows).  v. 24.  Correlatives.  8.
v. 10. 5, acc. of duration of time, v. 22. 1.  9. Large part
of the day.  10. v. 9. 1.  11. Comparative of θερμος, hotter.
12. v. 12. 5.  13. v. 9. 4, ' than the air ', v. 19.  14. Acc.
plur. of μεγας, great.  15. In proportion to, lit. according
to the reckoning of, v. 22 B.  16. v. 10. 6.  17. The lower
jaw (lit. the below jaw).  Gk. uses an adv. in between the
article and a noun as equivalent to an adj.  18. v. 9. 2
19. v. 10. 6.  20. v. 9. 4.

ὧν ἐν τῷ ποταμῷ το στομα ²¹ ἐχει μεστον βδελλων,
ἐκβας ²² δε εἰς ²³ την γην ἐκ του ὑδατος, ἐπειτα χασκει·
ἐνταυθα ὁ τροχιλος εἰσδυνων εἰς το στομα αὐτου
καταπινει τας βδελλας, ὁ δε κροκοδειλος οὐ βλαπτει
αὐτον. των μεν κροκοδειλων ἀγραι ²⁴ εἰσι πολλαι και
παντοιαι, ταυτην ²⁵ δε μονην γραφω. νωτον ὑος ὁ
θηρευτης ²⁶ δελεαζει ²⁷ περι ἀγκιστρον, και ῥιπτει εἰς
μεσον τον ποταμον,²⁸ αὐτος ²⁹ δε ἐπι ³⁰ του χειλους
του ποταμου ἐχων ³¹ ὑν ζωην ³² ταυτην τυπτει. ὁ δε
κροκοδειλος ἀκουει την φωνην και ἀσσει εἰς αὐτην,
ἐντυγχανων δε τῷ νωτῷ καταπινει· ὁ δε θηρευτης
ἑλκει αὐτον εἰς την γην.

ἐνταυθα δε πρωτον πηλῷ πλαττει τους ὀφθαλμους
αὐτου· τουτο δε ποιησας ³³ ῥαδιως αὐτον ἀποκτεινει.

## VOCABULARY

| | |
|---|---|
| ἀγκιστρον, a hook. | διατριβω, I spend. |
| ἀγρα, hunting. | δροσος, -ου, dew. |
| Αἰγυπτιος, -ου, an Egyptian. | εἰρηναιος, *adj.* of peace, |
| ἀκουω, I hear. | peaceful (Irene). |
| ἀποκτεινω, I kill. | εἰσδυνω, I enter. |
| ἀσσω, I dart or rush forward. | ἐκλεπω, I hatch. |
| βλαπτω, I hurt. | ἑλκω, I drag. |
| βδελλα, -ης, leech. | ἐνταυθα, then. |
| γραφω, I write. | ἐντυγχανω, I meet (*dat.*). |

21. v. 10.6. 22. ἐκβας, aor. partic. of βαινω, ' getting out '.
23. εἰς, prep. (with acc.) ' into ', ' on to '. 24. ἀγραι, here =
ways of catching. 25. ταυτην, sc. ἀγραν. ταυτην is acc. fem.
sing. of the demonstrative adj. οὑτος, ' this ', v. 24. 26.
θηρευτης, the man who hunts θηρες—i.e. a ' hunter'. 27.
δελεαρ is a bait. ∴ δελεαζω = ' use as a bait'. 28. Gk.
says, ' middle the river '; we say ' middle of the river '.
29. αὐτος, ' he himself', v. prons. 24. 30. ἐπι with the gen.
means ' on ', v. preps. 22 D. 31. ἐχων, pres. partic. ' having '. 32. Adj., ' alive ', ' living '. 33. ποιησας, aor. partic.
of ποιεω—' having done '.

ἔπειτα, *adv.* next, thereupon.

ἐσθίω, I eat

καταπινω, I drink down, or swallow.

καρτερος, *adj.* strong.

κινεω, I move.

κροκοδειλος, -ου, crocodile.

μεστος, *adj.* full (*gen.*).

μετρον, -ου, measure.

Νειλος, -ου, River Nile.

νομιзω, I think.

νωτον, -ου, back, chine.

ὀδους, ὀδοντος, tooth.

ὀξυς, ὀξεια, ὀξυ, *adj.* sharp, keen.

ὀρνις, -ιθος, bird.

οὐρα, -ας, tail.

οὐδεις, οὐδεμια, οὐδεν, no one, nothing.

οὐδε, nor.

παντοιος, *adj.* of all sorts.

παχυς, παχεια, παχυ, *adj.* thick.

πηλος, -ου, mud.

πλαττω, I mould (plastic), smear.

ῥαδιως, easily, *adv.*

ῥιπτω, I throw.

στηθος, -ους, breast (stethoscope).

τικτω, I bring forth.

τροχιλος, sand-piper or wagtail.

τυφλος, *adj.* blind.

ὑς, ὑος, pig (another form of συς), *acc.* is ὑν.

φευγω, I flee from (acc.).

χασκω, I gape.

χειλος, -ους, lip.

# CHAPTER XI

## THE VERB ; 1ST AND 2ND AORIST AND IMPERFECT ACTIVE, INFINITIVES AND PARTICIPLES

A working knowledge of the Ten Commandments should enable you to recognise your future at once. This may sound ambiguous, but you have seen λατρευ-ω become λατρευσ-ω, and κλεπτω become κλεψω (κλεπτ-σ-ω), and ἐργαζομαι (Middle; see c. 14) ἐργασομαι. It is but a step from the future to the past. The tense by which the Greeks indicated that someone did something in the past is called the AORIST. The same process of adding σ to the stem must be followed. There is also a different set of terminations in which the letter α predominates. But this time it is not merely a question of pinning a tail on the donkey. We have also to tie something on in front. This something is called the AUGMENT, a sign of the past tense in Greek, consisting usually of the letter ε attached as a prefix to the front of the verb. Thus χορευω, ' I dance'; χορευσω, future, ' I shall dance'; ἐ-χορευσα, aorist, ' I danced'. Here is the tense with its endings :—

> ἐχορευσα, I danced.
> ἐχορευσας, you danced (referring to a single person).
> ἐχορευσε(ν), he (or she) danced.

ἐχορευσαμεν, we danced.

ἐχορευσατε, you danced (referring to two or more).

ἐχορευσαν, they danced.

If, however, the verb begins with a vowel, the effect of the augment is to lengthen the vowel, in the same way that you saw a vowel in the stem lengthen when the verb became future—i.e. α and ε become η; ο, ι and υ become ω, ῑ, ῡ respectively. Thus ἁγιαζω in c. 8 became ἡγιασα, and ὁριζω, c. 3, would be ὡρισα. (N.B.—This means that if you have a past tense beginning with η, you may have to look up a word beginning either with α or with ε.)

Sometimes a verb is a *compound* verb—i.e., it consists of a main verb and a preposition (see c. 21). In that case the augment comes in between the preposition and the verb, replacing the final vowel if the preposition has two syllables—e.g. ' I rest ' (see note * on c. 8), κατα-παυω, ' he rested,' κατ-επαυσε. This is of the utmost importance to remember; if you have a word in a past tense, you must take away the augment in looking for the present tense, the form in which the verb will be found in a word list.

## IMPERFECT TENSE

When the Greeks wished to express a *continuous* action in the past, they used a tense called the imperfect, implying something begun, but not finished, in the past. This tense was formed from the *present* with the augment prefixed. Here are its forms—you will notice that the 1st person singular is identical with the 3rd person plural.

ἐχορευον, I was dancing.
ἐχορευες, you (sing.) were dancing.
ἐχορευε(ν), he (or she) was dancing.
ἐχορευομεν, we were dancing.
ἐχορευετε, you (plur.) were dancing.
ἐχορευον, they were dancing.

It is important to grasp the distinction between the aorist and the imperfect, especially as there are many translations of the latter. The aorist narrates a fact that is instantaneous, single, and finished; the imperfect describes an action that is prolonged, sustained, and repeated, or any one of these. Thus ἐχορευον may mean ' I was dancing ', ' I used to dance ', ' I began to dance ', ' I was for dancing ', and so on. Here is a sentence which well illustrates the difference between the imperfect and aorist tenses. The Persian aristocrat, Orontas, who had been considered friendly to the Greeks, is convicted of treachery. As he is led to execution, he is still accorded the honours due to his rank. " And when they saw him (those) who previously were in the habit of bowing down (imperfect) also then bowed down (aorist)." ἐπει δε εἰδον αὐτον οἱπερ προσθεν προσεκυνουν (προσεκυνε-ον) και τοτε προσεκυνησαν. (Notice the position of the augment in the compound verb.)

## EXERCISE. FIRST AORIST AND IMPERFECT

Translate :—

1. ἡ γυνη ἐφονευσε τον Ἀγαμεμνονα. 2. ἠκουσας τους του κριτου λογους. 3. οἱ παιδες ἐχορευον ἐν τῃ ὁδῳ. 4. οὐδεις ἐπραξε το ἐργον ἐκεινῃ τῃ ἡμερᾳ. 5. οἱ δουλοι προσεκυνησαν τῳ δεσποτῃ. 6. ἐξ ἡμερας ἐφυλασσετε την πολιν, ὦ φυλακες. 7. ὁ των θεων πατηρ κατεπινε τους παιδας. 8. αὐτοι οὐκ ἐκλεψαμεν τον χρυσον. 9. ὁ δεσποτης ἐκομιζε το δειπνον τῳ κυνι. 10. ἀει ἀπεβαλλομεν κακον κρεας. 11. οὐχ ὡρισατε τονδε τον νομον ἐμοι, ὦ θεοι. 12. το ῥευμα κατεσυρε την του ποιητου κεφαλην.

## KEY TO EXERCISE

1. The woman slew Agamemnon. 2. You heard the words of the judge. 3. The children were dancing in the road. 4. No one did the task on that day. 5. The slaves bowed down to the master. 6. For six days you were guarding the city, guards. 7. The father of the gods used to devour the (i.e. his) children. 8. We ourselves did not steal the gold. 9. The master was bringing the meal for the dog. 10. We were always throwing away bad meat. 11. You did not define this law for me, gods. 12. The stream was sweeping down the head of the poet.

## SECOND AORIST

The aorist you have learned is called the 1st or the weak aorist. It is formed regularly. But there is another large class of aorists called the 2nd or strong aorist. There are no rules for forming the stems of these. 2nd aorists are like the Cyclops of old : they are each a law unto themselves. You have to learn each one as you come to it. Their endings, however, are always those of the *imperfect* tense. Thus εἶδον, the 2nd aorist, from ὁραω, ' I see ', goes εἶδ-ον, -ες, -ε, -ομεν, -ετε, -ον. The augment, by the way, of εἶδον and εἶχον is irregular, ει replacing ι and η respectively. The 2nd Aor. Participle ends in -ων, and is declined like the noun γερων.

## EXERCISE. SECOND AORIST

Translate :—

1. ὁ κυων ἀπεβαλε το κρεας. 2. ὁ δεσποτης παρεβαλε το κρεας τῳ κυνι. 3. εἰδομεν την του κροκοδειλου σκιαν. 4. οἱ στρατιωται οὐκ ἐλαβον την πολιν. 5. τι ποτε (ever) ὑπελαβετε την σκιαν εἶναι ; 6. οὐκ εἶδες τον κυνα διαβαινοντα τον ποταμον. 7. ἐγω, ὠ πολιται, ἐπει ἐν τοις Λακεδαιμονιοις ἠν ἀει ἐξω εἶχον το δειπνον. 8. ἐκελευσα τον δουλον παιειν τον ὀνον.

## KEY TO EXERCISE

1. The dog threw away the meat. 2. The master threw down the meat before the dog. 3. We saw the shadow of the crocodile. 4. The soldiers did not take the city. 5. What ever did you suppose the shadow to be? 6. You did not see the dog crossing the river. 7. I, citizens, when I was among the Spartans, always had my dinner outside. 8. I ordered the slave to strike the ass.

## Two Fables from Æsop

Æsop was said to be a deformed Phrygian slave of about the sixth century B.C. He was freed by his Samian master, and came to the court of king Croesus, the fabulously wealthy despot of Lydia. Tradition says that Æsop went to Delphi, where he was put to death for sacrilege. We do not know

for certain whether Æsop wrote anything, but these
fables have been ascribed to him.

## Κυων και Δεσποτης

Εἶχε τις ποτε [1] κυνα [2] Μελιταιον [3] και ὀνον. [4] ἀει δε
προσεπαιζε [5] τῳ κυνι. και εἰ ποτε [6] δειπνον ἐξω [7]
εἶχε, ἐκομιζε τι αὐτῳ [8] και προσιοντι [9] παρεβαλε. [10] ὁ
δε ὀνος ἐζηλωσεν, ὡστε [11] προ-εδραμε [12] και αὐτος. [13]
και σκιρτων [14] ἐλακτισε [15] τον δεσποτην. και οὑτος

---

1. ποτε, ' once ', ' ever '. But as first word of a sentence,
it asks a question, ' When ? ' 2. Κυων, 3rd declension stem,
κυν- ; Lat. *canis*. The *Cynics* were a school of philosophers,
who snarled like dogs 3. Μελιταιον. See Acts 28. 1.
Maltese lapdogs were favourite pets of Roman ladies. 4.
ὀνος. See list of proverbs about the ass. 5. προσπαιζω.
Notice the position of the augment. παις, ' boy '; hence
παιζω, ' play ', προσπαιζω, ' play with '. 6. εἰ ποτε, if
ever = whenever. 7 ἐξω—i.e. not at home. 8. αὐτῳ.
Not *to* him, which would require a prep. with the accus.,
but *for* him. 9. προσιοντι. See participles in this chapter.
' For it (the dog) approaching '—i.e. ' As it approached '.
10. παρεβαλε, from παρα, ' alongside ', ' near ', and βαλλω,
' throw '. Here literal. What kind of aor. is παρεβαλε ?
Where is the augment ? What would the imperf. be ?
This word has an interesting history. From ' throw alongside ', comes the idea ' compare '; hence παραβολη, ' a com-
parison ', ' a parable '; then in Latin, *parabolari*, ' to speak
in parables ', and then just ' to speak ', which gives us the
French *parler*, and survives in the English ' parliament '.
11. ὡστε, ' so that ', leads to a Clause of Result. 12. προ-
εδραμε. A very irregular verb ; προ-τρεχω, fut. -δραμουμαι,
aor. -εδραμον. Run up, cf. the word δρομος, ' a place for
running '—e.g. Hippodrome. But the word ' drome ' is
(alas !) frequently used nowadays where no sense of
running is required. 13. και αὐτος, ' himself, too '. 14.
σκιρτων. Another pres. partic. Originally σκιρτα-ων,
' skipping ', ' leaping ', but the α has become swallowed up
in the ω. 15. λακτιζω, ' kick with the heel '. Cf. Acts 26,
14. προς κεντρα λακτιζειν, ' to kick against the pricks '.

ἠγανάκτησε [16] καὶ ἐκελευσε παιοντα [17] αὐτον ἀναγειν
προς τον μυλωνα [18] καὶ προς τουτον δησαι. [19]

### Κυων και Σκια

Κυων ὁς κρεας ἐφερε ποταμον διεβαινε.[20] ἐπει δε
εἰδε την ἑαυτου [21] σκιαν ἐπι του ὑδατος ὑπελαβεν [22]
ἑτερον κυνα εἰναι [23] κρεας κατεχοντα.[24] ἀπεβαλεν [10]
οὖν το ἰδιον [25] κρεας και ὡρμησε [26] το ἐκεινου λαβειν.[27]
ὡστε ἀπωλεσεν [28] ἀμφοτερα. το μεν [29] γαρ οὐκ ἦν, το
δε [29] τῳ ῥευματι [30] κατεσυρετο.[31]

---

16. ἠγανάκτησε, from ἀγανακτεω, 'I grow annoyed'.
Notice the effect of the augment on the vowel. 17. παιοντα.
Another partic. From παιω, 'I strike' (not connected
with παις !). There is no expressed object to ἐκελευσε,
'he ordered'; it is left to be understood. 'He gave
orders (for someone) striking it, to take it, etc.'—i.e. 'to
beat it and take it'. 18. μυλων, cf. Fr. *moulin*. 19. δησαι,
aor. infin., see below. There is no time difference between
the pres. and the aor. infin.

20. From βαινω and δια, go through or across. Notice
the position of the augment. 21. ἑαυτου, gen. of reflex.
pron., 'of himself'—i.e. 'his'. 22. ὑπο and λαμβανω, aor.
ἐλαβον, 'suppose'. A very frequent meaning of this word
is 'to answer'. 23. εἰναι, 'to be'; infin. of εἰμι, 'I
am'. You will have to supply the word 'it' in translating.
24. κατεχοντα. For form see c. 18. 25. ἰδιος, 'private',
'one's own'. Our word 'idiot' comes from the Gk.
ἰδιωτης, a person who took no part in public affairs, for
whom the Gks. had a great contempt. What is an 'idiom'?
26. ὡρμησε. What tense? What is ω when the augment is
removed? 27. Aor. infin. (which aor. ?) from λαμβανω. See
c. 25. 28. ἀπ-ολλυμι, 'lose or destroy'. Bunyan called
the Destroying One Apollyon. Aor. ἀπωλεσε. 29. ἀμφοτερα,
'both'; το μεν . . . το δε. 'The one . . . the other.'
30. ῥευματι. Rheum is 'a flowing' of the mucus, associated
with rheumatism. 31. κατεσυρετο, imperf. passive.

## VOCABULARY

ἀει, always.

δειπνον, dinner.

ἐξω, outside.

κομιζω, bring, carry.

ζηλοω, envy, grow jealous.

ἀναγω, take up.

μυλων, -ωνος, a mill.

δεω, bind.

κελευω, order.

κρεας, -ως (*n*.), meat.

ἐπει, when, since.

κατεχω, hold, possess.

ἀποβαλλω, throw away.

ὁρμαω, start towards.

ἐκεινος-η-ον, that (one), the other.

ὡστε, so that.

κατασυρω, sweep down.

ούν, accordingly.

ὁριζω, define.

### The Classical Ass

In a land of poor communications like Greece, the ass then, as now, played an important part. The habits of this refractory beast must have appealed to the Greek sense of humour, to judge from the numerous proverbial expressions which introduce it.

1. ὀνος λυρας ἀκουων.  An ass hearing the lyre—unappreciative. Pearls before swine.

2. περι ὀνου σκιας.  About an ass's shadow—a trivial cause for dispute.

3. ὀνου ποκαι.  An ass's wool-clippings—an impossibility. Pigeon's milk.

4. ἀπ᾽ ὀνου καταπεσειν.  To fall from an ass—to make a stupid blunder. Put one's foot in it.

5. ὀνος ὑεται.  An ass is rained on—insensitive. The hide of an elephant.

6. ὄνος ἄγω μυστη-  I celebrate the mysteries as
   ρια.                an ass. I do the donkey
                       work. Busman's holiday.

7. ὄνου ὑβριστοτερος.  More destructive than an
                       ass. A bull in a china
                       shop.

8. ὠτ' ὄνου λαβειν.  To get an ass's ears. To
                     be stupid, wear the
                     dunce's cap.

9. ὄνος εἰς ἀχυρα.  An ass into the chaff—gets
                    what he wants. A pig
                    in clover.

10. ὄνου γναθος.  The jaw of an ass. Said of
                  gluttons. A horse's ap-
                  petite.

11. ὄνος ἐν μελισσαις.  An ass in bees—in trouble.
                        Stirring up a hornet's
                        nest.

12. ὄνος ἐν πιθηκοις.  An ass among monkeys.
                       Said of somebody very
                       ugly.

13. ὄνος ἐν μυρῳ.  An ass in perfume. Wasted
                   luxury. A clown at a
                   feast.

14. εἰς ὄνους ἀφ' ἱππων.  To come down from horses
                          to asses. To come down
                          in the world.

## INFINITIVES

" Remember to keep holy the day of the Sabbath." Do you recollect the Greek word for ' to
keep holy '? Look it up again. What is the end-

ing? If a Greek wanted to say, "I wish to dance," he would use (say) θελω, for 'I wish', and for 'to dance', χορευειν. 'To keep holy', 'to dance' and so on, are called infinitives; and the ending (always keep your eye on the rudder!) -ειν, to be attached to the present stem.

But Greek had a whole set of infinitives—more than we have, in fact. A man may appear *to be going to say* something. You may observe a man *to be on the point of jumping* into the water. The Greeks had an infinitive for it. This is the future infinitive, formed as simply as was the future tense. Just insert a σ into the present infinitive. Thus χορευσειν means 'to be about to dance'—a cumbrous English expression for an idea readily expressed in Greek.

There is also an aorist infinitive. In most of the uses of the aorist infinitive there is little TIME difference between the present and the aorist infinitive. Very often it makes little difference to the sense whether the present or the aorist infinitive is employed. The exactness of the Greek language, however, *may* draw an interesting distinction between the present and the aorist infinitive, which it is difficult to bring out in English. The aorist often expresses a single act, whereas the present infinitive expresses a continuous one. Thus, "I love dancing" would be φιλω χορευειν, but "I want to dance (this dance)" would be θελω χορευσαι. Notice how to form the aorist infinitive:—

*1st Aorist*. ἐχορευσα; infinitive (no augment), χορευσαι. Greek is exceedingly fond of the 2nd aorist infinitive. The Greeks seemed, in those verbs which have a 2nd aorist, to use the aorist infinitive in preference to the present infinitive. The ending of the 2nd aorist infinitive is the same as that of the present -ειν, the difference being, of course, that it is added to the aorist stem and not the present.

You may observe this 2nd aorist infinitive in three words of the utmost importance which you have already had :—

λαμβανω, ' I take ', βαλλω, ' I throw ', and όραω, ' I see '.

λαμβανω, aorist, έλαβον; aorist infinitive, λαβειν.

βαλλω, aorist, έβαλον; aorist infinitive, βαλειν.

όραω, aorist, είδον; aorist infinitive, ίδειν.

## EXERCISE. INFINITIVES

Translate :—

1. ὁ ήλιος ἐστι καλος ἰδειν. 2. αἱ κοραι φιλουσιν ἐν κυκλῳ χορευειν. 3. ὡρμησεν ὁ κυων λαβειν το κρεας. 4. τι ἀει θελετε βαλλειν λιθους, ὡ παιδες ; 5. ἐκελευσε τον ἀδελφον ὁ τυραννος κλεψαι το φαρμακον. 6. ὁ κυων θελει προδραμειν προς τον δεσποτην. 7. κακον ἐστιν, ὡ τεκνον, λακτισαι τον ἀδελφον. 8. ὡρα νυν ἐστι καλους λογους λεξαι.

## KEY TO EXERCISE

1. The sun is beautiful to see. 2. The maids love to dance in a ring. 3. The dog started forward to take the meat. 4. Why do you always wish to throw stones, boys ? 5. The king ordered his brother to steal the drug. 6. The dog wishes to run up to the master. 7. It is a bad thing, child, to kick your brother. 8. It is now the season to speak fine words.

The following is a fragment from the *Danaê*, one of the many lost plays of Euripides. It is not unlike Masefield's poem ' I have seen dawn and sunset . . . but the most beautiful thing to me is . . . ', only in this poem it is children. Read it through several times, and see how much you can understand, before consulting the translation. The metre is the six-foot Iambic line (– –, and sometimes – –), the normal metre of Greek drama, into which the language fell so naturally, as English does into blank verse. ' Ī dŏ | nŏt thĭnk | that īt | wĭll raīn | tŏdāy ', only Greek adds another foot ' agaĭn '.


## CHILDREN

Φιλον μεν ἐστι φεγγος [1] ἡλιου τοδε,
καλον δε ποντου [2] κυμ᾽ [4] ἰδειν [3] εὐηνεμόν,[5]
γη τ᾽ ἠρινον [6] θαλλουσα,[7] πλουσιον [8] θ᾽ ὑδωρ,
πολλων τ᾽ ἐπαινον [9] ἐστι [10] μοι λεξαι [11] καλων·
ἀλλ᾽ οὐδεν οὑτω [12] λαμπρον,[13] οὐδ᾽ ἰδειν καλον
ὡς τοις ἁπαισι [14] και ποθῳ [15] δεδηγμενοις [16]
παιδων νεογνων [17] ἐν δομοις ἰδειν φαος.[18]

---

1. Light. 2. The sea. 3. To see. 4. κυμα (κυ-ω, ' I swell '), a swelling, usually of the sea = a wave. 5. Compound adj. no Eng. equiv., ' with a fair wind '. 6. Adj. from ἡρ (spring) lit. (blooming), ' a spring thing ' (acc. neuter). 7. Blooming. 8. Adj. of πλουτος = rich. Any traveller in Greece will appreciate this epithet for water. ἀριστον ὑδωρ (water is best) is a Gk. proverb. 9. Praise. 10. It is possible. 11. Aor. inf. of λεγω (λεγσαι becomes λεξαι). 12. So. 13. Bright. 14. To the childless (α = not, παις = child). 15. Yearning. 16. To those bitten (perf. part. pass. for δακνω = I bite). 17. Contr. for νεογενων, newly born. 18. Uncontracted form of φως = light.

*Translation* (not literal) :—

Sweet is the sunlight, and lovely the sea when the wind blows soft, and earth spring-blooming, and rich, fresh streams. Many beauties could I praise, but no sight is so bright or beautiful, as to the childless and heart-wrung with longing the light of children new-born about the house.

(Literal) :—

Dear on the one hand is this light of the sun, and beautiful to see the fair-winded wave of ocean, and (beautiful is) earth with the bloom of spring (upon her), and rich water, and of many beautiful (things) could I tell the praise. But nothing is so bright, or fair to see, as to the childless, and those bitten with yearning, to see the light of new-born babies in the house.

## PARTICIPLES

' A fellow feeling makes us wondrous kind.'
Methinks the poet would have changed his mind
If he had found some fellow feeling in his coat behind.

The operative words, as they say, are ' fellow feeling '. They do not seem to mean the same thing the second time. Why not ? The answer is partly that they are different parts of speech. ' Fellow ' in the first line is an adjective, qualifying ' feeling '. In the third it is a noun, object of ' found '. What about ' feeling ' ? In the first line it is the subject of the verb ' makes '. (What part of speech ?) In the third line, what does it do ? Well, it does two things. (*a*) It tells us something about the ' fellow ', thus doing the work of an adjective. (*b*) It is obviously connected with the verb ' I feel '. In other words, this word shares or participates in two parts of speech—a verb, and an adjective ; which is why it is called a participle.

We don't think much of participles in English. We have only two worthy of the name. There is the present participle—' He paused with his hand upon the door, *musing* a-while '—or the past participle—' There's that *cursed* knocker again ! ' We may consider the present participle to be active, and the past to be passive. But we are abominably casual about the time of our participles. We have to use our own discretion in order to find out the time of an action referred to in a participle. Look at these :—

    (1) He went out, *crying* bitterly.
    (2) *Saying* " Bah ! " she swept out.

In the first sentence we may have a moist trail of evidence to prove that the exit and the tears were simultaneous. But nobody will imagine in the second that the lady's departure was accompanied by a prolonged and continuous " Bah ! ", like a benighted sheep with a faulty sound-box. Yet there is nothing in the form of these two participles to suggest that their times, relative to that of their main verbs, are different.

The fact is, that we English are suspicious of a lot of fancy participles, and make one or two do all the work.

The Greeks, on the other hand, had stacks of them, " all carefully packed, with the name clearly

written on each ". What is more, they used them
with fantastic precision. In the active voice alone,
not only did they have a present and past, but also
a future and perfect participle. For the moment,
let us postpone the perfect. The future participle
is difficult to render in English, because we haven't
got one, in consequence of which we must have
recourse to the cumbrous English expression
" *About to* do something or other ". The thing to
remember about the present and aorist participles
is that :—

> (*a*) The present participle refers to an action
> going on at the same time as that of the main
> verb.
>
> (*b*) The aorist participle refers to an action
> preceding the time of the main verb.

It must also be remembered that the participle is an
adjective, and must therefore fully agree in number,
gender, and case with the word it qualifies.

> (*a*) διαβαινων τον ποταμον εἰδε κυνα.
> Crossing the river he saw a dog.
>
> (*b*) ἀκουσας τουτο ἀπεβη.
> Having heard this, he went away.

| | Masculine. | Feminine. | Neuter. |
|---|---|---|---|
| Present | χορευ-ων, -οντος | χορευ-ουσα, -ουσης | χορευ-ον, -οντος |
| Future | χορευ-σων, -σοντος | χορευ-σουσα, -σουσης | χορευ-σον, -σοντος |
| Aorist | χορευ-σας, -σαντος | χορευ-σασα, -σασης | χορευ-σαν, -σαντος |

The masculine and neuter genders are declined
like λεων (c. 9), except for the neuter nom., voc. and

acc. which ends -ον or -αν, and the plural -οντα or -αντα. The feminine goes like θαλασσα (c. 7).

## EXERCISE. PARTICIPLES

Translate :—

1. λιθους βαλλων ὁ παις εἰδε τον δεσποτην. 2. ἀκουσαντες του κιθαρῳδου, ἀπεβησαν. 3. λιθον λαβων ὁ παις ἐβαλε προς τον ἀδελφον. 4. κιθαριζων ὁ κιθαρῳδος οὐκ ἠκουσε του κωδωνος. 5. ἐκελευσας τον κιθαρῳδον κιθαριζειν τοις χορευουσιν. 6. ἀπιοντες οἱ παιδες ἐχορευσαν. 7. κελευσας τους ἀλλους ἀκουειν, τι αὐτος ἀπηλθες ; 8. ὁ ποιητης ἐλαβε τους παιδας τους χορευσοντας εἰς το θεατρον. 9. τοιαυτα ἀκουσασαι αἱ γυναικες ἐφυγον. 10. εἰδομεν το ζῳον την ἠπειρον διαβαινον.

## KEY TO EXERCISE

1. (While) throwing stones the boy saw his master. 2. Having heard the harp-player, they went away. 3. Taking up a stone, the boy threw (it) at his brother. 4. (While) playing the harp, the harp-player did not hear the bell. 5. You bade the harp-player to play to those dancing. 6. (While) departing the boys danced. 7. Having ordered the others to hear, why did you go away yourself ? 8. The poet took the boys who were going to dance into the theatre. 9. Hearing such things, the women fled. 10. We saw the animal crossing the mainland.

## "Caller Herring"

[Strabo was a Greek geographer who lived between 69 B.C. and A.D. 20. He wrote two important works : a History, up to the death of Caesar, now lost, and a Geography, almost entirely preserved in 17 books. Strabo's Geography was largely based on his own personal travels in Europe, Asia and Africa. Here (slightly adapted) is an anecdote about Iasus, a town in Asia Minor.]

Ἴασος ἐπι νησῳ κειται,[1] προσκειμενη τῃ ἠπειρῳ. ἐχει δε λιμενα, και το πλειστον του βιου τοις[2] ἐνθαδε ἐστιν ἐκ θαλασσης. και δη και[3] διηγηματα τοιαυτα πλαττουσιν εἰς αὐτην. ἐκιθαριζε γαρ ποτε κιθαρῳδος, ἐπιδειξιν παρεχων. και τεως μεν ἠκουον παντες, ὡς δ' ὁ κωδων ὁ κατα την ὀψοπωλιαν[4] ἐψοφησε, καταλιποντες ἀπηλθον[5] ἐπι το ὀψον πλην ἑνος δυσκωφου. ὁ οὐν κιθαρῳδος προσιων[6] εἰπεν, Ὠ ἀνθρωπε, πολλην σοι χαριν οἰδα[7] της προς με τιμης και φιλομουσιας. οἱ μεν γαρ ἀλλοι, ἁμα τῳ κωδωνος ἀκουσαι,[8] ἀπιοντες οἰχονται. ὁ δε Τι λεγεις; ἐφη· ἠδη γαρ[9] ἐψοφηκεν;[10] εἰποντος δε αὐτου,[11] Εὐ σοι εἰη,[12] ἐφη, και ἀναστας[13] ἀπηλθε και αὐτος.[14]

---

1. κειται, ' lies '; partic. κειμενος, προσ- ' near by '.  2. οἱ ἐνθαδε, lit. ' those there ' = inhabitants.  3. See c. 15, 1, 8.  4. ' The bell, the one to do with (κατα) the sale of fish '. ὀψον is a vague word in Gk., meaning any non-cereal food other than meat; hence it was often used for fish.  A bell rang here to announce the return of the fishermen.  5. ' Went away.'  Note this irregular verb, ἐρχομαι, aor. ἠλθον.  6. ' As he approached ', *present* partic.  7. Lit. ' I know gratitude—i.e. ' I feel gratitude for '—followed by gen.  8. ' Along with the hearing of the bell '—i.e. as soon as they heard the bell. ἀκουσαι is aor. infin., which, together with the neuter article το, makes a verbal noun in Gk., ' the hearing '.  9. γαρ is often difficult to translate and sometimes best omitted.  It often explains words to be supplied—e.g. ' (I ask) for . . .'.  10. Perfect tense.  *Has* it rung?  See next chapter.  11. ' Upon his saying (that it had).'  An expression like this with a partic. is often put into the gen. case.  It stands for " When he said . . ."  It is equivalent to the abl. abs. in Latin.  12. " Good for you!  (may it be) ".  13. " Having stood up."  Aor. partic. from ἀνιστημι.  14. See n. 13. in Κυων και δεσποτης.

## VOCABULARY

ἀκουω, hear (acoustics) (takes gen. case).

ἁμα, along with, at the same time as.

ἀνιστημι, rise up.

ἀπερχομαι, go away.

διηγημα, story.

δυσκωφος, hard of hearing, deaf.

εἰς, one.

ἐνθαδε, here.

ἐπιδειξις, recital.

ἠδη, already.

ἠπειρος (f), mainland (Epirus, N.W. Greece).

καταλειπω, I leave behind (aor., κατελιπον).

κιθαριζω, play the lyre.

κιθαρῳδος, singer, accompanying himself on the lyre

κωδων, bell.

οἰδα (irreg.), I know.

οἰχομαι, I am gone.

ὀψον, fish (see note).

ὀψοπωλια, fish-market.

παρεχω, provide.

πλαττω, invent.

πλειστος (superlative πολυς), most.

προσερχομαι, approach.

τεως, for a while.

τοιουτος, -αυτη, -ουτο, of such a kind.

φιλομουσια, love of music.

χαρις, thanks.

ψοφεω, ring, sound.

# CHAPTER XII

## THE VERB: PERFECT AND PLUPERFECT ACTIVE

THE perfect tense in Greek corresponds to our past tense preceded by the auxiliary 'have'. It expresses a *present* state resulting from a *past* act— e.g. τεθνηκε, is perfect: it means 'he has died', i.e. 'he is dead'. It must be remembered that the perfect tense views the action from the present only. If you have done any Latin, do not run away with the idea that the perfect (as in Latin) can serve to relate an action in the past. That is the aorist's job.

The perfect tense is formed by a sort of grammatical stutter, by putting in front of the verb the first letter of the verb, if it begins with a consonant, followed by the letter ε. Thus λυω, ' I loose ', has the perfect λελυκα, and ποιεω has πεποιηκα. This is called ' reduplication ', because it doubles the first letter. When the verb begins with an aspirated consonant—e.g. χορευω, φιλεω—the ' h ' of the initial letter is dropped in reduplication, its unaspirated equivalent being substituted. Thus χορευω becomes κεχορευκα, φιλεω πεφιληκα, and θαυμαζω τεθαυμακα. Verbs beginning with a vowel lengthen it as they do in the case of an augment. Verbs beginning with two consonants (unless the second be ρ, λ, or ν) or a double consonant (ξ, ζ, ψ) prefix an ε instead of reduplicating—e.g. ευρισκω, ' perfect '—ηὑρηκα

(Heureka! "I've found it!" as Archimedes said, when he jumped out of his bath). σπευδω, 'I hasten', becomes ἐσπευκα, and ζωγρεω, 'I capture', becomes ἐζωγρηκα.

## PERFECT TENSE

λελυκα, I have loosened.
λελυκας, you (singular) have loosened.
λελυκε(ν), he (or she) has loosened.
λελυκαμεν, we have loosened.
λελυκατε, you (plur.) have loosened
λελυκασι(ν), they have loosened.

The participle from this form has a first declension ending in the feminine, but a third declension ending in the masculine and neuter.

## PERFECT PARTICIPLE

| | *Masc.* | | *Fem.* | | *Neuter.* | |
|---|---|---|---|---|---|---|
| | *Sing.* | *Plur.* | *Sing.* | *Plur.* | *Sing.* | *Plur.* |
| N. | λελυκως | -κοτες | λελυκυια | -αι | λελυκος | -κοτα |
| A. | λελυκοτα | -κοτας | λελυκυιαν | -ας | λελυκος | -κοτα |
| G. | λελυκοτος | -κοτων | λελυκυιας | -ων | λελυκοτος | -κοτων |
| D. | λελυκοτι | -κοσι | λελυκυια | -αις | λελυκοτι | -κοσι |

It describes, of course, a state resulting from a past action; thus λελυκως means 'having loosed'— i.e. 'being a deliverer', and πεπωκως (from πινω, 'I drink') really means 'having drunk and still feeling the effects of it'.

## PLUPERFECT TENSE

There *is* another tense in the active, called the pluperfect. We are sure of your enthusiastic support when we counsel you *not* to learn this horror. It is included here in case you want at any time to refer to it. Although it means ' had ', and is the perfect tense viewed from the past, it does not occur with sufficient frequency in Greek to warrant your making a special study of it. It is a spluttering business, because it requires you to put an augment on top of a reduplication.

---

ἐπεπαιδευκη, I had trained.
ἐπεπαιδευκης, you (singular) had trained.
ἐπεπαιδευκει, he (or she) had trained.
ἐπεπαιδευκεμεν, we had trained.
ἐπεπαιδευκετε, you had trained (plur.).
ἐπεπαιδευκεσαν, they had trained.

The real meaning of the first person of this tense is, however, more like ' I used to be (someone's) extrainer '. The aorist is frequently used to translate the English ' had '.

## EXERCISE. PERFECT TENSE

Translate :—

1. νενικηκαμεν τους πολεμιους. 2. ἐζωγρηκασι τον των Ἀθηναιων στρατηγον. 3. τι ποτε γεγονεν ἐν τη πολει ; 4. πολλακις τεθαυμακα τι θελεις τοιαυτα λεγων. 5. ἀποβεβληκας ἐν τω ποταμω παντα τα ἱματια. 6. τοις νενικηκοσιν αὐτος ὁ στρατηγος ἀγγελλει την νικην. 7. ἀκηκοατε ὁτι ὁ ῥητωρ

ὤφληκε τὴν δίκην ; 8. τεθνηκότος τοῦ βασιλέως,
καινόν ἔχομεν ἡγεμόνα. 9. ὁρῶ τὰς γυναῖκας τὰ
πρόσωπα μεταβεβληκυίας. 10. τί κακὸν πεποίηκας
τοὺς πολεμίους ;

## KEY TO EXERCISE

1. We have conquered the enemy. 2. They have captured the general of the Athenians. 3. Whatever has
happened in the city ? 4. I have often wondered what
you mean (lit. wish) in saying such things. 5. You have
lost all your clothes in the river. 6. The general himself is
announcing the victory to those who have conquered.
7. Have you heard that the orator has lost his suit ? 8.
The king being dead, we have a new leader. 9. I see the
women have changed their faces. 10. What harm have
you done the enemy ?

### The Careless Talker

From Theophrastus's *Characters*.

Theophrastus was born in 370 B.C. at Eresus in
Lesbos. He came to Athens, and studied philosophy,
first under Plato and then under Aristotle, who
persuaded him to change his name from Tyrtamus
to Theophrastus (divinely eloquent). He became
one of the Peripatetic School of philosophers, who
derived their name from the practice of walking
up and down as they taught in the Lyceum or the
Garden, whose colonnades and porticoes provided
a famous resort for all men of learning and culture
all the world over. It must be remembered that
the term ' philosophy ' embraced in those days nearly
every branch of then existing knowledge, of which
one of the most important was what we now term
Science. Men of learning in those days seemed to
take all knowledge in their stride. The vast mass of

accumulated knowledge which Aristotle, for instance, had at his fingers' ends is truly staggering. Theophrastus himself wrote two hundred works, and is said to have had two thousand pupils, when he eventually became President of the Lyceum. Among his pupils was Menander, who has been already quoted. The chief fame of Theophrastus rested on a Botanical Work in two volumes, in which he catalogued many kinds of plants. His other and better known extant work is called the Characters—a series of short sketches in which he delineates with wonderful artistry and humour various "types" of city life. Perhaps this literary form had its origin in an after-dinner game beginning with questions—What is Meanness? What is Cowardice etc.? Each sketch begins with a definition, and then proceeds to illustrate from real life the behaviour of the Mean Man, the Coward, and so on. Here is that well-known scourge of modern times, the spreader of false rumours. From the Characters of Theophrastus we are able to gather a good deal about contemporary Athenian life, and we shall see that the Athenian of more than 2000 years ago does not differ much from his modern counterpart in any country. Theophrastus died probably about 287 B.C.

## ΛΟΓΟΠΟΙΙΑ

ἡ δε λογοποιια [1] ἐστι συνθεσις [2] ψευδων λογων και πραξεων ὡσπερ θελει ὁ λογοποιος. ὁ δε λογοποιος

---

1. λογοποιια, 'making of tales', 'manufacture of rumours'. 2. Cf. 'synthesis', 'a putting together'.

τοιουτος³ τις οἱος ἀπαντησας τῳ φιλῳ, εὐθυς κατα-
βαλων το ἠθος⁴ το ἐπι του προσωπου και μειδιασας,
ἐρωτησαι ' Ποθεν συ ; και Πως ἐχεις ; ⁵ και 'Εχεις τι
περι τουδε εἰπειν καινον ; ' ⁶ και οὐκ ἐασας ἀποκριν-
ασθαι (to answer), εἰπειν ' Τι λεγεις ; οὐδεν ἀκηκοας ; ⁷
μελλω ⁸ σε εὐωχησειν καινων λογων.' και ἐστιν
αὐτῳ ἡ στρατιωτης τις ἠ παις 'Αστειου του αὐλητ-
ου ⁹ ἠ Λυκων ὁ ἐργολαβος ¹⁰ ὁς παραγεγονεν ἐξ
αὐτῃς της μαχης. ''Απο τουτου γαρ' φησιν ' ἀκηκοα.' αἱ μεν οὐν ἀναφοραι ¹¹ των λογων τοιαυται
εἰσιν αὐτῳ ὡν οὐδεις οἱος τ' ἐστιν ¹² ἐπιλαβεσθαι (to
lay hands on). λεγει δε ὁτι οὑτοι ἀγγελλουσιν ὡς

---

3. τοιουτος . . . οἱος, ' of such a kind . . . as to '. Th.'s
Characters are all based on this formula. Usually a string
of infinitives follows. 4. See c. 3 and c. 10. Here it
means the 'customary expression'. His face lights up
when he sees a victim. 5. ' How *are* you ? ' but ancient,
as well as modern Gk., used ἐχω. 6. Cf. A. R. Burn, *The
Modern Greeks*, Nelson, 1944. " One finds also (i.e. in
Modern Greece) what amuses the English reader of Greek
Tragedy—the torrent of questions that welcomes each
new arrival on the scene. Where do you come from ?
Where are you going to ? What is your name ? How old
are you ? What is your profession ? Why have you come
here ? etc."; cf. also Acts 17, 21. 7. The perfect of ἀκουω,
ἀκηκοα, is irregularly formed, though its endings are, of
course, regular. 8. μελλω, ' I am going to ', is usually
followed in Gk by a fut. infin. 9. A son of the man who
played in the regimental band would be *bound* to know—
like the charwoman at the War Office ! 10. ' A contractor '.
A big man connected with the Ministry of Supply, who
had just come from the Front Line (from the battle, αὐτης,
itself). 11. ἀναφοραι. ἀνα + φερω = re-fer. His authorities,
to which he refers. Always unget-at-able ! 12. οἱος τ'
εἰμι, a fixed expression = ' I am able '. 13. ὁ βασιλευς,
the four-year-old son of Alexander, supported by the
general Polysperchon. His claim to the throne and defeat
of Cassander, son of the regent, would be as fantastic as it
would be distasteful to Theophrastus and his friends.

Πολυσπερχων και ὁ βασιλευς [13] νενικηκε και Κασαν-
δρον [14] ἐζωγρηκασιν. εἰποντος δε τινος [15] 'Συ δε ταυτα
πιστευεις ; ' ὑπολαμβανει [16] ὁτι ' Γεγονε το πραγμα·
παντες γαρ ἐν τῃ πολει βοωσι και συμφωνουσιν.[17]
ὁ λογος ἐπεντεινει. ταῦτα [18] γαρ λεγουσι παντες
περι της μαχης· πολυς ὁ ζωμος [19] γεγονε. σημειον [20]
δε μοι τα προσωπα των ἐν τοις πραγμασιν.[21] ὁρω
γαρ αὐτων παντων μεταβεβληκοτα.[22] παρακηκοα δε
και παρα [23] τουτοις κρυπτομενον (is in hiding) τινα
ἐν οἰκιᾳ ἠδη πεμπτην ἡμεραν,[24] ἡκοντα ἐκ Μακεδονιας,
ὁς παντα ταυτα οἶδε. δει δ' αὐτον σε μονον εἰδεναι.' [25]
πασι δε τοις ἐν τῃ πολει προσδεδραμηκε [26] λεγων.

---

14. Cassander was in favour at Athens at the time.
When Cassander was a young man Alexander is said to have
banged Cassander's head against a wall, because he laughed at
the Persian mode of prostration (see προσκυνεω, c. 8 and
11). 15. "Upon someone saying . . ." (see c. 11, Strabo,
n. 11). Gen. abs. 16. See c. 11, Æsop, n. 22. 17. "All
voice (the story) together." A symphony is an agreement
of sound. 18. ταῦτα, Crasis (c. 8) for τα αὐτα, 'the same
(things)'. Distinguish between the uses of αὐτος; ὁ αὐτος
ἀνηρ, 'the same man ', and ὁ ἀνηρ αὐτος, or αὐτος ὁ ανηρ, 'the
man himself '. 19. 'There's been buckets of soup.' Lit.
ζωμος, 'the gravy '—a slangy euphemism for 'bloodshed
—has become (pf. of γιγνομαι) widespread, πολυς '. 20.
Understand ἐστι. Lit. 'it's a sign (sema-phore) for me,
their faces '—' I can see it in the faces '. 21. οἱ ἐν τοις
πραγμασιν: those in affairs—' the high-ups '. 22. 'Having
changed ', here intrans., though the verb is usually trans.
23. παρα with dat. 'at the house of '. He is saying that a
messenger from Macedonia with all this news has been
locked up by the authorities, and deliberately kept incom-
municado. 24. 'Already for the fifth day '; the expression is equivalent to πεντε ἡμερας, which expresses extent of
time in the accus. case. 25. δει. Lit. 'It binds you alone
to know '—i.e. It is necessary for you alone to know.
' Don't tell anyone else ' is the talemonger's invariable
injunction. 26. See c. 11, Æsop, n. 12, This is the perf.
of προστρεχω, 'run up to '.

των τοιουτων ἀνθρωπων τεθαυμακα τι ποτε θελουσι
λογοποιουντες.  οὐ γαρ μονον ψευδη λεγουσιν ἀλλα
και ἀλυσιτελη [27] πλαττουσι.  πολλακις γαρ αὐτων
οἱ μεν [28] ἐν τοις βαλανειοις [29] περιστασεις [30] ποιουντες
τα ἱματια ἀποβεβληκασιν, οἱ δ' [28] ἐν τη στοᾳ [31] πεζο-
μαχιᾳ και ναυμαχιᾳ νικωντες ἐρημους δικας ὠφλη-
κασιν.[32]  πανυ δη ταλαιπωρον ἐστιν αὐτων το
ἐπιτηδευμα.[33]

## VOCABULARY

ἀγγελλω, report.
ἀπανταω, meet.
ἀποβαλλω (*pf.* -βεβληκα),
  lose.
ἀποκρινομαι, answer.
'Αστειος, an Athenian.
αὐλητης, -ου, flute-player.
βαλανειον (*n. pl.*), bath.
βασιλευς, -εως, king.

βοαω, shout, cry.
δικη, lawsuit.
ἐαω, allow.
εἰδεναι, *inf.* of οἰδα, know.
ἐπεντεινω, gain ground,
  spread.
ἐπιλαμβανομαι, catch hold
  of.
ἐπιτηδευμα, -ατος, way of life.

---

27. ἀ-, 'not', -λυσι, 'paying', -τελης, 'what is due '—
unprofitable.  28. οἱ μεν, ' some ' . . . οἱ δε, ' others '.
See c. 11, Æsop, n. 29.  29. The baths were always the
resort of idlers.  30. περιστασις, ' a standing round '—i.e.
a crowd.  While he assembles a crowd, someone gets
away with his cloak.  The clothes-stealer was a common
nuisance at the baths.  31. ἡ στοα, ' the porch '.  A well-
known public place in Athens.  It was decorated with
frescoes, depicting the victories of the Athenians over the
Persians at Marathon, etc.  A school of philosophers meeting there gained the name Stoic ; their professed indifference
to pain gave us the adj. ' stoical '.  32. ὀφλισκανω (pf.
ὠφληκα) ἐρημον δικην.  Notice the ending of the adj.  Some
2nd declens. adjs. have no separate fem. form.  Lit. ' I
lose an undefended suit '.  To fail to turn up when one's
case is called in the law-courts, and so let judgment go
against one by default.  Litigation was so frequent at
Athens that any citizen had to be ready at any time to
defend himself.  The rumour-monger has become so en-
grossed in imaginary victories that he has forgotten his
case.  33. ' Way of life.'

ἐρημος, -ον, deserted, of a law-suit at which one of the parties fails to appear (*der*. eremite).

ἐρωταω, ask (a question).

εὐθυς, immediately.

εὐωχεω, give a feast of.

ζωγρεω, take alive.

ἠ, either, or.

ἡκω, I have come—used as pf. of ἐρχομαι, come, go.

θαυμαζω, wonder.

ἱματιον, cloak.

καινος, -η, -ον, new.

Κασανδρος, son of Antipater, regent of Macedonia.

καταβαλλω, cast down, drop, relax.

κρυπτω, conceal.

Λυκων, business man at Athens.

μειδιαω, smile.

μαχη, battle.

ναυμαχία, sea-fight.

νικαω, conquer.

ὀφλισκανω (pf. ὠφληκα), lose.

παραγιγνομαι (pf. -γεγονα), come from.

παρακουω, hear on the side.

πεζομαχια, infantry battle.

πεμπτος, -η, -ον, fifth.

πιστευω, believe, trust.

ποθεν, whence?

πολλακις, often.

Πολυπερχων, a general.

πραγμα, -ατος, affair.

πραξις, -εως, deed.

προστρεχω, run up to.

πως, how?

ταλαιπωρος, -α, -ον, hard.

ψευδης, false.

ὡσπερ, just as.

## The Cicada

Here is a simple little poem, of unknown authorship, to the τεττιξ, often wrongly translated ' grasshopper ', that ' tick-ticks ' or rather ' tet-tinks ' all day, unseen among the asphodel, on any Greek hillside, especially at Pan's noon-time. Its metre is very simple—two short syllables, followed by three trochees, the last syllable being either long or short, e.g. ' Hŏw wĕ | blēss yŏu, | dēar cĭc | āda '—but the metre in English has an unfortunate resemblance to Hiawatha.

*Literal Translation.*[1]

| | |
|---|---|
| Μακαριζομεν σε τεττιξ | We bless you, cicada, |
| ὁτε δενδρεων ἐπ' ἀκρων | when on the tree tops |
| ὀλιγην δροσον πεπωκως | having drunk a little dew |

---

[1] A verse translation is given in the key.

*Literal Translation.*

| | |
|---|---|
| βασιλευς ὁπως ἀειδεις· | like a king you are singing; |
| σα γαρ ἐστι κεινα παντα, | For yours are those things all, |
| ὁποσα βλεπεις ἐν ἀγροις, | all that you see in the fields, |
| ὁποσα τρεφουσιν ὑλαι. | all that the woods nourish. |
| | |
| συ δε τιμιος βροτοισιν, | You are respected by mankind, |
| θερεος γλυκυς προφητης. | sweet prophet of summer. |
| φιλεουσι μεν σε Μουσαι, | The Muses love you, |
| φιλεει δε Φοιβος αὐτος, | and Phœbus himself loves you, |
| λιγυρην δ' ἐδωκεν οἰμην. | and he gave you a sweet voice. |
| το δε γηρας οὐ σε τειρει, | Old age doesn't wear you, |
| σοφε, γηγενης, φιλυμνε, | wise one, earth-born, music-lover, |
| ἀπαθης δ', ἀναιμοσαρκε,[2] | passionless, with bloodless flesh, |
| σχεδον εἰ θεοις ὁμοιος. | you are almost equal to the gods. |

Edmund Blunden has translated the poem (*Oxford Book of Greek Verse in Translation*, p. 225), the end being as follows :—

> " Tiny philosopher,
> Earth-child, musician,
> The world, flesh, and devil,
> Accost you so little,
> That you might be a god."

---

[2] Compound of αἱμα, 'blood' (anæmic, hæmorrhage) and σαρκ- root of σαρξ 'flesh' (sarcophagus, sarcology, etc.).

# CHAPTER XIII

## THIRD DECLENSION NOUNS (continued)

### VOWEL STEMS, DIPHTHONGS AND IRREGULARS

1. The other main type of the 3rd declension consists of *vowel stems*, of which by far the commonest have the termination -σις. There are twelve in Chap. 3. How many can you remember? And what does the termination denote? E.g. διαγνωσις, ἀναλυσις, κρισις, ὑποθεσις, φθισις, στασις.

They are declined thus : πολις, ' *city* ' (*politics*).

|  | Sing. |  | Plur. |
|---|---|---|---|
| N. | πολις | | πολεις (for ε-ες) |
| V. | πολι | | |
| A. | πολιν | | πολεις (for ε-ας) |
| G. | πολεως | | πολεων |
| D. | πολει (for ε-ι) | | πολεσι |

Notice the accusative singular termination -ιν, the genitive singular -εως, the accusative plural the same as the nominative plural, and the uncontracted genitive plural.

Here are some examples. They are all feminine.

|  | Gen. sing. | Eng. | Derivative |
|---|---|---|---|
| ἡ πιστις | πιστεως | belief, trust, faith | — |
| τερψις | τερψεως | delight | Terpsichore |
| λυσις | λυσεως | a loosing, freeing | analysis |
| δυναμις | δυναμεως | power | dynamic<br>dynamite<br>dynamo |

|  | Gen. sing. | Eng. | Derivative |
|---|---|---|---|
| φυσις | φυσεως | growing, evolution, nature | physics |
| ὑβρις | ὑβρεως | pride | hubris |
| μνησις | μνησεως | remembering, memory | { amnesia, amnesty |
| ὀψις | ὀψεως | sight | Cyclops, optical |
| αἰσθησις | αἰσθησεως | perception | aesthetic |
| ταξις | ταξεως | arranging | syntax |
| στασις | στασεως | revolt | — |

2. A few *masc. and fem.* nouns in -υς, and neuters in -υ are declined like πολις—e.g.

|  | Gen. sing. | Eng. | Derivative |
|---|---|---|---|
| πελεκυς | πελεκεως | axe | — |
| πρεσβυς | πρεσβεως | old man | presbyter |
| ἀστυ | ἀστεως | city | — |

But others in -υς and -υ are declined with stem in -υ, e.g.

|  | Gen. sing. | Eng. | Derivative |
|---|---|---|---|
| ὑς | ὑος | pig | — |
| ἰχθυς | ἰχθυος | fish | Ichthyosaurus (lizard-fish) |
| δρυς | δρυος | oak | — |
| δακρυ | δακρυος | tear | — |

Thus ἰχθυς and δακρυ are declined thus :—

|  | Sing. | Plur. | Sing. | Plur. |
|---|---|---|---|---|
| N.V. | ἰχθυς | ἰχθυες | δακρυ | δακρυα |
| Acc. | ἰχθυν | ἰχθυας or ἰχθυς | δακρυ | δακρυα |
| Gen. | ἰχθυος | ἰχθυων | δακρυος | δακρυων |
| Dat. | ἰχθυι | ἰχθυσι | δακρυι | δακρυσι |

3. Many nouns ending in -ευς (' the man who ') are declined thus :—

|  | *Sing.* |  | *Plur.* |
|---|---|---|---|
| N. | βασιλευς (king) | N. | βασιλης (note this— |
| V. | βασιλευ |  |   for ε -ες) |
| A. | βασιλεα | A. | βασιλεας (note that |
| G. | βασιλεως |  |   this does not |
| D. | βασιλει |  |   contract) |
|  |  | G. | βασιλεων |
|  |  | D. | βασιλευσι |

Similarly,     ἱππευς, horseman.
             ἱερευς, priest.
             γονευς, parent.
             Ἀχιλλευς, Achilles.
             φονευς, murderer.

4. Nouns ending in -ης. They are really contracted, and are most easily learnt from the uncontracted forms—e.g. τριηρης (trireme), and many proper names, such as Δημοσθενης and Σωκρατης, the σ dropping out between two vowels and contraction resulting.

|  | *Sing.* |  | *Plur.* |  |  |
|---|---|---|---|---|---|
| N. | τριηρης | N.V. | τριηρεις | Δημοσθεν-ης |  |
| V. | τριηρες |  | — | -ες |  |
| A. | τριηρη (for ε-α) | A. | τριηρεις | -η |  |
| G. | τριηρους (for ε-ος) | G. | τριηρων | -ους |  |
| D. | τριηρει (for ε-ι) | D. | τριηρεσι | -ει |  |

(For rules of contraction, see c. 20.)

5. We now have left only some irregular nouns, but they are common. Here are a few that you will frequently meet :—

| Nom. | Eng. | Sing. Acc. | Sing. Gen. | Sing. Dat. | Plur. Nom. | Plur. Acc. | Plur. Gen. | Plur. Dat. |
|---|---|---|---|---|---|---|---|---|
| αἰδως | sense of shame, modesty, respect | αἰδω | αἰδους | αἰδοι | — | — | — | — |
| ἠχω | echo | ἠχω / ἠροα / ἠρω | ἠχους | ἠχοι | — | — | — | — |
| ἡρως | hero | ἡρωα / ἡρωα / ἡρω | ἡρωος | ἡχοι / ἡροι / ἡρω | ἡρωες | ἡρωας | ἡρωων | ἡρωσι |
| θριξ | hair | τριχα | τριχος | τριχι | τριχες | τριχας | τριχων | θριξι |
| ναυς | ship | ναυν | νεως | νηι | νηες | ναυς | νεων | ναυσι |
| βους | ox | βουν | βοος | βοι | βοες | βους | βοων | βουσι |
| ὑδωρ | water | ὑδωρ | ὑδατος | ὑδατι | ὑδατα | ὑδατα | ὑδατων | ὑδασι |
| γυνη | woman | γυναικα | γυναικος | γυναικι | γυναικες | γυναικας | γυν αι-κων | γυναιξι |
| Ζευς | Zeus | Δια | Διος | Διι | — | — | — | — |
| κυων | dog | κυνα | κυνος | κυνι | κυνες | κυνας | κυνων | κυσι |

Translate :—

1. ἐπει ποταμοι εἰσι κενοι ὑδατος, οἱ ἰχθυες οὐ ζωσιν (live).

2. οἱ ἀγαθοι παιδες τῃ μητρι τερψιν φερουσιν, οἱ δε κακοι δακρυα.

3. ὁ βασιλευς ἐκελευσε τους ἱππεας σῳζειν παντας τους ὀϊας και τους αἰγας.

4. ἡ του Ἀχιλλεως ὑβρις ἐφερε μυρια κακα τοις Ἑλλησιν.

5. οἱ κυνες, ὡσπερ οἱ πρεσβεις, μαλιστα φιλουσι σιτον και ὑπνον.

### Key

1. When rivers are empty of water, fish do not live.
2. Good children bring delight to their mother, but naughty ones tears.
3. The king ordered the cavalry to save all the sheep and goats.
4. The pride of Achilles brought a thousand woes to the Greeks.
5. Dogs, like old men, like especially food and sleep.

### From Greek Writers

Translate :—

1. ἀνδρες [1] εἰσι πολις, οὐ τειχη [2] οὐδε νηες [3] ἀνδρων κεναι.

2. οἱ ἀμαθεις ὡσπερ ἐν πελαγει και νυκτι φερονται [4] ἐν τῳ βιῳ.

3. οἱ γονεις [5] και οἱ διδασκαλοι αἰδους [6] ἀξιοι εἰσιν.

4. παντ᾽ ἐκ-καλυπτων ὁ χρονος εἰς το φως ἀγει.

Sophocles.

---

1. Nom. plur. of ἀνηρ, c. 9. 4.   2. c. 10. 7.   3. c. 13. 5.
4. Pres. ind. pass. of φερω, 'I carry'.   5. c. 13. 3.   6. c. 13. 5.

## A Strong Hairwash.

την κεφαλην βαπτων τις[7] ἀπωλεσε[8] τας τριχας[9]
αὐτας,[10]
   και δασυς ὢν[11] λιαν ὠον ἁπας γεγονεν.[12]

## Woman.

δεινη μεν ἀλκη κυματων θαλασσιων,
δειναι δε ποταμων και πυρος θερμου πνοαι,
δεινον δε πενια, δεινα δ' ἀλλα μυρια,
ἀλλ' οὐδεν οὑτω δεινον, ὡς γυνη, κακον.—Euripides.

## Man.

ἀνηρ γαρ ἀνδρα και πολις σωζει πολιν.
ἁπασα δε χθων[13] ἀνδρι γενναιῳ πατρις.[14]

## Two Fragments of Sappho (atticised).

## Evening.

Ἑσπερε παντα φερων,[15] ὁσα[16] φαινολις ἐσκεδασ'[17]
ἠως,
φερεις ὀϊν, φερεις αἰγα,[18] φερεις ἀπο[19] μητερι παιδα.

## Night.

Ἀστερες[20] μεν ἀμφι καλην σεληνην

---

7. τις, indef. pron., v. 24.   8. ἀπωλεσε, 3rd sing. aor.
ind. act. of ἀπολλυμι, ' destroy ' or ' lose '.   9. c. 13. 5.
10. Reflexive ' themselves ', c. 24.   11. ὢν, pres. part. of
εἰμι, ' I am '.   12. γεγονε(ν), 3rd sing. strong perf. of
γιγνομαι, ' has become '.   13. c. 10.   14. c. 9.   15. Pres.
partic. of φερω.   16. ὁσα, c. 8 and 24, correlatives.   17.
aor. of σκεδαννυμι, ' I scatter '.   18. c. 9.   19. ἀπο, usually
a preposition, here equivalent to an adv. φερεις, ἀπο =
ἀπο-φερεις, ' thou bringest back '.   20. This lovely fragment
has only come down to us because it was quoted by an
ancient commentator to explain a certain line of Homer

ἀψ²¹ ἀποκρυπτουσι φαεινον εἶδος,
ὁπποτε πληθουσα μαλιστα λαμπει
γην ἐπι²² πασαν.

Sappho lived in Lesbos c. 600 B.C. Of her many poems
('speech mixed with fire' says one ancient critic, 'a few,
but roses' says another) only fragments remain. Her
language has 'the simplicity of plain speech raised to the
highest pitch of expressiveness,' says Dr. Bowra.

## VOCABULARY

ἀγω, I bring, bear.
ἀλκη, -ης, might, strength.
ἀμαθης, -ες, unlearned, ignorant.
ἀμφι (*prep.*), around.
ἀπας, stronger form of πας.
ἀποκρυπτω, I hide (apocrypha, things hidden away,
  secret).
βαπτω, I wash (baptise),
  dye.
γενναιος, -α, -ον, noble.
δασυς, -εια -υ, shaggy.
δεινος (*adj.*), strange, terrible.
διδασκαλος, -ου, teacher (from
  διδασκω, I teach).
εἶδος, -ους, appearance.
ἐκ-καλυπτω, I uncover, reveal    (Apocalypse = Re-
  velation).

Ἑσπερος, -ου, Evening Star,
  Hesperus.
ἠως, dawn (Eothen).
θαλασσιος, -ια, -ιον, of the sea
  (θαλασσα).
κεφαλη, -ης, head (brachycephalic).
λαμπω, I shine (lamp).
λιαν (*adv.*), very, exceedingly.
μαλιστα (*adv.*), especially,
  most, very much.
μυριοι, -αι, -α, 10,000,
  myriad, and so, countless.
ὀΐς (orig. ὀϜις, Lat. ovis),
  sheep.
ὁπποτε, whenever, (ὁποτε in
  Attic).
οὑτω, so (followed by an
  adj.), thus.

---

about the stars under a full moon. The metre is Sapphic—
her favourite one. The text here has been atticised. Sappho
wrote in the Æolic dialect thus :—

> Ἀστερες μεν ἀμφι καλαν σελανναν
> ἀψ ἀποκρυπτοισι φαεννον εἶδος
> ὁπποτα πληθοισα μαλιστα λαμπῃ
> γαν ἐπι παισαν

²¹ ἀψ = ἀπο adv. as 19.    ²² Order is ἐπι πασαν γην, 'over
the whole earth', for use of ἐπι with acc., v. 22.

πελαγος, -ους, sea.
πενια, -ας, poverty.
πληθω, I am full (plethora).
πνοη, -ης, breath, blast.
σωζω, I save.
φαεινος, -α, -ον, bright.

φαινολις (*poet. adj.*), light-
  bringing.
φως (contr. for φαος), φωτος,
  light.
ὡσπερ, just as.

# CHAPTER XIV

## THE MIDDLE VOICE

### Active and Passive

Most people are familiar with the active and passive voices in English. The active voice of the verb shows the subject as acting; and the same is true of Greek—e.g. The boy leads the dog, ὁ παις ἀγει τον κυνα; the passive voice shows the subject as acted upon—e.g. The dog is led by the boy, ὁ κυων ἀγεται ὑπο του παιδος.

### Middle

Greek, however, has also a middle voice, in which, roughly speaking, the subject acts, directly or indirectly, upon itself. This occurs in several ways, of which the following are the most important :—

*Reflexive.* ἐνδυω (like the English ' endue '), I clothe another (active).

ἐνδυομαι, I clothe myself in . . . .

*Indirect Reflexive.* Far more common than this, however, is the middle voice, used in the sense of doing a thing for one's self, or in one's own interest.

*E.g.*, φερω, I bring.
    φερομαι, I bring for myself = I win.
    μεταπεμπω, I send A after B.
    μεταπεμπομαι, I send A after B to bring him
               back to me—I send for B.

*Intransitive.* Sometimes the middle represents an intransitive meaning of a transitive verb—e.g.

> παυω τον ἱππον, I stop the horse.
> ὁ ἱππος παυεται, the horse makes itself to stop —i.e. stops (intrans.).

*Causative.* Sometimes, too, the middle implies getting a thing done for one's self—having it done.

> λυω, I free.
> λυομαι, I get freed for myself = I ransom.
> διδασκω, I teach.
> διδασκομαι, I get (my son) taught.

*Possessive.* Occasionally the middle voice conveys the force of a possessive pronoun, so that—

> λουω τους ποδας, I wash the feet (of others).
> λουομαι τους ποδας, I wash my own feet.

*Reciprocal.* Often in the plural the middle voice implies a reciprocal reflexive pronoun—

> ἀσπαζονται, they embrace one another.
> διαλεγονται, they talk with one another.

*Developed Meaning.* In many verbs it will be found that the development of the meaning of the middle voice has in the long run led to a sense far removed from that of the active.

> αἱρεω = αἱρω, I take.
> αἱρεομαι = αἱρουμαι, I choose, elect, prefer.
> γραφω, I write.
> γραφομαι, I get someone's name entered on a list=I accuse.
> δανειζω, I lend.

δανειζομαι, I get someone to lend to me = I borrow.

It is all a little frightening at first, but no one will expect you to deduce the sense of the middle from the active—so don't worry. As you learn more and more Greek verbs, you will see how the principle works out.

*Deponent Verbs.* Besides the above, however, there is a very large number of Greek verbs which are middle in their form but active in their meaning. These are called *deponent* verbs; the word means ' laying aside ', and you may think of them as laying aside the meaning that is appropriate to their form (as middle), and hence as having acquired a new active meaning.

Here, then, are the forms. You will have to learn them carefully and be sure of them, so that you can recognize them again, as it is hardly possible to find a page of Greek in which they do not occur everywhere. The future is again formed by the addition of a single letter—the aorist and imperfect tenses must have their augment; we will leave the perfect until later.

## MIDDLE VOICE

### Present Tense

| *Sing.* | *Plur.* |
|---|---|
| 1. λυομαι | λυομεθα |
| 2. λυει or λυῃ | λυεσθε |
| 3. λυεται | λυονται |

Infinitive λυεσθαι ; participle λυομενος, -η, -ον.

## Future Tense

1. λυσομαι                λυσομεθα
2. λυσει or λυσῃ      λυσεσθε
3. λυσεται              λυσονται

Infinitive λυσεσθαι; participle λυσομενος, -η, -ον.

## Aorist Tense

1. ἐλυσαμην                  ἐλυσαμεθα
2. ἐλυσω (originally ἐλυσαο)  ἐλυσασθε
3. ἐλυσατο                 ἐλυσαντο

Infinitive λυσασθαι; participle λυσαμενος, -η, -ον.

## Imperfect Tense

1. ἐλυομην                   ἐλυομεθα
2. ἐλυου (originally ἐλυεο)   ἐλυεσθε
3. ἐλυετο                   ἐλυοντο

# THE WRATH OF ACHILLES—I

One of the literary wonders of the world is the *Iliad* of Homer. The *Iliad* is an epic poem dealing with the exploits of the Greeks before Troy. It is written in hexameters in 24 books of some 600 lines each. Standing at the very dawn of history, it nevertheless shows no crudity of form or thought, no uncertainty of touch, no barbarism. It is a technical masterpiece, illuminated by flashes of genius never surpassed. Who wrote it? Who was Homer? One or many? When was it written? Was it committed to writing by its composer, or composers? These are baffling questions, to which none can give a certain answer. You will very soon be able to read the actual Greek of Homer.

In the meanwhile, the piece of Greek below deals
with some of the subject matter of the 1st Book of
the *Iliad*.   It has been specially written to give you
practice in the forms of the Middle Voice.

### The Greek leaders quarrel before Troy

Δεκα μεν ἐτη [1] ἐμαχοντο περι την Τροιαν οἱ Ἀχαιοι.[2]
τῳ δε δεκατῳ ἡδη ἐτει [3] οὐτε εἰσεβιασαντο εἰς την
πολιν, οὐτε κατεστρεψαντο τους Τρωας· ἠμυναντο
γαρ ἀει αὐτους οἱ τ᾿ ἀλλοι και [4] ὁ Ἑκτωρ.  κακως [5]
δε και [6] ἀλλως ἐγιγνετο τα των Ἀχαιων πραγματα·
ὁ γαρ Ἀγαμεμνων και ὁ Ἀχιλλευς, ἡγεμονες ὀντες
των Ἀχαιων, ὁμως διεφεροντο ἀλληλοις περι παρθενου
τινος.   ὁπως δε τουτο ἐγενετο, εὐθυς ἀκουσεσθε.[7]

### Chryses' plan to recover his daughter

Χρυσης, ὁ του Ἀπολλωνος ἱερευς, οὐ [8] την θυγατερα ἐλησατο ὁ Ἀγαμεμνων, ἐπει βουλεται ἀνακομιζ-
εσθαι την παρθενον, οὑτως βουλευεται.[9]  ῾αὐτος
παρα [10] τους Ἀχαιους βησομαι,[7] πολλα και [11] καλα
δωρα φερων.   εἰ δε δεξονται τα ἐμα δωρα, οὐκ ἐστιν

---

1. See c. 12, n. 25.   2. An early name for the fair-haired
race, which, coming down from the north, joined with the
Mediterranean peoples to form the Hellenes.   3. Dat. of
time *at* which something occurs.   4. οἱ τ᾿ ἀλλοι και.   See
c. 15, n. 24.   5. The adverbial ending is -ως; see also
ἀλλως, φιλιως and αἰσχρως.   6. και often means ' also '.
7. Many active verbs have a future deponent; cf. βησομαι
(βαινω) ληψομαι (λαμβανω).   8. οὐ. Notice the breathing
carefully; not οὐ, but οὑ, gen. of ὁς, ' whose '.   9. Don't
confuse βουλευομαι (' plan ') with βουλομαι (' wish ').   10.
The meaning of this prep. depends on the case that follows.
With the dat. it means ' along with '.   Lines that are παρ᾿
ἀλληλοις are ' alongside one another '.  (Now you won't
misspell it !)   With the acc. it means ' to '.   11. Two adjs.
with one noun must usually be coupled with ' and ' in Gk.

ὅπως οὐ [12] λυσομαι την κορην. εἰ δ᾽ αὖ μη [13]
λυσουσιν αὐτην, συγε, [14] ὦ ᾽Απολλον, (ὡδε γαρ
ἐλισσετο τον θεον) ἀποτεισει αὐτους.᾽

### Agamemnon rejects Chryses' plea—

ὦ σχετλιοι ᾽Αχαιοι ! δια τι οὐ φιλιως ἐδεξασθε τον
γεροντα ; αἰσχρως γαρ ἀπεωσασθε [15] αὐτον. παντων
δε μαλιστα συγ᾽, ὦ ᾽Αγαμεμνον. ποιοις λογοις
ἀπεκρινω προς τον γεροντα ! σκυθρωπος γαρ ἐφαινου
τῃ ὀψει και εἰπας [16] τοιαδε —
᾽ ἀρ᾽ οὐκ [17] αἰσχυνει, ὦ γερον, τοιαυτα λεγων ;
ἡμεις γαρ οἱ ᾽Αχαιοι οὐ ματην μαχομεθα. εἰ τινα
κορην ἐν τῃ μαχῃ φερομεθα, οὐποτε ἀποπεμπομεθα.᾽

### —and dismisses him with threats, to the displeasure of Apollo

᾽ ᾽Αλλ᾽ οὐδε ἐβουλομην ᾽, ἀπεκρινατο ὁ γερων, ᾽ ἀνευ
λυτρου κτησασθαι αὐτην· και δια τουτο ταυτα τα
δωρα παρεσκευασαμην.᾽

᾽ ῎Οπως μη ἡμεις (see that we don't) αὖθις ληψο-
μεθα [7] σε παρα ταις ναυσιν ᾽, ἐφη ὁ ᾽Αγαμεμνων. ᾽ νυν
μεν γαρ ὀλοφυρει, εἰτα δε οὐδεποτε παυσει ὀλοφυρο-
μενος· τοιαυτα κακα πεισει.᾽

Ταυτ᾽ ἀκουσας, ὦ ᾽Απολλον, πως οὐκ [18] ἠχθου και
ὑπεσχου ἀποτεισεσθαι [19] τους ᾽Αχαιους ;

---

12. Lit. ' It is not how not . . .' a Gk. idiom for ' assuredly '.
13. Negative after εἰ is μη, not οὐ.   14. Emphatic for συ.
15. This word has a curious double augment. ἀπωθεω,
ἀπεωσαμην, ' I thrust away from myself '.  ' Osmosis ', a
scientific term derived from this verb, denotes the penetrat-
ing power of some liquids.   16. The 2nd person is irregular ;
εἰπας for εἰπες.   17. Are you *not* = Lat. *nonne* ?  ἀρα μη
would mean—' You aren't ashamed, are you ? '   18. Lit.
' How not ? ' a way of saying, ' Of course . . .'   19. Verbs
of promising must always take a *future* infin. after them.
They refer, of course, to the future.

## VOCABULARY

αἰσχρος (adv. -ως), shameful.
αἰσχυνομαι, I am ashamed.
ἀλληλους, -ας, -α, one another.
ἀλλως (adv.), otherwise.
ἀμυνομαι, keep off from oneself.
ἀνακομιζομαι, get back for oneself.
ἀνευ (gen.), without.
ἀποπεμπομαι, send away from oneself.
ἀποτινομαι (fut. τεισομαι), get one to pay back = punish.
αὐ, αὐθις, again.
Ἀχαιος, Achæan.
ἀχθομαι, be vexed.
βαινω (fut. βησομαι), go.
βουλευομαι, plan.
βουλομαι, wish.
δεκα, ten.
δεκατος, tenth.
δεχομαι, receive.
διαφερομαι, differ, quarrel.
εἰσβιαζομαι, force one's way into.
εἰτα, then.
ἱερευς, -εως, m. priest.
κακως (adv.), badly.
καταστρεφομαι, I overturn for myself = I subdue.

κταομαι, I get for myself.
ληζομαι, win as booty.
λυομαι, I loose for myself, I ransom.
λισσομαι, I beseech.
λυτρον, -ου (n.), a ransom.
μαλιστα (adv.), most.
ματην (adv.), in vain.
μη, no, not.
ναυς, νεως, f. a ship.
ὀλοφυρομαι, bewail.
ὁμως, nevertheless.
ὁπως, how.
οὐποτε ⎫
οὐδεποτε ⎭ never.
ὀψις, -εως, f. face.
παρασκευαζομαι, get ready for oneself, prepare.
παρθενος, -ου, f. maiden.
πασχω (fut. πεισομαι), suffer
παυομαι, stop (intrans.).
ποιος, -α, -ον, what sort of?
σκυθρωπος, -η, -ον, scowling.
σχετλιος, rash, stubborn.
ὑπισχνουμαι (aor. ὑπεσχομην), promise.
φερομαι, take for oneself, win.
φημι (aor. ἐφη), say.
φιλιως (adv.), kindly
ὡδε, thus.

## THE WRATH OF ACHILLES—II

### Apollo's vengeance and the seer's advice

Οὑτως δε ὠργιζετο ὁ Ἀπολλων τοις Ἀχαιοις, ὡστε [1] πολλους νυκτωρ ἐξερχομενος διειργασατο.[2]

---

1. ὡστε. See. 11 Æsop. 11.    2. Notice an irreg. augment on -ἐργαζομαι, making the aor. -εἰργασαμην.

πολλαι δε ἐγενοντο αἱ πυραι [3] των ἀει [4] καιομενων. [5]
τελος [6] δε ὁ ᾽Αχιλλευς, ' Οὐποτε φευξομεθα ', ἐφη, ' τον
θανατον, εἰ μη ἐρωτησομεν δια [7] μαντεως τινος τον
θεον τι μεμφεται ἡμιν.' [8] ἐπειτα δε ὁ Καλχας (μαντις
γαρ ἠν) ἐμαντευσατο τοιαδε —

'Συ δη, ὠ ᾽Αγαμεμνον, οὐτ' ἐδεξω τα δωρα, οὐτ'
ἐλυσας την του ἱερεως θυγατερα. τοιγαρουν οὐδε
ἀπωσει [9] τον λοιγον. εἰ δε ἀποπεμψει [9] αὐτην, παντα
καλως εὐθυς ἐσται.'

## The dispute between Achilles and Agamemnon

ἠχθετο οὐν ὁ ᾽Αγαμεμνων και ἀπεκρινατο —' ᾽Επει
λισσεσθε ἐμε παντες, την μεν του γεροντος παρθενον
ἀποπεμψομαι, την δε Βρισηϊδα, την του ᾽Αχιλλεως
κορην, ἀντι τησδε ληψομαι. ἀλλως γαρ το ἀθλον [10]
ὁ [11] ἐν τη μαχη ἠνεγκαμην, [12] μονος των ᾽Αχαιων
οὐχ ἑξω.' [13] προς ταυτα [14] ὁ ᾽Αχιλλευς, ἰσην ὀργην

---

3. The invading Northerners burnt their dead, while the
Mediterranean races buried theirs. 4. ἀει, 'from time to
time'. There must have been a time when Apollo, who came
with the Achæans, was a strange and fearful god to the Greeks.
Then he is spoken of as the god who slays with ' the arrow
that flieth by night '. Only when the Greeks got to know
their Apollo better did they identify him with the sun and the
arts. 5. καιω (act.), ' I burn '; καιομαι (intrans.), ' I burn '.
Fut. καυσω, aor. ἐκαυσα; hence ' caustic '—encausticum—
the purple ink used by Roman Emperors, which seemed to
' burn into ' the paper; hence Fr. ' encre ', Eng. ' ink '!
6. τελος is often used adverbially, ' at last '. 7. δια + gen.
' through ', ' by means of '. 8. ἡμιν, ' us,' μεμφομαι takes the
dat. 9. Be careful of, ἀπωσει (ἀπωθεομαι) and ἀποπεμψει;
they are 2nd person, not 3rd. 10. What a pity that our
word ' athletics ' is so bound up with ἀθλον, a prize ! 11. ὁ
neuter relative pron.—not masc. 12. Irreg. aor. of φερομαι.
13. ἐχω becomes ἑξω in the future. Notice effect on οὐκ.
14. προς ταυτα, ' in reply to this '.

φαινων, εἶπεν, ' 'Αρ' ἀφαιρησει ¹⁵ με την ἐμήν παρθενον ; ἀλλα λεγω σοι τοδε· ἡμεις οὐχ ἑσπομεθα ¹⁶
μετα σου ¹⁷ Τροιανδε ¹⁸ των πολεμιων ἑνεκα ¹⁹ ἀλλα
της ληϊδος, ὡστε εἰ ἀφαιρησει τηνδε, οὐκετι ἐγωγε
ὑπερ σου βουλομαι μαχεσθαι. ὑμεις δε κακα πολλα
πεισεσθε, ἀλλ' ἐγω ἀφεξομαι του πολεμου.'

Οὑτως δε, κατα ²⁰ τον Ὁμηρον, ἡρξατο ἡ του
Ἀχιλλεως μηνις.

## VOCABULARY

ἀθλον, -ου (n.), prize.
ἀντι, prep. (gen.), instead of.
ἀπεχομαι, withhold oneself.
ἀρχομαι, begin.
ἀφαιρεομαι, take away from.
διεργαζομαι, kill.
ἑνεκα (gen.), for the sake of.
ἐξερχομαι, come out.
ἐπειτα, then.
ἑπομαι, follow.
καιομαι, I burn (intrans.).
ληϊς, -ιδος, f. booty.
λοιγος, plague, pestilence.
μαντις, -εως, m. seer.
μαντευομαι, to prophesy.
μεμφομαι (dat.), to blame.

μετα (gen.), with.
μηνις, -εως, f. wrath.
νυκτωρ (adv.), by night.
ὀργιζομαι, be angry.
οὐκετι, no longer.
πυρα, -ας, f. a pyre.
τελος (adv.), at last.
τοιγαρουν, therefore.
ὑμεις (pron.), you (pl.).
ὑπερ (prep. gen.), on behalf of.
φαινω, show.
φευγω (f. φευξομαι), flee.
Βρισηϊς, ιδος, f. Briseïs,
    captive maid of Achilles.
Καλχας, -αντος, m. Calchas, a
    Greek prophet.

---

15. ἀφαιρεομαι, takes two accusatives: (1) what you take
away, (2) whom you take it from.   16. Αογ. ἑπομαι.   17.
μετα + gen., ' with '.   18. -δε is attached to a word to
indicate direction towards it. Τροιανδε, to Troy. So
Ἀθηνασδε = Ἀθηναζε, to Athens.   19. ἑνεκα, ' for the sake
of ', always follows its gen.   20. κατα, ' according to '.

# CHAPTER XV

## THE PASSIVE VOICE

In the passive voice the subject is represented as acted upon—e.g.

ὁ παις παιδευεται—the boy is being trained. If the ' agent ', by whom an action is performed, is mentioned, the word ὑπο (' by ') precedes it, and it is put in the genitive case—e.g.

ὁ παις παιδευεται ὑπο του διδασκαλου.
The boy is being trained by the master.

*Agent and Instrument.* Distinguish carefully between the agent *by whom* a thing is done, and the instrument *with which* it is done. It was a secret agent *by whom* the plans were stolen (ὑπο+ genitive), but a blunt instrument *with which* (simple dative) the murder was done. Remember an agent must *live*, as the insurance man said when he was kicked out.

Instrument.  ἡ θαλασσα ταρασσεται τοις ἀνεμοις.
The sea is disturbed by the winds.

Agent.  ἡ θαλασσα ταραυσεται ὑπο του Ποσειδωνος.
The sea is disturbed by Poseidon.

### Tense Forms

It will occasion you much pleasure to know that you have already learnt the

## Present Passive
## Imperfect Passive

because these tenses are identical with the present
middle and the imperfect middle. The passive
forms, however, of the future and aorist are different
from those of the middle.

### Aorist

| Sing. | Plur. |
|---|---|
| ἐλυθην | ἐλυθημεν |
| ἐλυθης | ἐλυθητε |
| ἐλυθη | ἐλυθησαν |

### Future

| | |
|---|---|
| λυθησομαι | λυθησομεθα |
| λυθηση or -ει | λυθησεσθε |
| λυθησεται | λυθησονται |

Note that -θη- is a characteristic sign of tenses
peculiar to the passive, and that the endings of the
aorist passive are like the endings of an *active* tense.

## ORPHEUS AND EURYDICE.—I

Ἦν [1] δε ποτε ἀοιδος [2] τις,[3] Ὀρφευς [4] ὀνοματι, ὁς

---

1. Ἦν ' (*There*) was '. Gk. has no introductory word to
correspond with the Eng. preparatory ' there '. 2. ἀοιδος,
' minstrel '. If you remember that α + ο = ω, you will see
that this word is connected with ᾠδη = Eng. ' ode '. 3. τις,
' a certain '; the nearest thing the Gks. had to an indef.
article. Do not confuse with the other τις τι, meaning
' who ? what ? or why ? '. 4. Ὀρφευς. See the pretty
song in *K. Henry VIII*, 3. 1. 3, " Orpheus with his lute. . . ."
Also *Merchant of Venice*, 5. 1. 79. Orpheus was the reputed
founder of a mysterious association which had members all
over Ancient Greece. They had a secret ritual, and bound
themselves to a certain way of life. They believed in

οὖτω[6] καλως ἐκιθαριзε[7] τῃ λυρᾳ, ὣστε παντα τα
зῳα και τα δενδρα και δη και[8] τα ὀρη εἵπετο αὐτῳ
θαυμαзοντα. τουτου δε ἡ γυνη, ὡς ἐν τῳ κηπῳ
περιπατει,[9] ὑπο δρακοντος[10] δακνεται· ἐπει δε οὐκ
ἰατρευεται το ἑλκος,[11] τελος[12] ἀποθνῃσκει. ἀγεται τε
ὑπο του Ἑρμου,[13] του ψυχοπομπου, εἰς Ἀιδου.[14] και
τοιαυτα ὠλοφυρετο ὁ Ὀρφευς —

  ''Ὠμοι[15] ἐγω· δια τι[16] οὕτως, ὠ Εὐρυδικη, ὑπο
δρακοντος ἐδηχθης ; δια τι ὑφηρπασθης ἐμου ; εἰ
γαρ[17] και[18] ἐγωγε μετα σου ἐτρωθην, εἰπερ ἐξεστιν[20]

---

original sin, purification, and the transmigration of souls.
They eventually became connected with a similar brother-
hood founded by Pythagoras. 6. οὖτω . . ὣστε. ' So
. . . that (as a result).' The clause introduced by ὣστε is
called a consecutive clause, because it shows the consequence or result. 7. κιθαριзω, ' To play on the κιθαρα '—
the word which became both ' zither ' and ' guitar '. 8. και
δη και, ' and what is more ', is a phrase which adds something emphatic. 9. περιπατει. Aristotle founded a school
of Peripatetic philosophers, who used to walk up and down
the Lyceum at Athens while instructing their pupils.
Hence ' peripatetic ' means ' wandering ' or ' itinerant '.
10. δρακων, ' dragon ' or ' snake ', is derived from the aor.
part. of δερκομαι, ' look ', and means ' the one with the
piercing glance '. 11 ἑλκος, Latin ulcus; Eng. ' ulcer '
and so ' wound '. 12. τελος used as an adv. ' at last '. 13.
Ἑρμης, Hermes had many functions, being the god of
merchants, travellers and thieves. He was also the
official escort of the souls of the dead to Hades, ψυχοπομπος,
a task which kept him very busy. 14. εἰς Ἀιδου. εἰς
normally takes the accus. case, but sometimes the gen.
follows εἰς, when the word ' house ' is to be understood.
Hades in Gk. is a person, not a place. He was the king of
the underworld. So the Gks. talked of going to Hades's,
just as we might talk of going to Woolworth's. 15. ὠμοι,
' alas '. This word is said to be the ancestor of the Eng.
' Ah me ! ' 16. δια τι, ' owing to what ? = why ? '
although the word τι alone is frequently used in the sense
of ' why ' ? 17. εἰ γαρ, these words, which do not here

ὀφεσι [19] δις δακνειν. νυν δε [21] σφοδρα βαρυνομαι τω
σω πενθει· [22] τοιουτον δε ἀλγος ἐχω οἱου [23] οὑποτε
ἀπαλλαχθησομαι.'

Τελος δε ἐβουλευετο αὐτος καταβαινειν εἰς ῾Αιδου.
῾ Λυθησεται γαρ,' φησιν, ῾ ἡ Εὐρυδικη τῃ ἐμῃ λυρᾳ·
θελχθησονται δε ταις ἐμαις ᾠδαις οἱ τε ἀλλοι [24]
κατω θεοι και ὁ Πλουτων.' ὁπερ και ἐγενετο.
δια βραχεος [25] γαρ οἱ μεν [26] νεκροι ἠναγκαζοντο

---

bear their normal meanings, ' if ' and ' for ', are used in
Gk. to introduce a wish for the past, now impossible of
fulfilment. They are to be translated ' Would that . . .'
The aor. indic. which follows carries a meaning similar to
the English pluperfect ' Would that I had been wounded '.
18. και frequently means ' also ' as well as ' and '. 19.
ὀφεσι. Compare ophicleide in an orchestra, derived from
ὀφις, ' serpent ', and κλεις, -δος, ' key '. 20. ἐξεστιν, an
impersonal verb—i.e. one with no expressed subject—' (it)
is possible '. 21. νυν δε, ' but as it is '. 22. τω σω πενθει,
lit. ' by your grief ', but that is an idiomatic way of saying
in Gk., ' by my grief for you '. 23. οἱου, ' as ' corresponds
to τοιουτον, ' such '. The gen. is used to express ' from ',
the idea of separation contained in the verb. You will
meet other instances of this. 24. οἱ τε ἀλλοι κατω θεοι και
ὁ Πλουτων, ' The infernal gods and especially Pluto.' Notice
this Gk. way of mentioning others first with the object of
drawing attention to a single instance. This means literally
' Both (τε) the other gods below and Pluto '. Observe also
how an adverb may be put in between an article and a
noun, and have the effect of an adjective. οἱ κατω θεοι,
' the gods below '. So οἱ νυν στρατηγοι, ' present-day
generals '. 25. δια βραχεος, ' in a short (time) ': so, δια
πολλου, ' after a long (interval) '. 26. μεν . . . δε, lit. ' on
the one hand . . . on the other hand '. These words
always stand second in their clauses. The Greeks loved to
think of things as contrasted pairs. It is part of that
mental balance which their philosophers thought so important. You will find it too clumsy to translate μεν and
δε literally, and you may have to content yourself with
simply ' but ' in the second half. But you should bear the
meaning in mind.

ἐπακουειν, ὁ δε[26] κυων, ὁ Κερβερος,[27] κατειχετο του ὑλακτειν.[28]

## VOCABULARY

ἀγω, lead, take, drive.
ἀναγκαζω, force, compel.
ἀπαλλασσω, rid, free.
ἀποθνησκω, die, be killed.
βαρυνω, weigh down.
δις, twice.
εἰπερ, if, in fact.
ἐπακουω, listen to.
Εὐρυδικη, -ης, Eurydice, wife of Orpheus.
θελγω, charm, soften.
ἰατρευω, cure, heal.
καταβαινω, go down.
κηπος, -ου (m.), garden.
νεκρος, -ου (m.), body, corpse.
νεκροι, the dead.

Πλουτων, -ωνος (m.), Pluto, god of the underworld.
Ποσειδων, -ωνος (m.), Poseidon, god of the sea, Neptune.
σος, -η, -ον (poss. pron.), your, (of one person).
σφοδρα, exceedingly, very.
τιτρωσκω (aor. pass. ἐτρωθην), I wound.
ὑπο (gen.), by (of the agent).
ὑφαρπαζω, snatch away from.
ὡς (conj.), as, when.

## ORPHEUS AND EURYDICE.—II

Τελος δε εἰπεν ὁ Πλουτων ταδε —' και [1] ἡμεις τεγγο-μεθα τῃ σῃ λυπῃ· τοιγαρουν ληψει την γυναικα· εἰ δε βλεψεις ἐν τῃ ἀνοδῳ [2] προς την γυναικα, ἀφαιρε-θησεται παλιν [3] ἀπο σου.' ἡσθη [4] δε τουτοις τοις

---

27. Κερβερος, Cerberus, the fearsome three-headed hound who guarded the gates of Hell, could only be appeased by giving him something to eat. Only thus was it possible to slip by him. Hence the phrase, ' A sop to Cerberus.' 28. του ὑλακτειν, ' from barking '. The article and the infin. is equivalent to a verbal noun in English ending in -ing. See note 23 for the gen.

1. Και, see note 18 above. 2. ἀνοδος, ' the road up '; cf. the anode and the kathode in electrolysis. 3. παλιν, ' back again '. A palindrome is a word or sentence that runs backward as well as forward—e.g. Adam's words of self-introduction to his wife : '' Madam, I'm Adam.'' A famous Gk. palindrome is to be seen on many baptismal fonts ; thus, ΝΙΨΟΝΑΝΟΜΗΜΑΤΑΜΗΜΟΝΑΝΟΨΙΝ = νιψον

λογοις ὁ Ὀρφευς και ἐξηλθον, ὁ μεν ἐμπροσθε κιθαριζων, ἡ δε ὀπισθεν ἑπομενη.

ὦ ματαιοι [5] ἀνθρωποι! ἀρ' ἀει νικηθησεσθε ὑπο του
Ἐρωτος; [6] οὑτως και ὁ Ὀρφευς ἐν αὐτῃ τῃ ἐξοδῳ οὐ
κατειχεν ἑαυτον, ἀλλα ποθῳ της γυναικος περιεβλεψεν.
ἡ δε εὐθυς ἠφανισθη.[7]

και τουτῳ τῳ τροπῳ ὁ Ὀρφευς παλιν ἐχωρισθη
της γυναικος.[8] ἀκουσαντες δε οἱ των Θρᾳκων νεανιαι,
' Οὐ δητα', ἐφασαν, ' συ μονος χωρισθησει της γυναι-
κος· ἡμεις γαρ βουλομεθα μετεχειν της λυπης [9] μετα
σου. αἱ δε γυναικες οἰκοι καταλειφθησονται.'

προς δε ταυτα [10] ὠργιζοντο αἱ γυναικες, λεγουσαι,
' Ἀρ' οὐ δεινον εἰ [11] ἀοιδου τινος ἑνεκα ἀει νοσφισθη-
σομεθα των ἀνδρων; '

ὡστε προσεδραμον [12] προς τον Ὀρφεα και διε-
σπαραξαν αὐτου τα μελη·[13] ἡ δε κεφαλη ἐβληθη [14]

---

(aor. imper. of νιπτω, ' wash ') ἀνομηματα (' sins ',
' lawlessnesses ', ἀ + νομος), μη μοναν (for μονην), ὀψιν (' not
only ⟨my⟩ face '). 4. Aor. pass. from ἡδομαι. What is
a ' hedonist ' ? 5. Adj. from ματην, c. 14. 6. Ἐρως, son of
Aphrodite; the Gk. original of Cupid. Most Londoners
call their favourite statue in Piccadilly Circus, Eeros, but
the Greeks pronounced it E-rose. 6. περιεβλεψεν. The
final -ι of περι does not give place to an augment, nor can
it be elided. 7. From ἀ-φανιζω, ' to make to disappear '.
The story is reminiscent of that of Lot's wife. 8. της
γυναικος is called the gen. of separation—the case used
when one person or thing is removed *from* another. Other
examples occur here. See if you can find them. 9. της
λυπης is called the partitive gen., where a part or share of
the whole is involved. 10. προς ταυτα, see c. 14. 11. Is it
not shameful that . . . ? Notice the delicate Gk. εἰ (' if ')
instead of our blunter ' that '. 12. προσεδραμον, see c. 12,
n. 26. 13. μελη, from μελος, ' a limb '; don't confuse with
the other μελος, ' a melody '. 14. ἐβληθη, aor. pass. of
βαλλω.

εἰς τον ποταμον. και μην [15] ὡς κατα τον ποταμον [16] ἐφερετο, ἀει ἠδεν ἡ κεφαλη ἡ τμηθεισα [17] πανυ καλη [18] δη τῃ φωνῃ.

## VOCABULARY

ᾁδω, (ἀειδω), sing.
ἀπο, (gen.), away from.
βαλλω (aor. pass. ἐβληθην), throw.
βλεπω, look.
δεινος, -η, -ον, terrible, strange.
δη, indeed, of course.
διασπαρασσω, tear in pieces.
ἐμπροσθε(ν) (adv.), before, in front.
ἡδομαι (aor. ἡσθην), I am pleased.
ἡμεις (pers. pron.), we.
καταλειπω, leave behind.
κεφαλη, -ης, f. head.

λαμβανω (fut. ληψομαι), get, take.
μελος, -ους (n.), a limb.
μετα (gen.), with.
μετεχω, share in (takes gen.).
νοσφιζω, separate from.
ὀπισθε(ν) (adv.), behind.
πανυ (adv.), very, exceedingly.
περιβλεπω, look round.
τεγγω, melt, soften.
τμηθεις, -εισα, -εν (aor. pass. ptcple. from τεμνω), cut, severed.
χωριζω, separate, put apart.

## LOVE AMONG THE ROSES

We do not know exactly who wrote the poem about the Cicada. It is one of a number of poems that used to be ascribed to a poet named Anacreon. It is almost certain, however, that these poems, of which the following is another example, were the products of a later imitator of Anacreon. Anacreon

---

15. και μην, ' and lo ! '. This phrase is often used to attract the attention of the reader or hearer to something fresh. 16. κατα τον ποταμον, ' down stream '. What is the opposite ? See n. 2. 17. τμηθεισα, fem. aor. ptcple. pass. from τεμνω, ' I cut '. 18. Lit. ' with the voice very beautiful '. This is called a predicative position of the adj., and is common in Gk. It has almost the effect of adding a further statement, ' which was very beautiful '.

himself was born at Teos, and wrote many love-poems. He was a friend of Polycrates, the tyrant of Samos, and of Hipparchus, who ruled at Athens. He is said to have died through being choked by a grapestone. The spurious poems have not the virtues of the master, though Cowley and Tom Moore, the Irish poet, translated them.

This poem will give you practice in the forms of the aorist passive and aorist passive participle.

> Ἔρως ποτ' ἐν ῥόδοισι [1]
> κοιμωμενην [2] μελιτταν [3]
> οὐκ εἶδεν, ἀλλ' ἐτρωθη.
> τον δακτυλον [4] δε δηχθεις [5]
> της χειρος ὠλολυξε. [6]
> δραμων δε και πετασθεις [7]
> προς την καλην Κυθηρην, [8]
> Ὀλωλα, [9] μητερ, εἶπεν,

---

1. An extra ι is frequently added to the dative case in poetry. 2. κοιμα-ομενην, ‘sleeping’. A κοιμητηριον (cemetery) is a sleeping-ground. 3. μελισσα, see ‘The Ass,’ c. 11. σσ and ττ are interchangeable in Gk., the difference being one of dialect. 4. ‘ In the finger.’ The part of the body affected by a verb or an adj. is usually in the accus. case in Gk. This word means either ‘ finger ’ or ‘ toe ’. There is a pretty Homeric epithet of the Dawn, ῥοδοδακτυλος, ‘ rosy-fingered ’; cf. Pterodactyl. The foot, a dactyl, consisting of a long syllable and two short ones, was held to represent the joints of the finger. 5. Aor. pass. ptcple. from δακνω. See Orpheus 1. 6. Another onomatopœic word like ὀλοφυρομαι. 7. Tr. ‘ having flown ’, lit. ‘ spread wide his wings ’, from πεταννυμι, ‘ to spread ’. 8. A name for Venus, who was worshipped at the island of Cythera, off the south coast of Greece. 9. ‘ I am done for.’ This perf. tense from ὀλλυμι, ‘I destroy’, is always used in an intrans. way in Gk. It always has this significance of being ruined or finished.

ὄλωλα, κἀποθνῃσκω.
ὄφις μ' ἔτυψε μικρος
πτερωτος, ὁν καλουσι
μελιτταν οἱ γεωργοι.
ἡ δ' εἶπεν, Εἰ το κεντρον [10]
πονει [11] το της μελιττης,
ποσον, δοκεις, πονουσιν,
Ἐρως, ὁσους [13] συ βαλλεις ; [12]

## VOCABULARY

ὀλολυζω, cry aloud.  
πτερωτος, winged.  
καλεω, call.

δοκω, think  
ποσος, -η, -ον, how much ?

## PERFECT MIDDLE AND PASSIVE

Another tense whose forms are common to both middle and passive is the perfect. The endings, which are of great antiquity, are easy to learn : -μαι, -σαι, -ται, -μεθα, -σθε, -νται. As in the active perfect, the first syllable is reduplicated ; if the word begins with a vowel, the vowel is lengthened for reduplication.

*Agent.* With the 3rd person singular and plural of the perfect passive, and the perfect passive participle the agent may be indicated by the dative case instead of ὑπο with the genitive.

E.g. λελυται σοι, He has been freed by you.

---

10. See 11. Æsop. 15.   11. πονεω is used in two senses here : (a) ' hurt ', (b) ' suffer '.   12. Besides ' throw ', this verb means to strike ' with a missile '.   13. ὁσους, ' those whom ', ' as many as '.

## PERFECT MIDDLE AND PASSIVE

1. λελυμαι
2. λελυσαι
3. λελυται
1. λελυμεθα
2. λελυσθε
3. λελυνται

Participle λελυμενος, -η, -ον
Infinitve λελυσθαι

If, however, the verbal stem ends with a consonant instead of a vowel as in λυω, the perfect middle and passive become a little more complicated, because the final consonant causes modification of the endings. For instance, the perfect passive of πραττω is πεπραγ-μαι. If the 3rd person plural were like that of λυω, it would have to be πεπραγ-νται. But to a Greek γντ as a combination was an impossibility. Therefore they used in such cases the perfect participle, with εἰσι as an auxiliary.

These perfects with consonantal stems fall into five classes, according to the consonant modifying the ending. Below is a sample of each.

| πραττω, do. | πειθω, persuade. |
|---|---|
| 1. πεπραγμαι | 1. πεπεισμαι |
| 2. πεπραξαι | 2. πεπεισαι |
| 3. πεπρακται | 3. πεπεισται |
| 1. πεπραγμεθα | 1. πεπεισμεθα |
| 2. πεπραχθε | 2. πεπεισθε |
| 3. πεπραγμενοι εἰσιν | 3. πεπεισμενοι εἰσιν |
| Infin. πεπραχθαι | Infin. πεπεισθαι |
| Ptcple. πεπραγμενος | Ptcple. πεπεισμενος |

πεμπω, send.  ἀγγελλω, announce.

1. πεπεμμαι
2. πεπεμψαι
3. πεπεμπται
1. πεπεμμεθα
2. πεπεμφθε
3. πεπεμμενοι εἰσιν

Infin. πεπεμφθαι
Ptcple. πεπεμμενος

1. ἠγγελμαι
2. ἠγγελσαι
3. ἠγγελται
1. ἠγγελμεθα
2. ἠγγελθε
3. ἠγγελμενοι εἰσιν

Inf. ἠγγελθα
Ptcple. ἠγγελμενος

φαινω, show.

1. πεφασμαι
2. πεφανσαι
3. πεφανται
1. πεφασμεθα
2. πεφανθε
3. πεφασμενοι εἰσιν

Infin. πεφανθαι
Ptcple. πεφασμενος

# CHAPTER XVI

## THE -μι VERBS

BABY says, " Me want some ". He does so because he has reached a definite stage in the development of his growing consciousness. First of all, when he was quite helpless, he was interested in action only in terms of its effect on ' me '. Gradually, however, he becomes aware of his own identity and individuality; passivity passes into activity, and in this second stage ' me ' (the only personal pronoun he has) actively wants something. This, however, is only a transitory stage. It is not long before imitation and possibly parental correction lead him to make the proper distinction between the pronoun as subject and the pronoun as object. But the persons have to be sorted out in Baby's mind first.

The same is roughly true of the infancy of the Greek language. In the prehistoric stage of the language's development there was probably only one voice and one tense. This consisted of the stem, indicating generally the nature of the verb's action, and endings, consisting of personal pronouns affected by external causes. Most probably the earliest endings ran thus :—

> -μαι, me.
> -σαι, you (cf. συ).
> -ται, that one (cf. το).

But when baby Greek got to the second stage, distinguishing active from passive (the ' me-want-some ' stage), it used the endings it knew, only slightly modified. In fact, the -μαι, -σαι, -ται endings became -μι, -σι, -τι, the former being kept for the passive or middle. Later the 1st person pronoun, ἐγώ, came into use, and verbs in consequence acquired a new ending in -ω. This became by far the commonest ending, ousting in most verbs the old -μι ending. Yet even in Homer it can be seen that some verbs are wobbling uneasily between a -μι and an -ω termination, and by the time of the New Testament some of the most diehard μι's of the classical tradition have forsaken their old form. Even so does a language develop from age to age.

But some baby habits stick. And there stuck in the Greek language a number of verbs of the old -μι type, still lingering on from that second stage we have mentioned. They are all, as you would expect, transitive, with the exception of the two εἰμί(s), meaning ' I am ' and ' I go ', verbs so elemental in their meaning that it is hardly surprising that their endings are of great antiquity. It is generally true of all languages that the more simple in meaning the verb is, the more irregular are its forms, since they have had a longer passage of time to get knocked about in. Of course, the lapse of years had some effect, too, on the old -μι, -σι, -τι system, although it is still partly recognisable.

There are not many of these verbs, but, being of great antiquity, they are all the more important as their meanings are primary—e.g. I put, set, give, let go, show, say, etc. One can hardly open a page of Greek without coming across some part of either τίθημι or ἵστημι, especially in the aorist forms.

They are not easy, but if you wish to make any progress in Greek, you had better brace yourself to the effort of learning them, for you are hardly likely to make progress without.

They fall into four divisions according to the prevailing vowel, and there are also some odd ones, lying outside these categories : —

τιθημι, prevailing vowel—ε.
διδωμι, prevailing vowel—ο.
ἱστημι, prevailing vowel—α.
δεικνυμι, prevailing vowel—υ.

## ACTIVE

| | | I place. | I give. | I set up. | I show. |
|---|---|---|---|---|---|
| | | τιθημι | διδωμι | ἱστημι | δεικνυμι |
| PRESENT. | 1. | τιθημι | διδωμι | ἱστημι | δεικνυμι |
| | 2. | τιθης | διδως | ἱστης | δεικνυς |
| | 3. | τιθησι | διδωσι | ἱστησι | δεικνυσι |
| | 1. | τιθεμεν | διδομεν | ἱσταμεν | δεικνυμεν |
| | 2. | τιθετε | διδοτε | ἱστατε | δεικνυτε |
| | 3. | τιθεασι | διδοασι | ἱστασι | δεικνυασι |
| IMPERFECT. | 1. | ἐτιθην | ἐδιδουν | ἱστην | ἐδεικνυν |
| | 2. | ἐτιθης | ἐδιδους | ἱστης | ἐδεικνυς |
| | 3. | ἐτιθη | ἐδιδου | ἱστη | ἐδεικνυ |
| | 1. | ἐτιθεμεν | ἐδιδομεν | ἱσταμεν | ἐδεικνυμεν |
| | 2. | ἐτιθετε | ἐδιδοτε | ἱστατε | ἐδεικνυτε |
| | 3. | ἐτιθεσαν | ἐδιδοσαν | ἱστασαν | ἐδεικνυσαν |
| INFIN. | | τιθεναι | διδοναι | ἱσταναι | δεικνυναι |
| PTCPLE. | | τιθεις | διδους | ἱστας | δεικνυς |

### MIDDLE AND PASSIVE

| | | | | |
|---|---|---|---|---|
| **PRESENT.** | 1. τίθεμαι | δίδομαι | ἵσταμαι | δείκνυμαι |
| | 2. τίθεσαι | δίδοσαι | ἵστασαι | δείκνυσαι |
| | 3. τίθεται | δίδοται | ἵσταται | δείκνυται |
| | 1. τιθέμεθα | διδόμεθα | ἱστάμεθα | δεικνύμεθα |
| | 2. τίθεσθε | δίδοσθε | ἵστασθε | δείκνυσθε |
| | 3. τίθενται | δίδονται | ἵστανται | δείκνυνται |
| **IMPERFECT.** | 1. ἐτιθέμην | ἐδιδόμην | ἱστάμην | ἐδεικνύμην |
| | 2. ἐτίθεσο | ἐδίδοσο | ἵστασο | ἐδείκνυσο |
| | 3. ἐτίθετο | ἐδίδοτο | ἵστατο | ἐδείκνυτο |
| | 1. ἐτιθέμεθα | ἐδιδόμεθα | ἱστάμεθα | ἐδεικνύμεθα |
| | 2. ἐτίθεσθε | ἐδίδοσθε | ἵστασθε | ἐδείκνυσθε |
| | 3. ἐτίθεντο | ἐδίδοντο | ἵσταντο | ἐδείκνυντο |
| **INFIN.** | τίθεσθαι | δίδουθαι | ἵστασθαι | δείκνυσθαι |
| **PTCPLE.** | τιθέμενος | διδόμενος | ἱστάμενος | δεικνύμενος |

## NOTES ON THE CONJUGATION OF THE -μι VERBS

1. In the present and imperf. active the vowels are long in the singular, η, ω, η, ῡ, but short in the plural, ε, ο, α, ῠ.

2. The 3rd person sing. of the present -σι was originally made plural by adding -ν, making -νσι. α was prefixed to this ending, and the ν eventually disappeared. The α of -ασι coalesced with the α of the stem in ἵστημι, but it remained apart from ε, ο and υ in the other verbs.

3. In the imperf. the initial ι of ἵστημι becomes long by the augmentation.

4. Even τιθημι was beginning to lose its old -μι forms in classical times, and Greeks began to think of it as if it were τιθεω. The result is that the forms ἐτιθεις and ἐτιθει are quite common for the imperf. (see Contracted Verbs, c. 20). Similarly the imperf. of διδωμι should have been ἐδιδων, -ως, -ω, but that form had been replaced by ἐδιδουν, -ους, -ου, as if it came from a contracted verb, διδοω.

5. δυναμαι ('I am able') and ἐπισταμαι ('I understand'; the Greeks said 'over-stand', rather more sensibly!) are conjugated like ἱσταμαι, but generally have ἐδυνω and ἠπιστω instead of ἐδυνασο and ἠπιστασο in the 2nd person sing. of the imperf.

---

## EXERCISE ON THE -μι VERBS

Translate :—

1. τα προβατα οὐ δυναται φευγειν τον λυκον τον ἐρχομενον. 2. τι ἀφιης την ποιμνην, ὠ μισθωτε; 3. οὐκ ἐπισταμεθα την φωνην την του ἀλλου ποιμενος. 4. ὁ πατηρ μου ἐδεικνυ τα προβατα τοις παισι. 5. ὁ ᾿Αγαμεμνων ἱσταται ἡγεμων παντων των ῾Ελληνων. 6. οἱ φευγοντες ἐδιδοσαν παντα τοις λυκοις. 7. δει σε ἀφιεναι τον ἰχθυν. 8. οὐ δυναμενοι ἀλλῳ τινι διδοναι τον χρυσον, ἀει ἀπετιθεσαν. 9. τῳ πολλα ἐχοντι πολλα πολλακις διδοται. 10. συντιθεντος τους νομους του ἡγεμονος, εἰδωλον ἱστατο ὑπο των πολιτων

## KEY TO EXERCISE

1. The sheep are unable to escape the wolf which is coming. 2. Why do you let go your flock, hireling? 3. We do not understand the voice of the other shepherd. 4. My father was showing the sheep to the boys. 5.

Agamemnon is being set up as leader of all the Greeks.
6. Those running away were giving everything to the wolves.
7. It is necessary that you let go the fish.  8. Not being
able to give the gold to another person, they always used
to put it away.  9. To him that has much, much is
frequently given.  10. While the leader was putting together the laws (genitive absolute), an idol was being set
up by the citizens.

This passage from St. John x. 11 illustrates the
μι-verbs.

## Ὁ ΑΓΑΘΟΣ ΠΟΙΜΗΝ

Ἐγω εἰμι ὁ [1] ποιμην ὁ καλος.  ὁ ποιμην ὁ καλος την
ψυχην αὐτου τιθησιν [2] ὑπερ των προβατων.

Ὁ μισθωτος και οὐκ ὠν [3] ποιμην, οὐ οὐκ ἐστι τα
προβατα ἰδια,[4] θεωρει [5] τον λυκον ἐρχομενον, και
ἀφιησι [6] τα προβατα και φευγει.

Και ὁ λυκος ἁρπαζει αὐτα και σκεδαννυσι [7] τα προβατα.  ὁ δε μισθωτος φευγει, ὁτι [8] μισθωτος ἐστι,
και οὐ μελει [9] αὐτῳ περι των προβατων.

Ἐγω εἰμι ὁ ποιμην ὁ καλος· και γιγνωσκω τα
ἐμα,[10] και γιγνωσκομαι ὑπο των ἐμων, καθως γιγνω-
σκει με ὁ πατηρ, κἀγω γιγνωσκω τον πατερα, και
την ψυχην μου τιθημι ὑπερ των προβατων.

---

1. See c. 6.  Only late Gk. permitted the article with
the complement.  2. ' Puts ', but throughout this passage
in the sense of ' lays down '.  3. Pres. ptcple. of εἰμι, ' I
am—being '.  4. See c. 11, n. 25, here ' private property '.
5. θεωρεω, ' I watch ', gives us θεωρημα, ' something to be
investigated ', a theorem, and θεωρια, ' speculation ', as
opposed to ' practice '—i.e. theory.  6. ' Lets go.'  ἱημι
is one of the most important of the -μι verbs.  It is conjugated like τιθημι.  7. See c. 13.  The original New Testament uses a later and rarer word with this meaning.  8.
This word means both ' that ' and ' because '.  9. Impersonal verb, ' it does not concern him ' = ' he has no care
for '.  10. ἐμος, ' my ', nearly always has the article in
Gk.

Και ἄλλα προβατα ἐχω ἁ οὐκ ἐστιν ἐκ της αὐλης ταυτης· κἀκεινα δει με ἀγαγειν [11] και την φωνην μου ἀκουσονται, και γενησεται [12] μια [13] ποιμνη, εἰς ποιμην. δια τουτο ὁ πατηρ με ἀγαπᾳ [14] ὁτι ἐγω τιθημι την ψυχην μου ἱνα (in order that) παλιν λαβω (I may take) αὐτην.

Οὐδεις αἱρει [15] αὐτην ἀπ᾽ ἐμου, ἀλλ᾽ ἐγω τιθημι αὐτην ἀπ᾽ ἐμαυτου. ἐξουσιαν [16] ἐχω θειναι αὐτην, και ἐξουσιαν ἐχω παλιν λαβειν αὐτην. ταυτην την ἐντολην ἐλαβον παρα του πατρος μου.

## VOCABULARY

ἀγαπαω, I love.
αὐλη, -ης, fold, pen.
γιγνωσκω, realise, recognise.
ἐντολη, -ης, command.
ἐξουσια, -ας, power, permission.

καθως (conj.), just as.
λυκος, -ου, a wolf.
μισθωτος, a hired man, hired.
ποιμνη, -ης, a flock.
προβατα, -ων (n. pl.), sheep.
σκεδαννυμι, I scatter.

### Literary Fragments

Single lines and fragments of lost plays are preserved for us in large numbers, because they have been quoted by other authors in their books. Very often the reason for their preservation is none other than that the author wishes to illustrate some sentiment, rare word, or unusual construction. They provide, however, a peep, tantalisingly narrow, into a vast treasure-house to which we cannot gain access.

---

11. ἀγω, see c. 13. Aor., ἠγαγον; aor. inf., ἀγαγειν. 12. γενησομαι, fut. of γιγνομαι. 13. εἰς, see c. 11. Strabo (vocabulary), has fem. μια and neuter ἐν. 14. ἀγαπαω, see the noun, c. 7. 15. αἱρω, literally 'lift'; hence 'take away'. 16. ἐξουσια, the noun from ἐξεστι (see c. 15).

## Jack of All Trades

1. πολλ' ἠπιστατο ἐργα, κακως δ' ἠπιστατο παντα.

From the Margites (the Madman), a mock-heroic poem, ascribed to Homer.

## Time's Daughter, Justice

2. την τοι [1] Δικην λεγουσι παιδ' εἶναι χρονου.
   δεικνυσι δ' ἡμων [2] ὁστις [3] ἐστ' ἡ μη [4] κακος.

1. A particle—a class of words in Gk. which indicate the tone in which a remark is made—it might be translated, 'I tell you'. 2. Gen. of ἡμεις, see c. 15. 3. Who? τις; asks the question, who?, but when the question is governed by a verb (δεικνυσι), τις may become ὁστις. 4. Here = οὐ.

## Ruling Class

3.                             το τ' εὐγενες [1]
   πολλην διδωσιν ἐλπιδ' ὡς [2] ἀρξουσι [3] γης.

1. εὐγενης means well-born (cf. Eugene—eugenics). The neuter article and adj. often correspond to an abstract noun. Thus το εὐγενες, 'nobility', 'good birth'. 2. ὡς, besides meaning 'as' or 'when', frequently means 'that'. 3. ἀρχω, 'I rule' (but remember ἀρχομαι, 'I begin') is seen in Eng. in such words as arch-duke, arch-fiend. It is followed by the gen.

## Tomorrow We'll Be Sober

4. ἡ γαρ Κυπρις [1] πεφυκε [2] τω σκοτω [3] φιλη
   το φως [4] δ' ἀναγκην [5] προστιθησι σωφρονειν. [6]

1. The Cyprian—a name for Venus, who was worshipped at Cyprus. 2. There are many perfects of transitive verbs which are intrans. φυω means, 'I plant' or 'beget', but the intrans. πεφυκα means 'I have grown', or just 'I am'. 3. σκοτος (also σκοτια), 'darkness'. An old riddle used to run :—

"Scotland, how thee a double darkness mocks !
Thy name is σκοτια, and thy teacher (K)nox."

4. φως, 'light', φωσφορος (Phosphorus), the Morning Star, brings the light. What is photography? 5. Necessity, see ἀναγκαιος, c. 6. 6. σωφρονειν, 'to be temperate', 'safe-minded'. σωφροσυνη was a great Gk. virtue.

### Fatal Cleverness

5. το δ' ὠκυ [1] τουτο και το λαιψηρον [2] φρενων
εἰς συμφοραν [3] ἱστησι πολλα δη [4] βροτους.

1. ὠκυς, 'swift'; what, then, is το ὠκυ? 2. λαιψηρος,
'nimble'. 3. συμφορα, 'disaster'. 4. πολλα δη, 'oft, indeed'. The neuter plural frequently has an adverbial
sense.

### Time, the Healer

6. μελλων [1] ἱατρος και νοσῳ διδους χρονον
ἱασατ' [2] ἠδη μαλλον ἡ τεμνων [3] χροα.[4]

1. Besides meaning 'to intend', μελλω often means
'delay, linger'. 2. ἱαομαι = ἱατρευω. The aor. means
'has done so ere now' (ἠδη), and refers generally to all
occasions—probably the earliest and truest use of the aor.
3. See τμηθεις, c. 15. 4. χρως, -ωτος (also χροος), m. flesh.
Gk. surgery was perhaps more daring than successful.
For instance, an attempt to remove a fish-bone by opening
the larynx proved fatal. Plato considered that a doctor
needed a course of oratory to persuade the patient to adopt
the course of treatment which he recommended.

### Fame

7. φημη [1] τον ἐσθλον [2] κἀν μυχῳ [3] δεικνυσι γης.

1. φημη, 'good report'. 2. ἐσθλος, 'good, worthy'
3. μυχος, 'corner'. κἀν = και ἐν, 'even in '.

### Necessity Knows No Law

8. προς την ἀναγκην οὐδ' 'Αρης [1] ἀνθισταται.[2]

1. Ares = Mars, god of war. 2. Stands against, opposes.

### Women Good and Bad

9. ὁστις [1] δε πασας συντιθεις ψεγει [2] λογῳ
γυναικας ἐξης [3] σκαιος [4] ἐστι κοὐ σοφος·
πολλων γαρ οὐσων [5] την μεν [6] εὑρησεις κακην
την δ',[6] ὡσπερ αὐτη,[7] λημ' [8] ἐχουσαν εὐγενες.

1. Whoever. 2. ψεγω, 'blame'. 3. ἐξης, 'in order '—
i.e. in a class. 4. Lit. left-handed; hence, 'silly '; cf.

gauche. 5. Gen. absolute, see c. 11. 'There being many.'
6. τὴν μεν . . . τὴν δε, 'the one . . . the other'. 7. As
*she* is. 8. λημα, 'spirit'.

## -MI VERBS—THE AORISTS

More important, perhaps, than the present tenses
of the -μι verbs are the aorist systems linked with
these words. These are difficult to understand, but
they occur so frequently that it will amply repay
you for your trouble to give them close attention.
No aorist forms are given for the δεικνυμι verb, as
they are quite regular—thus δεικνυμι has an aorist
active ἐδειξα, future δειξω, aorist middle ἐδειξαμην,
aorist passive ἐδειχθην, future passive δειχθησομαι,
and so on.

*Aorist Active.* Note that in the singular τιθημι
and διδωμι both form an aorist ending in -κα instead
of in the usual -σα. In the plural it will be seen that
the endings of these two verbs are like the endings
of the imperfect tense—that is to say, they are 2nd
aorist endings.

ἱστημι has two aorists : 1st and 2nd. The 1st
is transitive, and means 'I set up'; the 2nd is
intransitive, and means 'I stood'. The 1st aorist
is quite regular, and goes like ἐχορευσα, but the
2nd aorist, whose endings you should carefully
memorise, is, on account of its meaning, more
important. In particular notice the infinitive and
participle of this tense.

*Aorist Middle.* In the middle voice the aorists
of τιθημι and διδωμι are 2nd aorists (with endings
like their imperfects). These verbs have no 1st
aorist middle. On the other hand, ἱστημι, while it
(*contd. p.* 160)

## AORIST SYSTEM -μι VERBS
### Active

| | | τίθημι. | δίδωμι. | ἵστημι. (Trans.) | ἵστημι (Intrans.). |
|---|---|---|---|---|---|
| | | | | 1. | 2. |
| INDICATIVE. | 1. | ἔθηκα | ἔδωκα | ἔστησα | ἔστην |
| | 2. | ἔθηκας | ἔδωκας | ἔστησας | ἔστης |
| | 3. | ἔθηκε | ἔδωκε | ἔστησε | ἔστη |
| | 1. | ἔθεμεν | ἔδομεν | ἐστήσαμεν | ἔστημεν |
| | 2. | ἔθετε | ἔδοτε | ἐστήσατε | ἔστητε |
| | 3. | ἔθεσαν | ἔδοσαν | ἔστησαν | ἔστησαν |
| INFIN. | | θεῖναι | δοῦναι | στῆσαι | στῆναι |
| PTCPLE. | | θείς, -εῖσα, -εν | δούς, -οῦσα, -ον | στησ-ας, στήσασα στῆσαν | στάς, στᾶσα, στάν |

### Middle

| | | 2nd Aorist Middle. | 2nd Aorist Middle. | 1st Aorist Middle. | 2nd Aorist Middle, 'I bought'. |
|---|---|---|---|---|---|
| INDICATIVE. | 1. | ἐθέμην | ἐδόμην | ἐστησάμην | [ἐπριάμην * |
| | 2. | ἔθου | ἔδου | ἐστήσω | ἐπρίω |
| | 3. | ἔθετο | ἔδοτο | ἐστήσατο | ἐπρίατο |
| | 1. | ἐθέμεθα | ἐδόμεθα | ἐστησάμεθα | ἐπριάμεθα |
| | 2. | ἔθεσθε | ἔδοσθε | ἐστήσασθε | ἐπρίασθε |
| | 3. | ἔθεντο | ἔδοντο | ἐστήσαντο | ἐπρίαντο |
| INFIN. | | θέσθαι | δόσθαι | στήσασθαι | πρίασθαι |
| PTCPLE. | | θέμενος, -η, -ον | δόμενος, -η, -ον | στησάμενος, -η, -ον | πριάμενος, -η, -ον] * see p. 160. |

## Passive

| INDIC. | ἐτέθην, etc. | ἐδόθην, etc. | ἐστάθην, etc. |
|--------|--------------|--------------|---------------|
| INFIN. | τεθῆναι | δοθῆναι | σταθῆναι |
| PTCPLE. | τεθ-εις,<br>-εισα, -εν | δοθ-εις,<br>-εισα, -εν | σταθ-εις,<br>-εισα, -εν |

## PERFECT

ἕστηκα (Intrans.)
' I stand '.

| | 1. | 2. |
|---|------|------|
| 1. | ἕστηκα | — |
| 2. | ἕστηκας | — |
| 3. | ἕστηκε | — |
| 1. | ἑστήκαμεν | ἕσταμεν |
| 2. | ἑστήκατε | ἕστατε |
| 3. | ἑστήκασι | ἕστασι |
| | ἑστηκέναι | ἑστάναι |
| | ἑστηκ-ως,<br>-υια, -ος | ἑστ-ως, -ωσα,<br>-ος |

## OTHER TENSES

**Future :**

| Act. | θησω | δωσω | στησω |
|------|------|------|-------|
| Mid. | θησομαι | δωσομαι | στησομαι |
| Pass. | τεθησομαι | δοθησομαι | σταθησομαι |

(Infinitives of Future regularly formed.)

**Perfect :**

| Act. | τεθηκα<br>(Trans.) | δεδωκα<br>(Trans.) | ἕστηκα<br>(Intrans. ' I stand '.) |
|------|--------|--------|--------|
| Ptcple. | τεθηκως, -υια,<br>-ος | δεδωκως, -υια,<br>-ος | ἑστηκως, -υια, -ος,<br>or ἑστως, -ωσα,<br>-ος. |
| Infin. | τεθηκεναι | δεδωκεναι | ἑστηκεναι, or<br>ἑστάναι |

has a 1st aorist middle ἐστησαμην (transitive, ‘ I set up for myself ’), has no 2nd aorist middle.   There *is* a verb, however, which goes like ἰστημι, which has got a 2nd aorist middle; the verb is ‘ I bought ’, ἐπριαμην, which has no present.   It is included here to show you how such a tense goes.

*Future*.   Futures exist in all voices, with regular endings.

*Aorist Passive*.   Notice the short vowels ε, ο, α, preceding the characteristic θ of the aorist passive.

*Perfect*.   While the perfects of τιθημι and διδωμι are regular and transitive, the perfect of ἰστημι is intransitive, and means ‘ I stand ’.   Another and shortened form of the plural is given, which is constantly used as an alternative in Gk.

## EXERCISE.   AORIST OF -μι VERBS

Translate :—

1. ἐφισταμεν τον δουλον ὡς παιδαγωγον των παιδων. 2. ἐδομεν πολυν χρυσον τοις δουλοις. 3. ἐπεστησαν τον Κυρον στρατηγον των Ἑλληνων. 4. ἐπεθηκε πολλας πληγας τοις κακοις παισι. 5. καλον θεις κλεπτειν, εἰτα κολαζεις τους ἁλισκομενους. 6. ἀπεθηκας τους τυρους εἰς τον ἀσκον. 7. ὁ Σωκρατης ἐστη πολυν χρονον ἀνευ ὑποδηματων. 8. οὐτε ἐπριατο ἱματια οὐτε ὑποδηματα. 9. παντα δοθησεται τοις μενουσι. 10. ἐφιετο ὡς ταχιστα ἀποδουναι παντα ἁ εἰχε.

## KEY TO EXERCISE

1. We are appointing the slave as an attendant of the boys. 2. We gave much gold to the slaves. 3. They appointed Cyrus general of the Greeks. 4. He inflicted

many blows on the bad boys. 5. (After) laying it down as
honourable to steal, then you punish those who are caught.
6. You put the cheeses away into the bag. 7. Socrates
stood for a long time without sandals. 8. He bought
neither clothes nor sandals. 9. Everything will be given
to those who wait. 10. He made it his aim to give away
as quickly as possible everything that he had.

## SPARTAN EDUCATION

### (Adapted from Xenophon's *Lacedæmonian Republic*.)

One of the best known of Athenian prose writers
was Xenophon. Born about 430 B.C., as a young
man he became a friend of Socrates, of whom he
wrote some affectionate Memoirs. In 401 he joined
the expedition of Cyrus, who was marching against
his brother Artaxerxes, to wrest from him the
throne of Persia. The death of Cyrus in the battle
and the murder of the Greek generals by Persian
treachery provided a chance for the young Xenophon
to exhibit his leadership and skill by organizing the
retreat of the famous Ten Thousand through the
mountains of Armenia to the Euxine Sea, where
they could take a vessel for Greece. We are indeed
lucky to possess the exciting narrative of these
adventures as told by the principal actor in the play,
Xenophon himself, who in the *Anabasis* gives a
thrilling log of all that happened to this mercenary
army. On his return to Greece, he accepted service
with the Spartans, and was exiled from Athens.
The Spartans provided him with an estate, where he
lived the next twenty years of his life as a country
gentleman, writing of his military adventures,

political and educational theories, sporting books on hunting, horses, dogs, and so on. He was a firm admirer of the Spartans (Lacedæmonians) and particularly of their system of Education, which is here described in a piece, adapted from his *Spartan Constitution*. The rigorous discipline, hard training, scanty fare, and frequent floggings were all directed towards producing in the Spartans a military race of invincible soldiers. The educational theory underlying such training was not altogether unknown in some of our public schools in the last century. It failed, of course, as more recently it has failed in National Socialist Germany. History has yet to produce an example of the success of this brutal form of specialized training.

Ἐγω μεντοι βουλομαι την παιδειαν των τ᾽ ἀλλων και των Λακεδαιμονιων σαφηνισαι. οἱ μεν γαρ ἀλλοι ἐπει ταχιστα [1] οἱ παιδες τα λεγομενα [2] συνιασιν, εὐθυς μεν ἐπ᾽ αὐτοις παιδαγωγους [3] θεραποντας ἐφιστασιν, εὐθυς δε πεμπουσιν εἰς διδασκαλων,[4] μαθησομενους [5] και γραμματα και μουσικην [6] και τα ἐν παλαιστρᾳ.

---

1. ' When quickest ', ' as soon as '.   2. ' The things said ' —i.e. what is said to the child.   3. The παιδαγωγος (' pedagogue ') was a slave who, at Athens, took the child to and from school and exercised a strict supervision over his habits and manners.   4. Why gen. ?   See c. 14.   5. Lit. ' about to learn '.   The future part. is often used to indicate a purpose—' in order to learn.'   6. This word has a wider significance than our word ' music '.   It comprises much of what we should class nowadays as Literature.   The Gks., and particularly Plato, laid equal stress in their education on the training of the body (what happened in the gymnasium—τα ἐν παλαιστρᾳ) and the training of the mind with literature.   Thus they aspired to produce the balanced man.

προς δε τουτοις [7] των παιδων ποδας μεν ὑποδημασιν [8]
ἀπαλυνουσι, σωματα δε ἱματιων μεταβολαις δια-
θρυπτουσι· σιτου γε μην αὐτοις γαστερα [9] μετρον
νομιζουσιν. ὁ δε Λυκουργος,[10] ἀντι μεν του ἰδιᾳ
ἑκαστον παιδαγωγους δουλους ἐφιστανα,[11] ἀνδρα
ἐπεστησε [12] κρατειν αὐτων ἐξ ὡνπερ [13] αἱ μεγισται
ἀρχαι καθισταντα, ὁς δη και παιδονομος καλειται.
οὑτος δε κατεστη [14] κυριος ὡστε ἀθροιζειν τους παιδας,
και, εἰ τις ῥᾳδιουργει, ἰσχυρως κολαζειν. ἐδωκε δ'
αὐτῳ και ὁ Λυκουργος των ἡβωντων [15] μαστιγο-
φορους, οἱτινες τιμωρησονται [16] τους παιδας ἀντι γε

7. 'In addition to this.' 8. Socrates used habitually
to go about without sandals, even in the depth of
winter. 9. 'They consider their belly the measure of
their food'—i.e. they give the children as much as they
can eat. 10. Lycurgus—the almost legendary founder
of the Spartan Constitution. The Greeks liked attaching
their laws to the name of some person, but we are not
sure that there ever was such a person as Lycurgus,
whose name suggests a tribal wolf-god. 11. 'Instead of
each one setting up. . . .' το with the infin. is equivalent
to a verbal noun (or gerund) in English, ending in -ing.
The subject of this infin. is often put into the *accusative* case,
as here ἑκαστον. 12. First aor. active from ἐφιστημι,
'appoint'. The passive and intrans. aor. from καθιστημι,
seen below, are used as the passive of the verb 'to appoint'.
13. The highest offices were not open to all those who lived
in Sparta. Only pure-blooded Spartans could have such a
privilege. The Perioeci 'dwellers round about' had few
rights, and the Helots, the serf population, none at all.
14. He was set up (intrans. aor.), κυριος, with authority.
15. οἱ ἡβωντες, the Youths' class, some of whom had
responsibility in the training and supervision of the younger
boys. ἡβη, youth; cf. Hebe, the personification of Youth,
who acted as wine-bearer to the gods. 16. ὁστις + the
future indic., lit. 'who shall punish . . .', is often used as
a purpose clause = in order to punish. What other way
have you already had of expressing purpose? See note 5
above. Severe floggings were administered as part of a
system intended to toughen the boys.

μην του ἁπαλυνειν τους ποδας ὑποδημασιν, ἀει
ἐφιετο ¹⁷ ἀνυποδησιᾳ κρατυνειν. και ἀντι γε του
τοις ἱματιοις διαθρυπτεσθαι, ἐνομισεν ἑνι ἱματιῳ δι᾽
ἐτους προσεθιζεσθαι, ὡς οὑτως βελτιον παρασκευαζο-
μενος προς ψυχη ¹⁸ και προς θαλπη. σιτον γε μην
ἐκελευσε δουναι ¹⁹ τοσουτον ὡστε ²⁰ ὑπο πλησμονης
μεν μηποτε βαρυνεσθαι, του δε ἐνδεεστερως ἐχειν μη
ἀπειρως ἐχειν.²¹ ὡς δε μη ὑπο λιμου ἀγαν πιεζοιντο,²²
ἀπραγμονως μεν αὑτοις οὐκ ἐδωκε ²³ λαμβανειν τον
ὀψον,²⁴ κλεπτειν δ᾽ ἐφηκεν ἐστιν ἁ ²⁵ τῳ λιμῳ
ἐπικουρουντας. ἐρει δ᾽ οὐν τις — τι ²⁶ δητα, εἰπερ το
κλεπτειν ἀγαθον ἐνομιζε, πολλας πληγας ἐπεθηκε τῳ
ἁλισκομενῳ ; ²⁷ ὁτι, φημι ἐγω, και τἀλλα ²⁸ ὁσα ἀνθρω-

---

17. ἐφιετο, imperf. mid. of ἐφιημι, ' he made it his aim '.
18. Plural of ψυχος—cold spells. Don't confuse with
ψυχη, 'life', 'soul', etc.　19. ' He gave orders to give—
i.e. that they (subject unexpressed) should give.　20. Such
a quantity as . . .　21. ἐχω with an adv. is equivalent
to εἰμι with an adj.　Xenophon is very fond of this construction, and uses it twice here, ' as not to be without experience of being in want '.　22. ' In order that
they should not be pinched by hunger.'　This is a final
clause of purpose, the third ˙ different way you have
had of expressing such an idea in this same piece.　It
is here used with the optative mood, concerning which
you should be well content for the present to remain in
blissful ignorance.　23. Here used in the sense of ' granted '.
24. Their ' extra ' over and above their plain rations.
Spartan fare was plain to the point of being nasty.　A
visitor who tasted the famous Spartan black broth is said
to have observed that he did not wonder that the Spartans
were not afraid to die, if such was the only food they had
to live on.　25. ἐστιν ἁ, two words used together in Gk., lit.
' there are things which '—an equivalent for ' some things ',
the object of κλεπτειν.　26. Notice these two uses of τις.
The first is an indef., ' someone,' but the second, in view of
the mark ; at the end, a question, ' Why ' ?　27. ' The one
caught.'　They advised them to steal if they were hungry, but

ποι διδασκουσι, κολαζουσι τον μη καλως ὑπηρετουντα. κἀκεινοι²⁹ οὖν τους ἁλισκομενους ὡς κακως κλεπτοντας τιμωρουνται. και καλον θεις³⁰ ὡς πλειστους³¹ ἁρπασαι τυρους παρ' Ὀρθιας,³² εἶτα μαστιγουν³³ τουτους ἀλλοις ἐπεταξε. βελτιον³⁴ γαρ ἐστιν, ὡς φασιν, ὀλιγον χρονον ἀλγησαντα,³⁵ πολυν χρονον εὐδοκιμουντα εὐφραινεσθαι.

## VOCABULARY

ἀγαν, too much, excessively.
ἀθροιζω, gather, muster.
ἀλγεω, grieve, feel pain.
ἁλισκομαι, be caught.
ἀνυποδησια, -ας, a going barefoot.
ἀπαλυνω, soften.
ἀπειρος, without experience.
ἀπραγμονως, without trouble.
ἀρχη, office, rule.
βελτιων, -ον, better.
γε μην, yet, nevertheless.

δητα, indeed.
διαθρυπτω, pamper (lit. break down).
διδασκω, teach.
ἑκαστος, -η, -ον, each.
ἐνδεεστερος, -α, -ον, comparative ἐνδεης, c. 9.
ἐπικουρεω, help against.
ἐπιτασσω, give orders to.
ἐπιτιθημι, put upon, inflict.
ἐρω, *fut.* of λεγω.
εὐδοκιμεω, have a good reputation.

---

punished them for being caught. 28. τἀλλα = τα ἀλλα, ' as regards the other things '; this neuter plural is in the accus., acc. of reference. 29. κἀκεινοι = και ἐκεινοι, they *too*. 30. θεις τιθημι is often used in the sense of ' reckon ' or ' deem '. Here the ptcple. has the force of although : ' Although having deemed it honourable.' 31. 'As many as possible.' 32. At the altar of Artemis Orthia, boys underwent endurance tests in being whipped. Some even died under the ordeal. From this passage it would appear that as a test of their cunning boys had to steal the sacrificial cheeses from her altar. 33. Infinit., ' to whip '. 34. Neuter of βελτιων, the comparative degree of ἀγαθος. 35. ἀλγησαντα is accus., agreeing with ' one ' understood, and subject of εὐφραινεσθαι. ' It is better, as they say, for one having suffered a short time (acc.) to enjoy having a good reputation for a long time.' This is called the accus. and infin. construction, and corresponds to a noun clause in English.

εὐφραινομαι, enjoy.

ἐφιημι (*act.*), command, (*mid.*) make it one's aim.

ἐφιστημι, set up, appoint.

ἡβαω, be youthful.

θαλπος, -ους (*n.*), heat.

θεραπων, -οντος (*m.*), attendant.

ἰδιᾳ (*adv.*), privately.

ἰσχυρος, -α, -ον, violent.

καθιστημι, appoint (*pass.* and *intrans.* tense, be appointed).

καλεω, call.

κολαζω, punish.

κρατυνω, make strong.

κυριος, -α, -ον, with authority.

Λακεδαιμονιος, Lacedæmonian, Spartan.

λιμος, -ου (*m.*), hunger.

Λυκουργος, Lycurgus.

μανθανω, μαθησομαι, learn.

μαστιγοφορος, -ου (*m.*), whipbearer.

μαστιγοω, I whip.

μεντοι, however.

μεταβολη, -ης (*f.*), change.

μουσικη, -ης (*f.*), music, literature.

ὀλιγος, -η, -ον, small, little.

Ὀρθια, -ας (*f.*), Orthia, name of Artemis.

παιδαγωγος, -ου (*m.*), slavetutor.

παιδεια, -ας (*f.*), education.

παιδονομος, -ου (*m.*), educational supervisor.

παλαιστρα, -ας (*f.*), gymnasium.

πεμπω, send.

πιεζω, press, pinch.

πληγη, -ης (*f.*), blow, lash.

πλησμονη, -ης (*f.*), fullness, satiety.

προς + *dat.*, in addition to.

προσεθιζομαι (*mid.*), accustom oneself.

ῥᾳδιουργεω, take it easy.

σαφηνιζω, explain, make clear.

συνιημι, understand.

ταχιστα (*superlative adv.*), soonest, most quickly.

τιμωρεομαι, punish.

τυρος, -ου (*m.*), cheese.

ὑποδημα, -ατος (*n.*), sandal.

ὑπηρετεω, serve.

ψυχος, -ους (*n.*), cold.

# CHAPTER XVII

## MORE -μι VERBS

Compounds.

1. You have already seen the -μι verbs in action, and you may have noticed that they seem to appear more in the form of compounds than as simple verbs. In this connection it is well to bear in mind that a preposition in front of a μι- verb changes in appearance a good deal as the verb changes. For example, κατα plus ἱστημι = καθιστημι, and since the 2nd aorist participle of ἱστημι is στας, that of καθιστημι is καταστας. The 2nd aorist indicative similarly is κατα plus ἐστην = κατεστην, while the perfect, κατα plus ἐστηκα, gives us καθεστηκα. These compound forms are very common indeed.

2. Like τιθημι is ἱημι (' I let go '). For clarity this is given as a simple verb, but a good many of its tenses are only to be found in Greek literature in compounds. As its correspondence with τιθημι is almost exact, it will be sufficient to give the 1st person singular only of each tense.

### I. ἱημι, ' I let go.'

Active.

Present :    ἱημι, etc., but 3rd person plural, ἱασι, not ἱεασι.

Imperfect :    ἱην, but 2nd and 3rd singular always ἱεις, ἱει.

Infinitive : ἱεναι.
Participle : ἱεις.

Middle and Passive

Present :     ἱεμαι, etc., regular like τιθεμαι.
Imperfect :   ἱεμην, etc.

Infinitive :  ἱεσθαι.
Participle :   ἱεμενος.

## AORIST SYSTEM

Active.

1st Aorist :   ἡκα, ἡκας, ἡκε, ἡκαμεν, ἡκατε, ἡκαν.
2nd Aorist :   No singular, εἱμεν, εἱτε, εἱσαν.

Infinitive :  εἱναι.
Participle :   εἱς.

Middle.

1st Aorist :   ἡκαμην, etc.
2nd Aorist :   εἱμην, εἱσο, εἱτο, εἱμεθα, εἱσθε, εἱντο.

Infinitive :  ἑσθαι.
Participle :   ἑμενος.

Passive.

Aorist :      εἱθην.              Infinitive :  ἑθηναι.
Participle :   ἑθεις.

## OTHER TENSES

Active.   Future : -ἡσω.   Perfect : εἱκα.
Middle.   Future : -ἡσομαι.
Passive.  Future : -ἑθησομαι.

3. There are no verbs resembling διδωμι.

4. A number of verbs resemble δεικνυμι, such as
ἀπολλυμι (' destroy '), ζευγνυμι (' yoke '), ὁμνυμι
(' swear '), σκεδαννυμι (' scatter '), ἀνοιγνυμι (' open '),
and μειγνυμι (' mix '). All these, however, resemble
δεικνυμι only in the present and imperfect tenses,
the aorist and the other tenses being quite regular.

5. The two εἰμι's (' I am ' and ' I go ') are obviously of great importance. They are like twins who, upon first acquaintance, appear to be indistinguishable, but when you become intimate with them you so readily recognize their peculiar features that you wonder how confusion was possible. There is no aorist or perfect of εἰμι (' I am ') because of its meaning. εἶμι (' I go ') has a future sense, and is usually employed as the future of ἔρχομαι. For the aorist ἦλθον is used, and for the perfect ἥκω (' I have come '), conjugated like χορευω.

### II. (a) εἰμι, ' I am.'

| Present. | Future. | Imperfect. |
|---|---|---|
| 1. εἰμι | ἐσομαι | ἦν or ἦ |
| 2. εἶ | ἐσῃ or ἐσει | ἦσθα |
| 3. ἐστι | ἐσται | ἦν |
| 1. ἐσμεν | ἐσομεθα | ἦμεν |
| 2. ἐστε | ἐσεσθε | ἦτε |
| 3. εἰσι | ἐσονται | ἦσαν |

Infinitive : εἰναι     ἐσεσθαι     —
Participle : ὤν, οὖσα, ὄν     ἐσομενος     —

### (b) εἶμι, ' I go.'

| Present. | Imperfect. |
|---|---|
| 1. εἶμι | ἦα or ᾖειν |
| 2. εἶ | ᾖεισθα |
| 3. εἶσι | ᾖει |
| 1. ἰμεν | ᾖμεν or ᾖειμεν |
| 2. ἰτε | ᾖτε or ᾖειτε |
| 3. ἰασι | ᾖσαν or ᾖεσαν |

Infinitive : ἰεναι         —
Participle : ἰων, ἰουσα, ἰον    —

6. φημι (' I say '), though in some respects resembling ἰστημι, must be considered an irregular verb. Notice in particular that the participle which you would expect, φας φασα φαν, is not used in Attic Prose, its place being usually taken by φασκων.

### III. φημι, ' I say.'

| Present. | Imperfect. |
|---|---|
| 1. φημι | ἐφην |
| 2. φης | ἐφησθα |
| 3. φησι | ἐφη |
| 1. φαμεν | ἐφαμεν |
| 2. φατε | ἐφατε |
| 3. φασι | ἐφαυαν |

Infinitive : φαναι     Future : φησω
Participle : φασκων,    Aorist (very rare : usually
      -ουσα, -ον        imperfect) : ἐφησα.

Homer has some middle forms of φημι used in the same sense as the active : Infinitive φασθαι, participle φαμενος, imperfect ἐφαμην, and, especially, 3rd person ἐφατο or φατο.

7. καθημαι (' I sit ') and κειμαι (' I lie ' or ' I am placed ', used as the passive of τιθημι) are perfect passives of -μι verbs used with a present sense.

IV. καθημαι, ' I sit.'    κειμαι, ' I lie.'

| Present (Perfect Form). | Imperfect. | |
|---|---|---|
| 1. καθημαι | ἐκαθημην | or καθημην |
| 2. καθησαι | ἐκαθησο | καθησο |
| 3. καθηται | ἐκαθητο | καθηστο |
| (but ἧσται in | | or καθητο |
| simple verb) | | |
| 1. καθημεθα | ἐκαθημεθα | καθημεθα |
| 2. καθησθε | ἐκαθησθε | καθησθε |
| 3. καθηνται | ἐκαθηντο | καθηντο |

Infinitive :   καθησθαι    Participle : καθημενος

The simple verb ἧμαι is used mainly in poetry.

---

| Present. | Imperfect. |
|---|---|
| 1. κειμαι | ἐκειμην |
| 2. κεισαι | ἐκεισο |
| 3. κειται | ἐκειτο |
| 1. κειμεθα | ἐκειμεθα |
| 2. κεισθε | ἐκεισθε |
| 3. κεινται | ἐκειντο |

Infinitive :   κεισθαι    Future :   κεισομαι
Participle :   κειμενος

8. A difficult -μι verb is οἶδα (' I know '). It is one of many intransitive perfect forms in Greek with a present meaning (see πεφυκα and ἑστηκα). Its infinitive and participle show its perfect form. The pluperfect, which is used to represent the past, is full of variant forms. Note that there is only -σ- in the plural of this tense in the shorter form, to distinguish it from the imperfect of εἶμι (' I go ').

## V. Οἶδα, 'I know.'

|  | Perfect<br>(Present meaning) | | Pluperfect<br>(Past meaning) | |
|---|---|---|---|---|
| 1. | οἶδα | ᾔδη | or | ᾔδειν |
| 2. | οἶσθα | ᾔδεισθα | | |
| 3. | οἶδε | ᾔδει | | |
| 1. | ἴσμεν | ᾔσμεν | or | ᾔδειμεν |
| 2. | ἴστε | ᾔστε | or | ᾔδειτε |
| 3. | ἴσασι | ᾔσαν | or | ᾔδεσαν |

Infinitive : εἰδέναι            Future : εἴσομαι
Participle : εἰδώς, εἰδυῖα, εἰδός.

## EXERCISE. MORE -μι VERBS

Translate :—

1. ἄπιμεν εἰς τας σκηνας. 2. ἔσεσθε λοχαγοι της στρατιας. 3. το ὀρος ἠν ὑπερυψηλον τοις ἀναβαινουσι. 4. ἀφηκαμεν τας ἀγκυρας εἰς τυ ὑδωρ. 5. οὐ ῥᾳδιως εἰσομεθα το του ποταμου βαθος. 6. ἴστε ὁτι οὐ καταδυσεσθε. 7. ἠσθα στρατηγος παντων των Ἑλληνων. 8. παντες οἱ βοες ἠσαν εἰς τον ποταμον. 9. ἴσασι γαρ ὁτι δυνανται διαβαινειν. 10. ' τι φῃς συ ; ' ἐφασαν. ὁ δε ' Ὀδυσσευς εἰμι ' ἐφη.

## KEY TO EXERCISE

1. We shall depart into the tents. 2. You will be captains of the army. 3. The mountain was exceedingly high for those going up it. 4. We let down the anchors into the water. 5. We shall not easily know the depth of the river. 6. You know that you will not sink. 7. You were general of all the Greeks. 8. All the oxen went into the river. 9. For they know that they can cross. 10. ' What do you say ? ' they said. And he said, ' I am Odysseus.'

## A BRIGHT IDEA

(From Xenophon's *Anabasis*, Bk. III, c. 5.)

(The Greeks come to an impassable river; a Rhodian's scheme for crossing it is rejected.)

Ἐπει δε ἐπι τας σκηνας [1] ἀπηλθον, οἱ μεν ἀλλοι περι [2] τα ἐπιτηδεια ἠσαν, στρατηγοι δε και λοχαγοι συνησαν.[3] και ἐνταυθα πολλη ἀπορια ἠν. ἐνθεν μεν [4] γαρ ὀρη ἠν ὑπερυψηλα, ἐνθεν δε [4] ὁ ποταμος τοσουτος το βαθος [5] ὡστε μηδε το δορατα ὑπερεχειν πειρωμενοις του βαθους.[6]

Ἀπορουμενοις [7] δ' αὐτοις προσελθων τις ἀνηρ Ῥοδιος εἰπεν, Ἐγω θελω, ὠ ἀνδρες, διαβιβασαι ὑμας κατα τετρακισχιλιους [8] ὁπλιτας. ἀλλα πρωτον δει ὑμας ἐμοι ὠν [9] δεομαι ὑπηρετειν, και ταλαντον [10]

---

1. τας σκηνας. Probably vaguely for 'quarters' here. Actually their 'tents' (see c. 3) had been burned by the Persians. 2. περι, 'engaged on', 'busy with'. 3. συνησαν. Notice the two contrasted imperfs., the first from εἰμι, 'be', and the second from συνειμι, 'come together'. 4. ἐνθεν μεν . . . ἐνθεν δε, 'on the one side . . . on the other side'. The Greeks were marching up the left bank of the Tigris (ὁ ποταμος), with the high mountains of Kurdistan (τα ὀρη) on their right, gradually closing in on them, to make progress impossible. 5. το βαθος, 'in depth'. In giving measurements the dimension is usually put into the accus. case. 6. του βαθους. The gen. is used after πειραομαι, when it means 'to make trial of'. The soldiers failed to find the bottom of the river by testing it with their spears. 7. This word is usually used in the active voice with this meaning. The dat. is governed by προσελθων. 8. κατα τετρακισχιλιους. By four thousands—in companies of 4000. κατα often has this distributive sense. 9. ὠν δεομαι, 'what I want'; ὠν is the gen. case of the neuter plural relative pron. = 'the things which'. δεομαι, 'I stand in need of', is always followed by the gen. of the thing wanted. 10. ταλαντον, 'a talent'—a fairly large sum, corresponding to about £240 of English money before 1914. μισθον is in apposition to it = 'as a reward'.

μισθον ποριζειν. ἐρωτωμενος δε ὁτου[11] δειται, ᾿Ασκων, ἐφη, δισχιλιων δεησομαι· πολλα δ᾿ ὁρω προβατα και αἰγας και βους και ὀνους, ἃ ἀποδαρεντα[12] και φυσηθεντα ῥᾳδιως παρεξει την διαβασιν. δεησομαι δε και των δεσμων οἱς[13] χρησθε περι τα ὑποζυγια· τουτοις[14] ζευξας τους ἀσκους προς ἀλληλους, ὁρμισας ἑκαστον ἀσκον, λιθους ἀρτησας και ἀφεις[15] ὡσπερ ἀγκυρας εἰς το ὑδωρ, διαγαγων[16] και ἀμφοτερωθεν δησας, ἐπιβαλω[17] ὑλην και γην ἐπιφορησω· ὁτι μεν οὐν[18] οὐ καταδυσεσθε αὐτικα μαλα εἰσεσθε·[19] πας γαρ ἀσκος δυο ἀνδρας ἑξει[20] του μη καταδυναι. ὡστε δε μη ὀλισθανειν ἡ ὑλη και ἡ γη σχησει.[20]

᾿Ακουσασι[21] ταυτα τοις στρατηγοις το μεν ἐνθυμημα[22] χαριεν ἐδοκει εἰναι, το δ᾿ ἐργον ἀδυνατον.

---

11. ὁτου, gen. of ὁστις ἡτις ὁτι, ' who ? what ? '. 12. Tr., ' Which, being skinned and blown up '. It is the skins, of course, that are to be blown up. Xenophon has, naturally enough, forgotten that ' animals ', and not 'skins,' is the subject of his verb. 13. οἱς : χραομαι (irreg., ' 1 use ') takes the dat. case. 14. τουτοις, ' by means of these ', the instrumental dat. 15. ἀφεις, aor. active participle of ἀφιημι. 16. διαγαγων, ' carrying the skins across '. 17. ἐπιβαλω, fut. tense. 18. μεν οὐν, ' however '. 19. αὐτικα μαλα, ' in a moment—presently '. εἰσεσθε, fut. of οἰδα. 20. ἑξει and σχησει. There are two futs. of ἑχω, both with the same meaning : ἑξω and σχησω. ἑχω often has the meaning of ' keep from ' or ' restrain ', in which sense it is usually followed by the gen. ' Every skin will keep two men from sinking '. For το with the infin. = -ing, see c. 16—Spartan education, n. 11. Notice the μη, which does not seem to be wanted. The Gk. habit of looking at the result of an action often had an effect on their idiom. The *result* of using the skins was that the men did *not* sink. Hence a superfluous or redundant μη. So also in the next sentence : ' The wood and earth will keep them so that they do not slip '. 21. ἀκουσασι, dat. plur. of the aor. participle. 22. ἐνθυμημα, ' something considered '; hence, ' a plan '—a piece of reasoning. An ' enthymeme ' in English is a kind of logical syllogism, in particular a faulty one.

ἦσαν γαρ οἱ κωλυσοντες [23] περαν πολλοι ἱππεις, οἱ
εὐθυς ἐμελλον τους πρωτους παυειν ταυτα ποιουντας.

## VOCABULARY

ἀδυνατος, -η, -ον, impossible.

ἀμφοτερωθεν, from both sides.

ἀποδερω (aor. pass. ἀπεδερην), cf. δερμα, take the skin off, flay.

ἀπορεω, be at a loss.

ἀπορια, -ας (f.), perplexity.

ἀρταω, tie, bind.

δεομαι (gen.), want, need.

δεσμος, cable, bond.

διαβασις, -εως (f.), a crossing.

διαβιβαζω, convey across.

διαγω, carry across, spend (of time).

δισχιλιοι, two thousand.

δορυ, -ατος (n.), a spear.

ἐπιβαλλω, cast upon.

ἐπιφορεω, put upon.

καταδυνω, sink (transitive).

καταδυσομαι (fut.), κατεδυν (aor.) (intransitive).

κωλυω, prevent.

λοχαγος (m.), captain.

μισθος (m.), pay, reward.

ὀλισθανω, slip.

ὁπλιτης, -ου (m.) hoplite, heavy-armed soldier.

ὁρμιζω, to anchor.

πειραομαι, try, test.

περαω, I cross.

τοσουτος, τοσαυτη, τοσουτο, so great, so much.

ὑλη, -ης (f.), wood.

ὑπερεχω, protrude above.

ὑπερυψηλος, -ον, exceedingly high.

ὑπηρετεω, to furnish to.

φυσαω, to blow out.

χαριεις, -εσσα, -εν, pleasing.

χραομαι (dat.), use.

---

23. οἱ κωλυσοντες, ' those who were going to stop them '.

# CHAPTER XVIII

## THE ADJECTIVE

IF you have mastered the declension of nouns, you should have no difficulty with adjectives, as there are no new forms to be learnt. What matters is that you should be able to recognise an adjective and its case when you meet one. Most adjectives are of three terminations, and are a combination of the 1st and 2nd declensions, being declined like κακος or, if the termination -ος is preceded by a vowel or ρ, like μικρος (c. 7). But there are others of two terminations, the masculine and feminine being the same, and a few of one termination only. This applies also to adjectives of the 3rd declension. Let us take the types in order.

## 2nd Declension Types

1. **Contracted.** e.g. χρυσους (golden), being contracted for χρυσεος. The nom. and acc. sing. are different, but other cases go like κακος. Similarly, ἀργυρους (silver) goes like μικρος.

|  | *Sing.* | | | *Sing.* | | |
|---|---|---|---|---|---|---|
|  | *Mas.* | *Fem.* | *Neuter.* | *Mas.* | *Fem.* | *Neuter.* |
| N.V. | χρυσ-ους | χρυσ-η | χρυσ-ουν | ἀργυρ-ους | ἀργυρα | ἀργυρουν |
| Acc. | χρυσουν | χρυσην | χρυσουν | ἀργυρουν | ἀργυραν | ἀργυρουν |
| Gen. | χρυσου | χρυσης | χρυσου | ἀργυρου | ἀργυρας | ἀργυρου |
| Dat. | χρυσῳ | χρυση | χρυσῳ | ἀργυρῳ | ἀργυρᾳ | ἀργυρῳ |

2. **Compound adjectives in -ος are mostly of Two Terminations, thus :—**

| Mas., Fem. | Neuter. | Meaning |
|---|---|---|
| ἀθανατος | ἀθανατον | immortal |
| ἐφημερος | ἐφημερον | v. c. 7 |
| ἀθεος | ἀθεον | v. c. 5 |
| ἀπειρος | ἀπειρον | inexperienced (in), v. c. 16 |
| βαρβαρος | βαρβαρον | v. c. 6 |
| but εὐνους | εὐνουν | well-disposed (decl. like χρυσους, but without the fem. forms). |

3. Two very common adjectives (μεγας, great, and πολυς, much) which are irregular in the nom. and acc. sing., but regular in all other cases, thus :—

| | Mas. | Fem. | Neuter. | Mas. | Fem. | Neuter. |
|---|---|---|---|---|---|---|
| N.V. | μεγας | μεγαλη | μεγα | πολυς | πολλη | πολυ |
| Acc. | μεγαν | μεγαλην | μεγα | πολυν | πολλην | πολυ |
| Gen. | μεγαλου | μεγαλης | μεγαλου, etc. | πολλου | πολλης | πολλου etc. |

### 3rd Declension

1. **One Termination.**

ἀπαις (Gen. ἀπαιδος), ' childless '; decl. like παις.
ἀγνως (Gen. ἀγνωτος), ' unknown ' or ' unknowing '.
πενης (Gen. πενητος), ' poor '.

2. **Two Terminations.**

(a) Adjectives that are compounded of two words have only two terminations, e.g. σωφρων, because it is compounded of σως (' sound ', ' safe ', ' healthy '), and φρην (' mind '). For meaning v. σωφροσυνη (c. 3). Similarly declined is εὐδαιμων, ' happy ' (in the true sense, i.e. having ' a good spirit ' inside you).

|  | *Sing.* | | *Plural.* | |
| --- | --- | --- | --- | --- |
|  | *Mas. Fem.* | *Neuter.* | *Mas. Fem.* | *Neuter.* |
| *Nom.* | σωφρων | σωφρον | σωφρονες | σωφρονα |
| *Acc.* | σωφρονα | σωφρον | σωφρονας | σωφρονα |
| *Gen.* | σωφρονος | | σωφρονων | |
| *Dat.* | σωφρονι | | σωφροσι | |

(*b*) Mostly stems in -ες, and declined in mas. and fem. like τριηρης or Σωκρατης, e.g. ἀληθης, ' true .'

|  | *Sing.* | | *Plural.* | |
| --- | --- | --- | --- | --- |
|  | *Mas. Fem.* | *Neuter.* | *Mas. Fem.* | *Neuter.* |
| *Nom.* | ἀληθης | ἀληθες | ἀληθεις | ἀληθη |
| *Acc.* | ἀληθη | ἀληθες | ἀληθεις | ἀληθη |
| *Gen.* | ἀληθους | | ἀληθων | |
| *Dat.* | ἀληθει | | ἀληθεσι | |

Similarly are declined εὐγενης, ' well-born ' (eugenics), εὐτυχης, ' fortunate ', ψευδης, ' false ' (pseudo-), συγγενης ' related to '.

(*c*) Stems in -ι, -τ, -δ, or -ρ are declined like πολις (c. 13), e.g. φιλοπολις, ' patriotic '.

|  | *Sing.* | | *Plural.* | |
| --- | --- | --- | --- | --- |
|  | *Mas. Fem.* | *Neuter.* | *Mas. Fem.* | *Neuter.* |
| *N.V.* | φιλοπολις | φιλοπολι | φιλοπολεις | φιλοπολη |
| *Acc.* | φιλοπολιν | φιλοπολι | φιλοπολεις | φιλοπολη |
| *Gen.* | φιλοπολεως | | φιλοπολεων | |
| *Dat.* | φιλοπολει | | φιλοπολεσι | |

*but* εὐελπις, ' hopeful ', is declined like ἐλπις (c. 9, 3), —i.e. acc. εὐελπιδα, etc.

3. **Three Terminations.**

Stems in -υ. Masc. and neuter are 3rd declension (like πελεκυς and ἀστυ, except that the gen. sing.

ends in -ος, and the neut. plur. in -εα (not contracted)). The fem. is 1st declension—e.g. ἡδυς,
'pleasant', βραχυς, 'short' (brachycephalic), γλυκυς,
'sweet' (glucose), ὀξυς, 'sharp' (oxygen), ταχυς,
'swift'.

|  |  | Mas. | Fem. | Neuter. |
|---|---|---|---|---|
| Sing. | N.V. | ἡδυς | ἡδεια | ἡδυ |
|  | Acc. | ἡδυν | ἡδειαν | ἡδυ |
|  | Gen. | ἡδεος | ἡδειας | ἡδεος |
|  | Dat. | ἡδει | ἡδειᾳ | ἡδει |
| Plur. | N.V. | ἡδεις | ἡδειαι | ἡδεα |
|  | Acc. | ἡδεις | ἡδειας | ἡδεα |
|  | Gen. | ἡδεων | ἡδειων | ἡδεων |
|  | Dat. | ἡδεσι | ἡδειαις | ἡδεσι |

4. Irregular.

μελας, 'black' (melancholy).

|  | Mas. | Fem. | Neuter. |
|---|---|---|---|
| Nom. | μελας | μελαινα | μελαν |
| Acc. | μελανα, etc. | μελαιναν, etc. | μελαν, etc. |

ταλας, 'wretched'.

|  | Mas. | Fem. | Neuter. |
|---|---|---|---|
| Nom. | ταλας | ταλαινα | ταλαν |
| Acc. | ταλανα, etc. | ταλαιναν, etc. | ταλαν, etc. |

χαριεις, 'pleasing'.

|  | Mas. | Fem. | Neuter. |
|---|---|---|---|
| Nom. | χαριεις | χαριεσσα | χαριεν |
| Acc. | χαριεντα, etc. | χαριεσσαν, etc. | χαριεν, etc. |

### Declension of Participles

Participles are so common in Greek that it is well to take their declension together, even though you have met some of them separately already.

Three are 3rd declension in the masc. and neut. and 1st declension in the fem.—viz.

(1) Present participle active (e.g. λυων, ' loosing ').

(2) Aorist participle active (e.g. λυσας, ' having loosed ').

(3) Aorist participle passive (e.g. λυθεις, ' having been loosed ').

All these three are declined like λεων in the masc. and neut., and like μουσα in the fem., thus :—

| | Sing. | | | Plur. | |
|------|------|------|------|------|------|
| *Mas.* | *Fem.* | *Neuter.* | *Mas.* | *Fem.* | *Neuter.* |
| N. λυων | λυουσα | λυον | λυοντες | λυουσαι | λυοντα |
| A. λυοντα | λυουσαν | λυον | λυοντας | λυουσας | λυοντα |
| G. λυοντος | λυουσης | λυοντος | λυοντων | λυουσων | λυοντων |
| D. λυοντι | λυουση | λυοντι | λυουσι | λυουσαις | λυουσι |

### Contracted Participles.

| 1. τιμαω | τιμων | τιμωσα | τιμων |
|------|------|------|------|
| 2. φιλεω | φιλων | φιλουσα | φιλουν |
| 3. δουλοω | δουλων | δουλουσα | δουλουν |

Similarly,  λυσας     λυσασα     λυσαν
              λυσαντα    λυσασαν    λυσαν, etc.

and          λυθεις     λυθεισα    λυθεν, etc.

*Note.*—And the adj. πας (*all*), πασα,  παν,
                    παντα,   πασαν, παν, etc.

The perf. ptcple. λελυκως goes thus :—

| Nom. Sing. | λελυκως | λελυκυια | λελυκος |
|---|---|---|---|
| Acc. Sing. | λελυκοτα | λελυκυιαν | λελυκος |
| Gen. Sing. | λελυκοτος | λελυκυιας | λελυκοτος |
| Dat. Plur. | λελυκοσι | λελυκυιαις | λελυκοσι |

Present participles of -μι verbs (v. chap. 16), go more or less like λυσας, thus :—

| Nom. Sing. | διδους (' giving ') | διδουσα | διδον |
|---|---|---|---|
| Acc. Sing. | διδοντα | διδουσαν | διδον, etc. |
| Nom. Sing. | δεικνυς (' showing ') | δεικνυσα | δεικνυν |
| Nom. Sing. | τιθεις (' placing ') | τιθεισα | τιθεν |

You will meet these forms so often that it will pay you to learn them thoroughly.

Translate :—

1. ἡδεια τοις ναυταις ἐστιν ἡ της χθονος ὀψις ἐκ χειμωνος σωζομενοις.

2. ὁ ἱερευς κηρυξας την του νοσηματος λυσιν παση τῃ πολει μελαιναν ὑν ἐθυσε (θυω = I sacrifice) τῳ Διι.

3. εὐτυχει πολις εἰ οἱ πολιται εἰσι σωφρονες και εὐνοι.

## KEY

1. Sweet to sailors is the sight of land when they are being saved from a storm.

2. The priest, having proclaimed release from the disease to the whole city, sacrificed a black pig to Zeus.

3. A city is fortunate if the citizens are sensible and patriotic.

## Lines from Greek Drama

The following iambic lines (you have had many already) from Greek drama will not only give you practice in adjectives, but help you to read plays later. As they are poetry, the order of words, which, as always in Greek, is the order of thought, is not always what you might expect in prose, but if you *pay attention to the terminations*, you should be able to translate them correctly. It is helpful to learn them by heart, feeling the beat of the six-foot line, thus :—

1. των εὐτυχούν|των [1] ‖ πάν|τες εἴσ|ι σύγ|γενείς.
2. βραχεια τερψις ἐστιν ἡδονης κακης.
3. ὁ γραμματων ἀπειρος [2] οὐ βλεπει βλεπων.
4. και πολλ' ἀπ' ἐχθρων μανθανουσιν οἱ σοφοι.
5. φθειρουσιν ἠθη χρησθ' ὁμιλιαι κακαι.
6. εἰ θεοι τι δρωσι [3] φαυλον, οὐκ εἰσιν θεοι.
7. θεου θελοντος [4] δυνατα παντα γιγνεται.
8. ἐνεστι γαρ πως τουτο τῃ τυραννιδι
   νοσημα, τοις φιλοισι μη πεποιθεναι. [5]

## From Prose Writers

9. ἡ μεγαλη πολις ἐρημια μεγαλη ἐστι [6] (said of Megalopolis).

---

1. εὐτυχουντων, gen. plur. of present ptcple. of εὐτυχεω. *v.* Contracted verbs 20. 2. We say ' unskilled in ', Gk., says, ' unskilled of '. 3. δρωσι, contracted from δραουσι, *v.* 20. 4. Gen. abs. ' if god wishes '. 5. πεποιθεναι, strong perf. inf. from πειθω, ' I persuade '. Strong perfects are usually intransitive, therefore this means ' to trust '. Why μη and not οὐ ? *v.* 28 (end). 6. Megalopolis was a city in Arcadia founded by Epaminondas, the Theban, after the defeat of Sparta at Leuctra in 370 B.C. His idea was to build an ' enormous city ' to hold the forty scattered communities of Arcadia as a protection against Sparta, but it was not a success. The walls were 6 miles in circuit, but the city was largely uninhabited, and so a ' desolation '. British archæologists have excavated it and found the foundations of a hall large enough to hold 10,000 people.

10. το μεν σωμα θνητον, ή δε ψυχη άθανατος.

11. ή φιλια περιχορευει την οίκουμενην,[7] κηρυτ-
τουσα δη[8] πασιν ήμιν[9] έγειρεσθαι έπι τον
μακαρισμον.—Epicurus.

12. παντες φυσει παντα[10] όμοιως[11] πεφυκαμεν[12]
είναι και[13] βαρβαροι και Έλληνες.—Antiphon.

13. (From the newspaper *Hellas*, 16 ΦΕΒΡΟΥΑΡΙΟΥ,
1945.) :

### Νεαι Ελπιδες

Έχομεν[14] ήδη άνα[15] χειρας το πληρες κειμενον[16]
της συμφωνιας μεταξυ των Άντιπροσωπων
(representatives) της Έλληνικης Κυβερνησεως
και της Άντιπροσωπειας (delegation) του
ΕΑΜ[17]—ΕΛΑΣ.[18]

---

7. Sc. γην, ' the inhabited ', common Gk. expression for
' the world '.   8. δη, particle difficult to translate.   It often,
as here, has the force of underlining the word it follows—
' proclaiming loudly '.   Sometimes it is ironical.   9. ήμιν,
' to us ', *v*. Pronouns 24.   10. παντα, adverbial acc. ' in everything '.   11. Adv. from όμοιος, *v*. 5.   12. πεφυκα is the perfect
of φυω (' I grow '), and used intransitively to mean ' I have
grown to be ', and so, ' I am by nature '.   Here the inf.
είναι depends on it.   13. και . . . και, ' both . . . and '.
This is a remarkable admission of the equality of man by a
Greek of the fifth century B.C.   14. This sentence from the
newspaper *Hellas* is good classical Gk. with the exception
of the two words with Eng. translations.   15. άνα, prep.
' through ', originally ' up ', *v*. 22.   16. κειμενον in classical
Gk., ' thing lying ', and so ' fixed ' here = ' text '.   17.
E.A.M. stands for έθνικον άπελευθερωτικον μετωπον, National
Liberation Front.   18. E.L.A.S. stands for Έλληνικος λαικος
άπελευθερωτικος στρατος, National Popular Liberation Army.

## VOCABULARY

ἀθανατος, -ον, not mortal, immortal.

δυνατος, -η, -ον, possible, powerful.

ἐγειρω, I awaken. Mid. I awake.

ἐνειμι, I am in.

ἐρημια, desolation (ἐρημος, adj. desolate).

εὐτυχεω, I am fortunate (εὐ, well; τυχη, fortune) .

ἐχθρος, enemy, also (as adj.) hateful.

ἡδονη, -ης, pleasure (hedonist).

ἠθος, -ους, no Eng. equivalent. Therefore we have taken over the word as ' ethos '. Sometimes = disposition, character, manners. Adj. ἠθικος. τα ἠθικα, ' a treatise on morals ' (e.g. Aristotle's Ethics).

θνητος, -η, -ον, mortal (θνησκω, θανατος).

κηρυττω \ I proclaim (κηρυξ,
κηρυσσω / a herald).

κυβερνησις, -εως, a steering guiding (κυβερνητης is a pilot). So in Mod. Gk. = Government (Lat. Gubernator, etc.).

μακαρισμος, -ον, a pronouncing happy (μακαριος), a blessing, here ' the praises of a happy life '.

μεταξυ, between (gen.).

νοσημα, -ατος, disease (νοσεω, I am sick).

οἰκεω, I inhabit.

ὁμιλια, -ας, converse, intercourse (ὁμιλεω, I associate with). [' Homily ' is a sermon to a crowd].

περιχορευω, I dance round.

πληρης, -ες (adj.), full.

πως (adv.), somehow.

συμφωνια, -ας, harmony (symphony, ' a sound together ').

τυραννις, -ιδος, tyranny.

φαυλος, -η, -ον (adj.), base, disgraceful.

φθειρω, I destroy, corrupt.

# CHAPTER XIX

## DEGREES OF COMPARISON, AND ADVERBS

THE grammatical terms 'comparative' and 'super-lative' reveal their meaning from examples in English. If you want to say shortly that John is more wealthy than Peter, but Michael is the most wealthy of the three, you can say that John is wealthi*er* than Peter, but Michael is the wealthi*est*. In the same way in Greek you can either say that J. is μαλλον (*v.* c. 7) πλουσιος than P., but M. is μαλιστα πλουσιος, or (as is more common) J. is πλουσιωτερος than P., but M. is πλουσιωτατος. In other words, you can change the termination of the adj. to express *the comparative degree* when *two* things are being compared, and the *superlative* degree when *more than two* are involved. So far the English (and Latin) usage resembles the Greek, but 'than Peter' can be expressed in two ways in Greek, which are equally common.

(1) by the conjunction ἡ (meaning 'than') without altering the construction of the word that follows it, e.g. J. is πλουσιωτερος ἡ Πετρος, or

(2) when the first person or thing to be compared is in the nom. or acc. case, by omit-ting ἡ and putting the second member to be compared into the gen, e.g. J. is πλουσιωτερος Πετρου.

## Rules for Forming the Comparative and Superlative

1. The commonest way is by the termination -τερος (declined like μικρος) for the comp., and -τατος (declined like κακος) for the superl., affixed to the masc. stem of the adj.—e.g.

| | | | |
|---|---|---|---|
| θερμος, ' warm '; | θερμο-τερος, | θερμο-τατος | (stem θερμο-) |
| μακρος, ' long '; | μακρο-τερος, | μακρο-τατος | (stem μακρο-) |
| αληθης, ' true '; | αληθεσ-τερος, | αληθεσ-τατος | (stem αληθες-) |
| οξυς, ' sharp '; | οξυ-τερος, | οξυ-τατος | (stem οξυ-) |

*but* in the case of adjs. ending in -ος, which have the preceding vowel short the ο becomes ω.

e.g. σοφος, ' wise ';      σοφωτερος, σοφωτατος
       αξιος, ' worthy ';    αξιωτερος, αξιωτατος.

2. In some adjs. the ο is dropped altogether.

e.g. φιλος, ' friendly '; φιλτερος, φιλτατος

     [also sometimes φιλαιτερος, φιλαιτατος]
     γεραιος, ' old '; γεραιτερος, γεραιτατος,

but αρχαιος, ' ancient '; σπουδαιος, ' earnest '; δικαιος, ' just ', follow rule 1.

3. Stems ending in -ον insert ες before the termination, thus :—

ευδαιμων, ' fortunate '; ευδαιμον-εστερος, ευδαιμον-εστατος
σωφρων (*v.* σωφροσυνη, ch. 3), σωφρον-εστερος, σωφρον-εστατος.

4. A few adjs. (mostly ending in -υς or -ρος) adopt a different procedure altogether. They drop the vowel of the stem, and for the comparative add

-ιων, and for the superlative -ιστος. Stems in -ρο drop the -ρ also.

E.g. ἡδυς, ' sweet '; ἡδιων, ἡδιστος
ταχυς, 'swift'; θασσων (for ταχ-ιων), ταχιστος
μεγας, ' big '; μειζων (for μεγ-ιων), μεγιστος
αἰσχρος, ' shameful '; αἰσχιων, αἰσχιστος
ἐχθρος, ' hostile '; ἐχθιων, ἐχθιστος

These comparatives are thus declined, eliding the
ν and contracting in acc. sing. (masc. and fem.) and
in nom. and acc. plur.

|  | Sing. | | Plur. | |
|---|---|---|---|---|
|  | Mas., Fem. | Neuter. | Mas., Fem. | Neuter. |
| N.V. | μειζων | μειζον | μειζονες or μειζους | μειζονα or μειζω |
| Acc. | μειζονα or μειζω | μειζον | μειζονας or μειζους | ,, ,, |
| Gen. | μειζονος | | μειζονων | |
| Dat. | μειζονι | | μειζοσι | |

5. Some of the commonest adjs. behave irregularly, employing different stems, as in English ' good, better, best ', ' bad, worse, worst '. Sometimes this is the result of words in commonest use getting their less important syllables slurred over, and harsh sounds getting worn away soonest. Here are some irregulars, which are so common that it is worth studying them carefully. Otherwise you may not recognise them in a sentence.

| Positive. | Comparative. | Superlative. | Derivative. |
|---|---|---|---|
| ἀγαθος, ' good ' | ⎧ ἀμεινων<br>⎨ βελτιων<br>⎩ κρεισσων | ἀριστος<br>βελτιστος<br>κρατιστος | aristocrat |
| κακος, ' bad ' | ⎧ κακιων<br>⎩ χειρων | κακιστος<br>χειριστος | |
| καλος, ' beautiful ' | καλλιων | καλλιστος | |
| ὀλιγος,' little ',<br>' few ' | ⎧ ἡσσων<br>⎨ ἐλασσων | ὀλιγιστος<br>ἐλαχιστος | [ἡκιστα only as<br>adverb, ' in the<br>least degree,'<br>' not at all '.] |
| μικρος, ' little ' | ⎧ μικροτερος<br>⎩ μειων | μικροτατος, microphone | |
| πολυς, ' much ',<br>' many ' | πλειων or<br>πλεων | πλειστος, pleonastic | |
| ῥᾳδιος, ' easy ' | ῥᾳων | ῥᾳστος | — |
| — | προτερος<br>(former) | πρωτος<br>(first) | protoplasm,<br>etc. |
| — | ὑστερος<br>(later) | ὑστατος<br>(last) | — |
| — | — | ἐσχατος<br>(last) | eschatology |

## ADVERBS

The normal way to form adverbs is to cut off the last syllable of the gen. sing. of the adj. and add -ως. Their comps. are the same as the neut. *sing.* of the comp. adj., and their superls. as the neut. *plur.* of the superl. adj.—e.g.

| Adj. | Gen. | Adv. | Comp. | Superl. |
|---|---|---|---|---|
| σοφ-ος, | -ου | σοφως | σοφωτερον | σοφωτατα |
| ἡδ-υς, | -εος | ἡδεως | ἡδιον | ἡδιστα |
| κακ-ος, | -ου | κακως | κακιον | κακιστα |
| σωφρ-ων, | -ονος | σωφρονως | σωθρονεστερον | σωφρονεστατα |

## A Few Irregulars

| εὐ, ' well ' | ἀμεινον | ἀριστα |
|---|---|---|
| ἀγχι, ' near ' | ἀσσον | ἀγχιστα |
| μαλα, ' much ' | μαλλον (' rather ') | μαλιστα (' especially ')<br>(v. p. 1 of this<br>chap.) |
| ἀνω, ' up ' | ἀνωτερω | ἀνωτατω |

N.B.—(1) The neut. acc. of an adj. (sing. or plur. is often used as adv.—e.g. πολυ and πολλα, ' much '; μεγα, ' greatly '; μονον, ' only '.

(2) ὡς or ὁτι with a superl. express ' as —— as possible '—e.g. ὡς ταχιστα = ' as quickly as possible '.

## Lines from Plays

Translate :—

1. κρεισσον σιωπαν ἐστιν ἡ λαλειν ματην.
2. αἰσχιον ἐστιν οὐδεν [1] ἡ ψευδη λεγειν.
3. οὐδεις ἀναγκης μειζον [2] ἰσχυει νομος.
4. αἱ δευτεραι πως φροντιδες σοφωτεραι.
5. ὁ πλειστα πραττων πλεισθ' [2] ἁμαρτανει βροτων.
6. ἠν Οἰδιπους [3] το πρωτον [4] εὐτυχης ἀνηρ,
   εἰτ' ἐγενετ' [5] αὐθις ἀθλιωτατος βροτων.

## Epigrams

7. πας τις ἀπαιδευτος [6] φρονιμωτατος ἐστι σιωπων,
   τον λογον ἐγκρυπτων, ὡς [7] παθος αἰσχρο-
   τατον. [8]—Palladas.
8. ἐστιν ὁ μεν [9] χειρων, ὁ δ' [9] ἀμεινων ἐργον [10]
   ἑκαστον· [10]
   οὐδεις δ' ἀνθρωπων αὐτος ἁπαντα [10] σοφος.—
   Theognis.

---

1. οὐδεν is the subject. 2. μειζον and πλειστα—here adv. 3. A reference to the unhappy fate of Œdipus. The Delphic Oracle had foretold that he would kill his father and marry his mother. When he did both of these things, not knowing who his parents were, he put his eyes out. The story is told by Sophocles in his play Οἰδιπους Τυραννος. 4. Adverbial use, ' at first '. 5. Aor. of γιγνομαι. 6. ἀ-, ' not '; παιδευτος, ' educated '. 7. ὡς, ' just as '. 8. Poetical form for αἰσχιστον. 9. ὁ μεν . . . ὁ δε, ' the one . . . the other '. 10. Acc. after ἀμεινων, ' better at '; sometimes called the ' acc. of the part concerned '. Similarly, ἁπαντα, ' wise in everything '.

## From Greek Writers

9. χρησμος Ἀπολλωνος ἠν ἐν Δελφοις·
σοφος Σοφοκλης, σοφωτερος δ᾽ Εὐριπιδης,
ἀνδρων δε παντων Σωκρατης σοφωτατος.[11]

10. πλεον ἡμισυ παντος, ὡς Ἡσιοδος λεγει.

11. ἀριστον [12] ὑδωρ, ὡς Πινδαρος λεγει.

12. δεινοτατον ἐστι τους χειρους των βελτιονων [13]
ἀρχειν.

13. ἐσται [14] ἡ ἐσχατη πλανη χειρων της πρωτης.
—New Testament.

14. ἐλευθερως δουλευε· δουλος οὐκ ἐσει.[14]—Menander.

15. ἡ πολις, την καλλιστην πολιτειαν ὡς ταχιστα [15]
και ἀριστα λαβουσα,[16] εὐδαιμονεστατα
διαξει.

## VOCABULARY

ἁμαρτανω, I miss the mark,
' err ', perhaps ' do wrong '
(but it does not mean
' sin ' in classical Gk.).
Ἀπολλων, -ωνος, Apollo.
Δελφοι, -ων (*plur. noun*),
Delphi.
διαγω, I pass (time). Supply
βιον (frequently omitted).
δουλευω, I am a slave (δουλ-ος).
ἐγκρυπτω, I hide.

ἡμισυ, half.
ἰσχυω, I am strong, powerful.
λαλεω, I talk.
πλανη, error, wandering
(planet, why so called ?).
πολιτεια, -ας, citizenship,
government (policy).
σιωπαω, I am silent.
φρονιμος, -ον, wise.
φροντις, -ιδος (*f.*), thought.
χρησμος, -ου, oracle.

---

11. Sc. ἐστι. The Delphic Oracle had declared Socrates the
wisest of men. When asked why, he said that, while other
men thought they were wise and were not, he knew he wasn't.
12. Sc. ἐστι. This is inscribed on the Pump Room at Bath.
13. Acc. and inf. construction (*v. c.* 26). τους χ. των β.
ἀρχειν, ' that the . . . should rule the', is a noun clause
equivalent to the subject of ἐστι. 14. Fut. of εἰμι, ' I am '.
15. *v.* Adverbs in this chapter. 16. Aor. ptcple. of λαμβανω.

# CHAPTER XX

## CONTRACTED VERBS

**Vowels.** Vowels are the fluids of a language. They are likely to alter their shape according to the vessel (or verb) in which you use them. They are also liable to run into one another. Look at Chapter 12. In the piece from Theophrastus you have the words βοωσι, ποιουντες, and νικωντες. In Chapter 14 αἱρεομαι you were told = αἱρουμαι, and in Chapter 15 κοιμαομενην = κοιμωμενην. In Chapter 16 you had ἐπικουρουντας, and in Chapter 17 ἀπορουμενοις and ἐρωτωμενος. What is the reason for these strange antics on the part of the vowel?

**Contracted Verbs.** If the stem of a verb ends with a diphthong (as ευ in χορευ-ω), η, ω or υ (as υ in κωλυ-ω) ; or a consonant (as ττ in πραττω), the endings will be regular. These you have already learnt (let us hope). If, on the other hand, the stem of the verb ends in α, ε, or ο, this vowel tends to melt and run into the vowel of the regular ending. The vowel resulting from this amalgamation of the stem and the ending is called a ' contracted ' vowel, and a verb evincing this regrettable tendency to fuse at the joint is called a ' contracted ' verb. In the poetry of Homer, and poetry imitating an archaic style, and in the Ionic dialect employed by Herodotus, we are at a stage of Greek where the contraction has not yet taken place. In the poem on the Tettix, for example (c. 12), in the words φιλεει, φιλεουσι and even the noun δενδρεων, contraction has not yet taken place.

**How to Learn.** There are three possible ways to deal with contracted verbs. You may come to the conclusion that the vagaries of the vowel in a contracted verb are incalculable anyway, and that as long as you keep a rough idea of the personal ending of a verb you cannot go far wrong in being prepared for any old vowel to turn up. That is an understandable but dangerously casual view to take. After all, there is a divinity that shapes these ends, rough-hew them how we will. But offend that deity, and you will find Nemesis lurking among the subjunctives and optatives. The second view is that these contracted verbs represent three more mountainous obstacles to surmount, and that one had better get down to the solid learning of them in all their arid detail without further ado. This is heroic, but rather unnecessarily laborious. The third way, and the one we recommend, is to learn the principle of contraction so thoroughly that its application to any verb form (or noun form for that matter, for the same rules apply to some nouns) is the work of a split second. Just as it becomes an automatic reaction to anyone with an elementary knowledge of colour to see not merely orange and green, but at the same moment the constituent red and yellow or blue and yellow, so you should be able instinctively to resolve the vowel of a contracted verb into the constituent vowels of stem and ending.

**Tenses not Affected.** As the future, aorist, and perfect stems do not end with a vowel, it will be

seen that there is no contraction in these tenses.
It has already been pointed out in Chapter 8, on
the future tense, that where a verb stem ends in
a short vowel, the method of forming the future,
aorist and perfect, is to lengthen the vowel, α and ε
both changing to η, and ο to ω, and to add σ for the
future and aorist, and κ for the perfect.   Thus the
unaffected tenses of the three model contracted
verbs will be as follows :—

| PRES. | FUT. | AOR. | PERF. | AOR. PASS. |
|-------|------|------|-------|------------|
| τιμα-ω | τιμησω | ἐτιμησα | τετιμηκα | ἐτιμηθην |
| φιλε-ω | φιλησω | ἐφιλησα | πεφιληκα | ἐφιληθην |
| δουλο-ω | δουλωσω | ἐδουλωσα | δεδουλωκα | ἐδουλωθη |

**Principles of Vowel Mixing.**   The three vowels of
the stem are α, ε, and ο.   The changes they undergo
in contraction are best learnt as a series of equations,
thus :—

' α ' *stems*.

   α + ο, ου or ω = ω ;       α + ει or η = ᾳ
   α + ε or η     = α ;       α + οι      = ῳ

' ε ' *stems*.

   ε + ο = ου.   ε before any long vowel or
   ε + ε = ει      diphthong disappears.

' ο ' *stems*.

   ο + ει, η or οι   = οι ;   ο + ε, ο, or ου = ου
   ο + ω or η = ω.

Note that Iota subscript in contraction has always
the same force as the full Iota.

# CONTRACTED VERBS

τιμα-ω, 'honour'; φιλε-ω, 'love'; δουλο-ω, 'enslave'

### Present Active

| | | | | | | |
|---|---|---|---|---|---|---|
| 1. | (α-ω) | τιμω | (ε-ω) | φιλω | (ο-ω) | δουλω |
| 2. | (α-εις) | τιμᾳς | (ε-εις) | φιλεις | (ο-εις) | δουλοις |
| 2. | (α-ει) | τιμᾳ | (ε-ει) | φιλει | (ο-ει) | δουλοι |
| 1. | (α-ομεν) | τιμωμεν | (ε-ομεν) | φιλουμεν | (ο-ομεν) | δουλουμεν |
| 2. | (α-ετε) | τιμᾱτε | (ε-ετε) | φιλειτε | (ο-ετε) | δουλουτε |
| 3. | (α-ουσι) | τιμωσι | (ε-ουσι) | φιλουσι | (ο-ουσι) | δουλουσι |

### Imperfect Active

| | | | | | | |
|---|---|---|---|---|---|---|
| 1. | (α-ον) | ἐτιμων | (ε-ον) | ἐφιλουν | (ο-ον) | ἐδουλουν |
| 2. | (α-ες) | ἐτιμᾱς | (ε-ες) | ἐφιλεις | (ο-ες) | ἐδουλους |
| 3. | (α-ε) | ἐτιμᾱ | (ε-ε) | ἐφιλει | (ο-ε) | ἐδουλου |
| 1. | (α-ομεν) | ἐτιμωμεν | (ε-ομεν) | ἐφιλουμεν | (ο-ομεν) | ἐδουλουμεν |
| 2. | (α-ετε) | ἐτιμᾱτε | (ε-ετε) | ἐφιλειτε | (ο-ετε) | ἐδουλουτε |
| 3. | (α-ον) | ἐτιμων | (ε-ον) | ἐφιλουν | (ο-ον) | ἐδουλουν |

| Present Infinitive Active | Present Infinitive Active | Present Infinitive Active |
|---|---|---|
| (α-*ειν)   τιμᾶν | (ε-ειν)   φιλεῖν | (ο-*ειν)   δουλοῦν |

| Present Participle Active | Present Participle Active | Present Participle Active |
|---|---|---|
| (α-ων)    τιμῶν | (ε-ων)    φιλῶν | (ο-ων)    δουλῶν |
| (α-ουσα)  τιμῶσα | (ε-ουσα)  φιλοῦσα | (ο-ουσα)  δουλοῦσα |
| (α-ον)    τιμῶν | (ε-ον)    φιλοῦν | (ο-ον)    δουλοῦν |

| Present Mid. and Pass. | Present Mid. and Pass. | Present Mid. and Pass. |
|---|---|---|
| 1. (α-ομαι)   τιμῶμαι | 1. (ε-ομαι)   φιλοῦμαι | 1. (ο-ομαι)   δουλοῦμαι |
| 2. (α-ει, -η)  τιμᾷ | 2. (ε-ει, -η)  φιλεῖ | 2. (ο-ει, -η)  δουλοῖ |
| 3. (α-εται)   τιμᾶται | 3. (ε-εται)   φιλεῖται | 3. (ο-εται)   δουλοῦται |
| 1. (α-ομεθα)  τιμώμεθα | 1. (ε-ομεθα)  φιλούμεθα | 1. (ο-ομεθα)  δουλούμεθα |
| 2. (α-εσθε)   τιμᾶσθε | 2. (ε-εσθε)   φιλεῖσθε | 2. (ο-εσθε)   δουλοῦσθε |
| 3. (α-ονται)  τιμῶνται | 3. (ε-ονται)  φιλοῦνται | 3. (ο-ονται)  δουλοῦνται |

* As this ειν is itself a contraction of ε-εν, no iota appears in the infinitives, τιμα -ε -εν = τιμαν, δουλο -ε -εν = δουλουν.

## CONTRACTED VERBS—continued

| Imperfect Mid. and Pass. | Imperfect Mid. and Pass. | Imperfect Mid. and Pass. |
|---|---|---|
| 1. (α-ομην) ἐτιμωμην | 1. (ε-ομην) ἐφιλουμην | 1. (ο-ομην) ἐδουλουμην |
| 2. (α-ου) ἐτιμω | 2. (ε-ου) ἐφιλου | 2. (ο-ου) ἐδουλου |
| 3. (α-ετο) ἐτιμᾶτο | 3. (ε-ετο) ἐφιλειτο | 3. (ο-ετο) ἐδουλουτο |
| 1. (α-ομεθα) ἐτιμωμεθα | 1. (ε-ομεθα) ἐφιλουμεθα | 1. (ο-ομεθα) ἐδουλουμεθα |
| 2. (α-εσθε) ἐτιμᾶσθε | 2. (ε-εστι) ἐφιλεισθε | 2. (ο-εσθε) ἐδουλουσθε |
| 3. (α-οντο) ἐτιμῶντο | 3. (ε-οντο) ἐφιλουντο | 3. (ο-οντο) ἐδουλουντο |
| **Present Infin. Mid. and Pass.** | **Present Infin. Mid. and Pass.** | **Present Infin. Mid. and Pass.** |
| (α-εσθαι) τιμᾶσθαι | (ε-εσθαι) φιλεισθαι | (ο-εσθαι) δουλουσθαι |
| **Present Participle Mid. and Pass.** | **Present Participle Mid. and Pass.** | |
| (α-ομενος, -η, -ον) τιμώμενος, -η, -ον | (ε-ομενος, -η, -ον) φιλουμενος, -η, -ον | (ο-ομενος, -η, -ον) δουλουμενος, -η, -ον |

## EXERCISE. CONTRACTED VERBS

Translate :—

1. οἱ Λακεδαιμονιοι ἐδειπνουν ἐν ταις ὁδοις. 2. ὁ Μητιοχος ἐπωπα τους ἀρτους. 3. ἡγουμεθα τους στεφανους συρφετον εἰναι. 4. οἱ Ἀθηναιοι πολλακις ἐνικων τους Λακεδαιμονιους. 5. ὁ Θεαγενης ἐδηλου το ἀγαν φιλοτιμον. 6. ὁ ἀθλητης ἀξιοι νενικηκεναι. 7. λογοι ἀει ποιουνται ὑπο των ῥητορων. 8. πολλακις ἐνικα ὁ ἡρως την πυγμην. 9. δουλοι ὑπο του δεσποτου, ὠ νεανια. 10. τιμᾳ ὑπο του ποιητου, ὠ ἀθλητα. 11. οἱ ἀγαν πολιτικοι οὐκ ἐφιλουντο ὑπο των πολλων. 12. τουτο ἐδηλουτο τοις παισιν ὑπο του διδασκαλου. 13. ἐρωντες της πατριδος, ὠ πολιται, οὐ μαχεσθε ὑπερ αὐτης ; 14. κακον ἐστι δουλουσθαι τοις πολεμιοις. 15. τις οὐκ ἐπιθυμει φιλεισθαι ὑπο παντων ; 16. τιμωμενος ὑπο των κριτων ἠθροισε πολλους στεφανους. 17. ἀγαν ἐτιμω, ὠ Θεαγενες. 18. ὁ Περικλης εἰωθεν ἡγεισθαι τῳ δημῳ. 19. οὐκ ἀει ἐπηνου ὑπο των ἡγεμονων, ὠ Περικλεις. 20. ἀγαν ῥᾳδιον ἐστιν ἐπιφθονως χρησθαι * τῃ δυναμει.

## KEY TO EXERCISE

1. The Spartans used to dine in the roads. 2. Metiochus supervises the bread. 3. We consider the garlands to be rubbish. 4. The Athenians often used to conquer the Spartans. 5. Theagenes used to display excessive ambition. 6. The athlete claims to have won. 7. Speeches are always being made by orators. 8. The hero often won the boxing. 9. You are being enslaved by the master, young man. 10. You are honoured by the poet, athlete. 11. Excessively political people were not loved by the many. 12.

---

* In the verb χρωμαι (χρα-ομαι) η is everywhere found where there would be an α in τιμωμαι (τιμαομαι).

This was being shown to the boys by the teacher.   13.
(While) loving your country, citizens, do you not fight on
behalf of it?   14. It is evil to be enslaved to the enemy.
15. Who does not desire to be loved by all?   16. Being
honoured by the judges, he amassed many garlands.   17.
You were honoured too much, Theagenes.   18. Pericles is
accustomed to lead the people.   19. You were not always
praised by the leaders, Pericles.   20. It is too easy to use
power unpopularly.

## POT-HUNTER AND POOH-BAH

### (From Plutarch)

Plutarch, who lived from A.D. 48 to about A.D.
120, was a native of Chæronea in Bœotia. His
two main works are the *Parallel Lives* and the
*Moralia*, the first a series of biographies of famous
Greeks and Romans compared with one another,
the second a collection of eighty-three essays on a
wide range of subjects, from " Advice to Married
Couples " to " The Face of the Moon ". The
" Lives " of Plutarch have become familiar to
English readers from North's translation. Shake-
speare, Wordsworth and Browning all drew from
Plutarch's well. The Essayists, especially Montaigne
and Francis Bacon, were profoundly influenced by
the *Moralia*. The following passage, which has been
somewhat adapted, not only gives some useful
practice in the contracted verbs, but also illustrates
Plutarch's chatty and anecdotal style.

Οὐδε γαρ του Θεαγενους [1] το ἀγαν φιλοτιμον και

---

1. Theagenes was a native of Thasos, and was reputed
to be a son of Hercules. At the tender age of nine he
carried home on his shoulders one of the bronze statues in
the market-place. His superhuman strength and speed won

φιλονεικον ἐπαινουμεν. οὖτος γαρ οὐ μονον την
περιοδον² ἐνικα ἀλλα και πολλους ἀγωνας, οὐ παγ-
κρατιῳ³ μονον ἀλλα και πυγμη και δολιχῳ.⁴ τελος
δε, ὡς ἡρῳα ἐπιταφιου τινος ἐδειπνει,⁵ προτεθεισης
ἁπασι κατα το εἰωθος της μεριδος,⁶ ἀναπηδησας
διεπαγκρατιασεν.⁷ και οὑτως ἐδηλου ὁτι ἀξιοι αὐτος
μονος νικαν οὐδ᾽ εἰα οὐδενα ἀλλον κρατειν αὐτου
παροντος.⁸ ὁθεν ἡθροισε χιλιους και διακοσιους

for him not only 1200 prizes, but also, as may be readily
inferred from this passage, many enemies. One man
visited a statue of Theagenes for the express purpose
of occasionally whipping it, until the outraged effigy got
its own back by falling one night on its owner and killing
him. Nor did the aggrieved relatives have the last word
when they threw the statue into the sea, for a famine
ensued which, according to Delphi, could only be averted
by the restoration of Theagenes. Shortly afterwards the
triumphant image was miraculously hauled up in some
fishermen's nets. In spite of Plutarch's strictures, it would
appear that the gods are on the side of the big biceps!
2. "The whole round" comprises the four big games
meetings, the Olympic, Pythian, Isthmian and Nemean.
3. The Pancratium was a brutal kind of 'all-in' contest,
with no inhibitions or Queensberry rules. In the "boxing"
(πυγμη) leathern thongs were wound round the fists of the
combatants. In both kinds of contest the fight went on
uninterruptedly until one of the competitors owned himself
beaten. 4. The "long" race was about two and a quarter
miles. What does the anthropologist term 'dolichocephalic'
mean? 5. Lit. "He was eating the 'hero' feast of some
funeral-games celebration." As early as Patroclus in the
Iliad, games contests were held to celebrate the passing of
a hero. Theagenes was attending the banquet which would
naturally accompany such a celebration. 6. "A share
having been placed before all"—Genitive Absolute; see
c. 11, Strabo, n. 11; c. 12, Theophrastus, n. 15. 7. "He
went through the whole Pancratium." This is not very
clear. It takes two to make a Pancratium, and Plutarch
does not tell us who his opponent was. It almost looks as
if Theagenes assaulted his fellow-guests. 8. It is true
that a garland of leaves was the only prize for victory in

στεφανους, ὧν συρφετον [9] ἡμεις ἡγουμεθα τους πλεισ-
τους. οὐδεν οὖν τουτου διαφερουσιν οἱ προς πασαν
ἀποδυομενοι [10] πολιτικην πραξιν, ἀλλα μεμπτους τε
ταχυ ποιουσιν ἑαυτους τοις πολλοις ἐπαχθεις τε
γιγνονται. εἰ μεν γαρ τις των τοιουτων κατορθοι,
ἐπιφθονος γιγνεται. εἰ δ' αὖ σφαλλεται, ἐπιχαρτος.
και το θαυμαζομενον [11] αὐτων ἐν ἀρχῃ της ἐπιμελειας
εἰς χλευασμον ὑπονοστει και γελωτα. τοιουτον [12] το
' Μητιοχος μεν γαρ στρατηγει, Μητιοχος δε τας
ὁδους, [13] Μητιοχος δ' ἀρτους ἐπωπᾳ, Μητιοχος δε

---

the festivals. Too much should not be made of this, however, as the home town of the victor frequently rewarded
him lavishly. At Athens an Olympic victor received a
purse of 500 drachmas and a free dinner in the Town Hall
for the rest of his life, an honour which, incidentally,
Socrates claimed he should receive, when his accusers
required him to fix his own penalty. The crown at the
Olympic games was of wild olive, at the Pythian, bay, at
the Isthmian, parsley and pine, and at the Nemean, parsley.
9. " Rubbish " because they were easy or empty victories.
10. " Stripping for "— i.e. getting ready for. Plutarch
still has the games in mind. The Greeks, sensibly enough,
had no qualms about complete nudity, and the wearing of
any sort of clothing at games would perhaps have surprised
them as much as the reverse would us. Indeed, the only
event in which the competitors wore clothes (i.e. armour)
was a comic event. 11. " That which was admired "—
their readiness to assume the burden of office. 12. " Of
such a kind as . . ." where we should say " for instance."
Thucydides tells us that the democracy in the time of
Pericles was practically a rule by one man, Pericles.
Metiochus, whom Pericles defended in the law-courts, seems
to have been Pericles' right-hand man, responsible for
carrying out the chief's decisions. According to the
anonymous Comic Poet whom Plutarch quotes, he was
Lord This and That, and Lord High Everything Else.
His habit of " seeing to " everything would one day make
him say " oimoi "— i.e. be sorry for himself. 13. Object
of ἐπωπᾳ. Not only was he in the War Office, but he was
Minister for Transport.

τάλφιτα,[14] Μητιοχος δε παντ' ἀκειται, Μητιοχος δ'
οἰμωξεται.'

των Περικλεους οὑτος εἰς ἡν ἑταιρων, τη δι' ἐκεινον
δυναμει [15] ἐπιφθονως χρωμενος και κατακορως.   δει [16]
δε τον πολιτικον ἐρωντι τῳ δημῳ προσφερεσθαι και,
εἰ μη παρεστι, ποθον ἑαυτου ἐναπολειπειν.

## VOCABULARY

ἀθροιζω, amass, collect.
ἀκεομαι, see to, remedy.
ἀλφιτα (n.pl.), barley.
ἀναπηδαω, leap up.
ἀξιοω, think right, claim.
ἁπας, -σα, -ν, every, all
  (longer form of πας).
ἀποδυομαι, take clothes off,
  strip.
ἀρτος (m.), bread.
δειπνεω, dine, have a dinner.
δηλοω, show, make clear.
διακοσιοι (adj.), two hundred.
διαπαγκρατιαζω, perform the
  whole Pancratium.
διαφερω (gen.), differ from.
εἰωθα (perf.), I am accustomed; (n. ptcple.) το
  εἰωθος, custom.
ἐναπολειπω, leave behind in
  one.
ἐπαινεω, praise.
ἐπαχθης, -ες, annoying, offen-
  sive.
ἐπιμελεια, office, ministry.
ἐπιταφιος (sc. ἀγων), com-
  memorative celebration.

ἐπιφθονος (adv. -ως), un-
  popular, odious.
ἐπιχαρτος (adj.), rejoiced
  over, an object of malig-
  nant joy.
ἐπωπαω, supervise.
ἐραω (gen.), love.
ἡγεομαι, consider, (with dat.)
  lead.
ἡρῳον (n.), a hero's feast.
Θεαγενης, Theagenes, a remarkable athlete.
κατακορως, immoderately, to
  excess.
κατορθοω, succeed.
μεμπτος, -η, -ον, contemp-
  tible.
μερις, -ιδος (f.), share, portion.
ὁθεν, whence.
οἰμωζω (fut.), -ξομαι, lament,
  regret.
οὐδε, nor, neither, not even.
παγκρατιον (n.), an ' all-in '
  boxing contest.
παρειμι, be present.
Περικλης, -εους, Pericles,
  famous Greek statesman.

---

14. For τα ἀλφιτα, he was Minister of Food, and Agriculture as well.  15. For χραομαι, taking the dative, see c. 17,
n. 13.  16. δει, "It is right that. . ." is followed by the
accus. of the person and the infin. of the verb.

περιοδος (f.), sequence, series.

προσφερομαι, 'find' a person to be so and so in one's relations towards him.

προτιθημι, put before.

πυγμη, boxing.

στεφανος (m.), a garland.

στρατηγεω, be a general.

συρφετος (m.), sweepings, rubbish.

σφαλλομαι, fail.

ὑπονοστεω, sink to, come down to.

φιλονεικος, contentious, fond of winning; το -ον, the competitive spirit.

φιλοτιμος, ambitious; το -ον, vaulting ambition.

χιλιος (adj.), thousand.

χλευασμος (m.), scorn, mockery.

## THE CONTRACTED FUTURE

1. If the stem of a verb ends in λ, μ, ν or ρ, the Future Tense is frequently formed by adding not -σ but -ε to the stem—e.g. μενω (I remain), Fut. μενε-ω. This, of course, contracts and is conjugated like the Present tense of φιλεω. In the same way the Future of some verbs ending in one of the above consonants (called 'liquids') in the Middle is conjugated like φιλουμαι—e.g. φαινομαι (I appear), Fut. φανουμαι.

2. καλεω (I call), and τελεω (I complete), in some dialects of Greek have Futs. καλεσω and τελεσω. But in Attic Greek the -σ- dropped out, and the fut. καλω and τελω is conjugated like φιλεω. In many of these verbs the form of the Future is indistinguishable from that of the Present. In Attic the Future of ὁλλυμι is ὁλω, and of μαχομαι, μαχουμαι.

3. All words that end in -ιζω or -ιζομαι form Futures with a contracted ε instead of σ—e.g. νομιζω, νομι-εω = νομιω, and . . . κομιζομαι, κομιουμαι.

4. One or two verbs with α in the stem, making a future in -ασω, dropped the σ and contracted the future like the present tense of τιμαω—e.g. σκεδαν-

νυμι—(I scatter), Fut. σκεδαω (σκεδω); ἐλαυνω (I drive), Fut. ἐλαω, ἐλω.

## FURTHER NOTES ON CONTRACTED VERBS

1. A few verbs have -η instead of -α all the way through, though conjugated like τιμαω—e.g. διψαω (I am thirsty, cf. dipsomaniac), infin. διψην, etc.; ζαω (I live) and χραομαι (I use).

2. Two-syllabled verbs in -εω, like πλεω (I sail) and πνεω (I breathe), contract ε + ε to ει and ε + ει to ει, but leave ε + ο or ου, uncontracted— i.e. πλεω, πλεις, πλει, πλεομεν, πλειτε, πλεουσι.

# CHAPTER XXI

## IMPERATIVES

' Καὶ λέγω τούτῳ,' said the centurion, ' Πορευθητι, καὶ πορευεται· καὶ ἄλλῳ, Ἐρχου, καὶ ἐρχεται· καὶ τῷ δουλῳ μου, Ποιησον τουτο, καὶ ποιει' (Matt. viii. 9 or Luke vii. 8). One suspects that the centurion must have frequently been in this imperative mood, grammatically as well as mentally. At any rate, he uses three forms of it here. The Imperative Mood, then, expresses a command. In Greek, not only is the Present Tense of the Imperative used, but also quite as commonly the Aorist Tense. There was a distinction, though it is not one of time. The distinction is the same as that which applied to the Infinitives. Strictly speaking, the Aorist Imperative should be used for an instantaneous command relating to a specific action, the Present for a general injunction, or one calling for continuous action. Doubtless, however, the distinction became blurred in the course of time, and it will be noted that our centurion hops about quite unconcernedly from Aorist to Present, and back to Aorist again, although he can hardly have intended any difference from a grammatical point of view between ' come ', ' go ', and ' do '.

Here, then, are the Imperatives. Only the 2nd persons are given in full, for they are obviously the most common. Greek did employ a 3rd person singular and plural of the Imperative, to be trans-

lated in English, ' Let him, her, or it loose, honour,
love, etc. Let them loose, etc.' You are recommended to learn the 2nd persons thoroughly, but
the 3rd persons are not of such frequent occurrence
as to warrant your spending much time on them.
The 3rd person forms of λυω are given here, and it
will not be difficult to infer the corresponding forms
for the other verbs. The Irregular Imperatives must
be noted very carefully, as they are important.

A <u>Present</u> (not Aorist) Imperative is negatived by
putting μη before the verb. This is called a Prohibition. An instantaneous and specific prohibition
involves the use of μη with the Aorist Subjunctive,
and that must be learned later.

Learn first the regular Imperatives pp. 206-7, and
then return to these, from the -μι verbs.

1. ἵημι    ἵει    ἵεσο (ἵου)    ἕς    οὗ    -ἕθητι
        ἵετε    ἵεσθε      ἕτε    ἕσθε    -ἕθητε

2. εἰμι (' I am ')
    Present Imper. Sing. 2. ἴσθι    Plur. 2. ἔστε
                     3. ἔστω          3. ὄντων (or
                                       ἔστωσαν)

3. εἰμι (' I go ')
    Present Imper. Sing. 2. ἴθι    Plur. 2. ἴτε
                     3. ἴτω          3. ἰοντων

4. φημι
    Present Imper. Sing. φαθι    Plur. φατε

5. καθημαι    Sing. καθησο    Plur. καθησθε, κειμαι
                   κεισο             κεισθε

6. οἶδα    Sing. ἴσθι    Plur. ἴστε.

# THE IMPERATIVE MOOD

| Verb. | Present. | | Aorist. | | |
| --- | --- | --- | --- | --- | --- |
| | Active. | Middle and Passive. | Active. | Middle. | Passive. |
| λυω | S. λυε<br>P. λυετε | λυου<br>λυεσθε | λυσον<br>λυσατε | λυσαι<br>λυσασθε | λυθητι<br>λυθητε |
| τιμαω | S. τιμα<br>P. τιματε | τιμω<br>τιμασθε | τιμησον<br>τιμησατε | τιμησαι<br>τιμησασθε | τιμηθητι<br>τιμηθητε |
| φιλεω | S. φιλει<br>P. φιλειτε | φιλου<br>φιλεισθε | φιλησον<br>φιλησατε | φιλησαι<br>φιλησασθε | φιληθητι<br>φιληθητε |
| δουλοω | S. δουλου<br>P. δουλουτε | δουλου<br>δουλουσθε | δουλωσον<br>δουλωσατε | δουλωσαι<br>δουλωσασθε | δουλωθητι<br>δουλωθητε |
| τιθημι | S. τιθει<br>P. τιθετε | τιθου<br>τιθεσθε | θες<br>θετε | θου<br>θεσθε | τεθητι<br>τεθητε |

| | | | | | |
|---|---|---|---|---|---|
| διδωμι | S. διδου | διδοσο | δος | δου | δοθητι |
| | P. διδοτε | διδοσθε | δοτε | δοσθε | δοθητε |
| ἱστημι | S. ἱστη | ἱστασο | 1. S. στησον<br>2. S. στηθι | 1. S. στησαι<br>2. S. —— | σταθητι |
| | P. ἱστατε | ἱστασθε | P. στησατε<br>P. στητε | P. στησασθε<br>P. —— | σταθητε |
| δεικνυμι | S. δεικνυ | δεικνυσο | δειξον | δειξαι | δειχθητι |
| | P. δεικνυτε | δεικνυσθε | δειξατε | δειξασθε | δειχθητε |

## IMPERATIVE THIRD PERSON SINGULAR AND PLURAL

| | | | | | |
|---|---|---|---|---|---|
| λυω | S. λυετω | λυεσθω | λυσατω | λυσασθω | λυθητω |
| | P. λυοντων<br>or<br>λυετωσαν | λυεσθων<br>or<br>λυεσθωσαν | λυσαντων | λυσασθων | λυθεντων<br>or<br>λυθητωσαν |

## EXERCISE. IMPERATIVES

Translate :—

1. τιμα τον πατερα σου και την μητερα σου. 2. δος την βασιλειαν τῳ ξενῳ. 3. μη δηλου την θησαυρον τοις πολιταις. 4. εὐθυς ἰθι προς την πολιν και ταυτα ἀγγειλον τοις πολιταις. 5. παιδες μικροι φιλουντων ἀλληλους. 6. πειθου τοις του βασιλεως λογοις. 7. παυεσθε μαχομενοι τοις Λακεδαιμονιοις, ὠ Ἀθηναιοι. 8. ἀνδρειοι ἐστε, ὠ στρατιωται. εὐθυς δειξατε τοις πολεμιοις την ἀρετην. 9. ἰστε ὁτι οὑποτε ἀποδωσω το ἀργυριον. 10. εἰ δακνει σε ὁ ἰχθυς, ἀφες. 11. καθησθε, ὠ παιδες, και σιωπατε. 12. εὐδαιμων ἰσθι, ὠ παι, παντα τον βιον. 13. λυετε τους ἱππους ἐκ των ἀγρων. 14. μη φαθι τουτο· αἰσχρον γαρ ἐστι. 15. ἀγε· στηθι ἐν τῃ ὁδῳ· μεγαλῃ δε τῃ φωνῃ βοα.

## KEY TO EXERCISE

1. Honour thy father and thy mother. 2. Give the kingdom to the stranger. 3. Do not show the treasure to the citizens. 4. Go at once to the city and announce these things to the citizens. 5. Let little children love one another. 6. Obey the words of the king. 7. Stop fighting the Spartans, Athenians. 8. Be brave, soldiers. Show your courage at once to the enemy. 9. Know that I shall never give back the money. 10. If the fish is biting you, let it go. 11. Sit down, boys, and be quiet. 12. Be happy, my boy, all your life. 13. Release the horses from the fields. 14. Do not say this, for it is disgraceful. 15. Come, stand in the road, and shout with a loud voice.

## Inveni Portum

1. Ἐλπις και συ Τυχη μεγα [1] χαιρετε· τον λιμεν' εὑρον·

οὐδεν ἐμοι χ' [2] ὑμιν· παιζετε τους μετ' [3] ἐμε.

1. As adv., a 'long' farewell.  2. For και.  3. See c. 22.
A Latin translation of this anonymous epitaph is to be
found on the statue of Lord Brougham at Cannes.

> Inveni portum : Spes et Fortuna valete;
>   Sat me lusistis; ludite nunc alios.

---

> Perhaps : So farewell, Hope, for ever,
>     Fond Fortune, fare thee well,
>   For I have found a harbour,
>     To shelter from the swell;
>   And others will come after,
>     Your jest and sport to be.
>   But I am nought to you again,
>     And ye are nought to me.—T. W. M.

## Point d'Appui

2. δος μοι που στω [1] και κινησω την γην.—Archimedes.

1. Subjunctive, 'I am to stand.'  See c. 27.

Archimedes was illustrating the principle of the
lever.  A fulcrum and a *locus standi* would give
him power to wobble the earth.  Luckily no one
was prepared to make these concessions to the
reckless scientist.

## Mehr Licht !

3. μικρον απο του ηλιου μεταστηθι.—Diogenes.

Diogenes the Cynic philosopher is said to have
lived in a tub.  Alexander the Great came to visit
him, and asked what favour he could bestow on
him.  This is Diogenes' reply.

## Benefits Forgot

4. χαριν λαβων μεμνησο [1] και δους επιλαθου.[2]

1. μεμνημαι, a perf. with pres. meaning, is conjugated like
καθημαι.  2. It will be observed that parts derived from the

2nd aor. have endings like the pres.—e.g. the aor. of λαμβανω is ἐλαβον, the aor. imper. λαβε. The aor. of ἐπιλανθανομαι is ἐπελαθομην (mid.). This is the aor. mid. imper.

## Be Sober, be Vigilant

5. ναφε και μεμνασ᾽ ἀπιστειν.—Epicharmus.

Epicharmus, a comic poet of the fifth century B.C., lived in Sicily, where the sound η was broadened to α. An Athenian would have pronounced this νηφε and μεμνησο. This has been suggested as the motto of a NAAFI canteen !

## Compulsory Maths.

6. ἀγεωμετρητος μηδεις [1] εἰσιτω (see c. 7).

1. Not only is μη used to negative an imper., but compounds of οὐ like οὐδεις (‘ no one ’), οὐποτε (‘ never ’), etc., change their οὐ to μη.

## Proper Study

7. γνωθι [1] σεαυτον.

1. Imper. from ἐγνων, aor. of γιγνωσκω. This advice was written up in the temple of Delphi, together with the other great maxim, μηδεν ἀγαν, ‘nothing in excess’ (see note above for μηδεν).

## Après Nous le Déluge

8. ἐμου θανοντος [1] γαια [2] μιχθητω [3] πυρι·
οὐδεν μελει [4] μοι· τἀμα [5] γαρ καλως ἐχει.

1. Gen. abs. 2. Another form of γη. 3. 3rd person aor. pass. imper. of μιγνυμι or μειγνυμι. 4. An impers. verb — i.e. one without a subject for which we supply the word ‘ it ’—‘ it concerns ’. οὐδεν is here a kind of adv., ‘ in no way ’. 5. = τα ἐμα, ‘ my affairs ’. This verse was frequently quoted by the Roman Emperors Tiberius and Nero.

## Divine Protection

9. ἐνδυσασθε τὴν πανοπλιαν του Θεου—Eph. vi. 11.

## On the Spartans Who Fell at Thermopylae [1]

10. ὦ ξειν᾽,[2] ἀγγειλον [3] Λακεδαιμονιοις ὅτι τῃδε
    κειμεθα τοις κεινων [4] ῥημασι πειθομενοι.
    Simonides.

1. The story of Leonidas, who with 300 Spartans kept the Persians at bay in 480 B.C., is too well known to require repeating. The simplicity and restraint of this epitaph of Simonides have been universally admired. 2. ξεινος (voc. ξεινε), a form of ξενος, a word of many meanings: ' stranger ', ' friend ', ' host ', ' guest '. Here it refers to a bypasser. 3. ἀγγειλον, aor. imper. of ἀγγελλω—though some read here ἀγγελλειν—an infin. for imper., a construction common in French : ' Ne pas parler au Wattman '. 4. = ἐκεινων. See c. 24. 4.

## Blind Bartimeus

11. Ye that have eyes, yet cannot see,
    In darkness and in misery
    Recall those mighty voices three—

    ' Ἰησου,[1] ἐλεησον [2] με '—
    ' Θαρσει, ἐγειραι '—' Ὑπαγε,[3]
    Ἡ πιστις σου σεσωκε σε.'—Longfellow.
    See Mark x. 46–52.

1. Vocative. 2. Aor. imper. of ἐλεεω. This word is known to Catholics in the transliterated form ' Kyrie, eleison '. 3. ὑπαγω was used in late Gk. frequently in an intrans. sense, as ' move along ', ' go away '.

## The Lord's Prayer

12. Οὕτως οὖν προσευχεσθε ὑμεις· Πατερ ἡμων ὁ ἐν τοις οὐρανοις, ἁγιασε.ͺτω [1] το ὀνομα σου, ἐλθετω

---

1. 3rd person aor. pass. imper.

ἡ βασιλεια σου, γενηθητω[2] το θελημα σου, ὡς ἐν οὐρανῳ, και ἐπι γης· τον ἀρτον ἡμων τον ἐπιουσιον δος ἡμιν σημερον· και ἀφες[3] ἡμιν τα ὀφειληματα ἡμων, ὡς και ἡμεις ἀφιεμεν τοις ὀφειλεταις ἡμων· και μη εἰσενεγκης[4] ἡμας εἰς πειρασμον, ἀλλα ῥυσαι[5] ἡμας ἀπο του πονηρου.[6]—Matt. vi. 9–13.

2. The aor. ἐγενηθην (a pass. form) is late Gk. for the classical ἐγενομην. 3. Aor. imper. of ἀφιημι. 4. This is the aor. subjunct. of εἰσφερω—another way in Gk. of saying, Don't do something or other, see c. 28. 5. ῥυσαι, aor. mid. imper. from ῥυομαι, 'draw away', 'rescue'. 6. It is not easy to say whether this is neuter ' evil ', or mas., ' the evil one '.

## EUCLID. Στοιχειων α′ ιε′

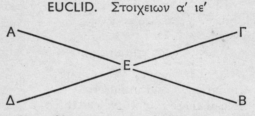

Ἐαν δυο εὐθειαι τεμνωσιν[1] ἀλληλας, τας κατα κορυφην[2] γωνιας ἰσας ἀλληλαις ποιουσιν.

So departmental is education today that it is frequently overlooked that Euclid was a Gk. philosopher who lived about 300 B.C. and whose series of essays in deduction provided the only geometrical textbook for generations of schoolboys until 1886. Eucleides called his work Στοιχεια, which means ' the elements '. He regarded them as the elements of deductive proof. The above proposition is from Bk. I, No. 15 (in Gk. numerals α′ ιε′).

1. τεμνωσιν. Subj., required by the word ἐαν, ' if '. You may, however, translate it exactly as if it were the indic. How many Eng. words can you think of with the root TEM or TOM in, meaning ' cut '? 2. Lit. ' at the peak ' or ' vertex '. We talk about ' vertically opposite angles '.

Δυο γαρ εὐθειαι αἱ ΑΒ, ΓΔ τεμνετωσαν[3] ἀλληλας κατα το Ε σημειον· λεγω ὁτι ἰση ἐστιν ἡ μεν ὑπο[4] ΑΕΓ γωνια τῃ ὑπο ΔΕΒ, ἡ δε ὑπο ΓΕΒ τῃ ὑπο ΑΕΔ.

Ἐπει γαρ εὐθεια ἡ ΑΕ ἐπ' εὐθειαν την ΓΔ ἐφεστηκε,[5] γωνιας ποιουσα τας ὑπο ΓΕΑ, ΑΕΔ, αἱ ἀρα[6] ὑπο ΓΕΑ, ΑΕΔ γωνιαι δυσιν[7] ὀρθαις ἰσαι εἰσιν. παλιν, ἐπει εὐθεια ἡ ΔΕ ἐπ' εὐθειαν την ΑΒ ἐφεστηκε,[5] γωνιας ποιουσα τας ὑπο ΑΕΔ, ΔΕΒ, αἱ ἀρα ὑπο ΑΕΔ, ΔΕΒ γωνιαι δυσιν ὀρθαις ἰσαι εἰσιν. ἐδειχθησαν δε και αἱ ὑπο ΓΕΑ, ΑΕΔ δυσιν ὀρθαις ἰσαι· αἱ ἀρα ὑπο ΓΕΑ, ΑΕΔ ταις ὑπο ΑΕΔ, ΔΕΒ ἰσαι εἰσιν. κοινη ἀφῃρησθω[8] ἡ ὑπο ΑΕΔ. λοιπη ἀρα ἡ ὑπο ΓΕΑ λοιπη τῃ ὑπο ΒΕΔ ἰση ἐστιν· ὁμοιως δη δειχθησεται, ὁτι και αἱ ὑπο ΓΕΒ, ΔΕΑ ἰσαι εἰσιν.

Ἐαν ἀρα δυο εὐθειαι τεμνωσιν ἀλληλας, τας κατα κορυφην γωνιας ἰσας ἀλληλαις ποιουσιν· ὁπερ ἐδει δειξαι.[9]

## VOCABULARY

ἀπιστεω, disbelieve.
ἀρα, after all, you see.
ἀφιημι, let go, forgive.
βασιλεια (f.), kingdom.
γωνια (f.), angle.

δυο, two.
ἐαν (conj.), if.
εἰσφερω, bring into.
ἐλεεω, pity, have mercy on.
ἐνδυομαι, put on.

---

3. 3rd pers. plur. of the pres. imper. 4. Euclid always uses ὑπο when denoting angles : ἡ ὑπο ΑΕΓ γωνια is short for ἡ ὑπο ΑΕΓ περιεχομενη γωνια—i.e. the angle enclosed by ΑΕΓ. 5. Lit. ' stands on '. 6. ἀρα is a particle meaning ' then ', ' you see '. 7. δυσιν is a late dat. plur. of δυο. ὀρθη, ' right ', is, of course, short for ὀρθη γωνια, ' right angle '. 8. This is a rare form which you have not been given. It is the 3rd sing. imper. of the perf. pass. of ἀφαιρεω. ' Let (it) be taken away '. 9. = Q.E.D. (quod erat demonstrandum), lit. ' which it was necessary to show '. Note the active infin. δειξαι in the Gk.

ἐπιλανθανομαι, forget.
ἐπιουσιος, sufficient for the coming day (*adj.*), from ἡ ἐπιουσα (ἡμερα), the on-coming (day).
εὐθεια (*f.*), line.
θαρσεω, cheer up.
θελημα (*n.*), will, wish.
κοινος, -η, -ον, common.
κορυφη (*f.*), apex, vertex.
λοιπος, -η, -ον, remaining.
μεθιστημι (*intrans.* tenses), shift, move.
μεμνημαι (*perf.*), I remember.
νηφω, be sober.
ξεινος, ξενος (*m.*), stranger, host, guest.
ὀφειλετης, debtor.
ὀφειλημα. (*n.*), debt.
παιζω, play with, mock.
πανοπλια (*f.*), a full suit of armour.

πειθομαι, I obey (c. *dat.*).
πειρασμος (*m.*), temptation.
πονηρος, -α, -ον, wicked, evil.
πορευομαι (*aor.* ἐπορευθην), go, march.
προσευχομαι, pray.
πυρ (*n.*), fire.
ῥημα (*n.*), command, ordinance.
ῥυομαι, rescue, deliver.
σημειον (*n.*) (see c. 12), point.
σημερον (*adv.*), today.
στοιχειον (*n.*), element.
σωζω, save.
τηδε, here.
τυχη (*f.*), fortune.
ὑπαγω, move, go one's way.
χαιρω, farewell, rejoice.

# CHAPTER XXII

## PREPOSITIONS

(Also rules for expressing Time and Space, and
prepositions compounded with verbs.)

PREPOSITIONS are so common in Greek that it has
been impossible to avoid them in the previous
extracts. In the Crocodile story, for instance
(ch. 10), they occur sixteen times. Some (e.g.
ἐν, ἐξ, etc.) take only one case, some (e.g. κατα, δια,
etc.) two, and others (e.g. ἐπι, παρα, etc.) three.
The important thing in the case of these two latter
classes is to notice what case they take when you
meet them, because *the meaning of the preposition is
decided by the case which it governs*.   Originally they
were a sort of *adverbs of place*, used to make the
meanings of the cases more clear.   Therefore εἰς,
' into ', only takes an acc., ἐξ, ' out of ', a gen., and
ἐν, ' in ', dat.   But παρα, ' alongside of ', can be used
with all three cases, and has a different meaning
with each.

At first sight this may sound confusing, but if
you once understand the fundamental meaning of
the cases, difficulties disappear.   This is best seen
in reference to the ideas of Place and Time.

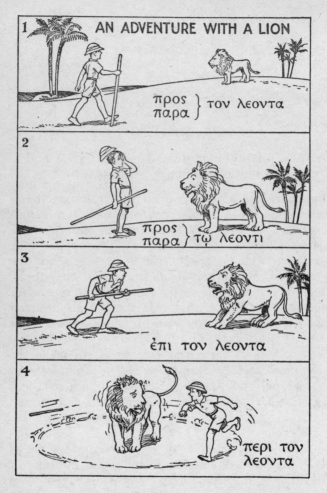

AN ADVENTURE WITH A LION

1 προς } τον λεοντα
παρα

2 προς } τῳ λεοντι
παρα

3 ἐπι τον λεοντα

4 περι τον λεοντα

5 μετα του λεοντος

6 ἀνα τον λεοντα

7 ὑπερ του λεοντος

8

ἐπι του λεοντος

9

κατα του λεοντος

10

ὑπο τῳ λεοντι

11 εἰς τον λεοντα

12 ἐν τῳ λεοντι

13 ἐκ του λεοντος

14 { ἀπο του λεοντος
{ παρα

## Meaning of the Cases in Reference to Place and Time

### (a) *Place.*

The acc. means originally *motion to.*
    ,, gen.        ,,        *motion from.*
    ,, dat.        ,,        *rest at.*

ἤλθομεν τὴν πολιν means (in poetry, at any rate) 'we came to the city'.   So does ἤλθομεν εἰς τὴν πολιν.

ποιας γης ἤλθες means ' from what kind of land did you come ? '

αἰθερι ναιων means ' dwelling in the sky' (Homer), but in prose writers prefer, ἐν αἰθερι.

Similarly,

παρα τους πολεμιους means ' towards the enemy'.

παρα των πολεμιων means ' from the enemy '.

παρα τοις πολεμιοις means ' near or by the enemy '.

### (b) *Time.*

The acc. implies *extension over.*   τρεις ἡμερας ἐμεινα, ' I remained three days '.   (Also of space—e.g. ἰεναι τὴν αὐτην ὁδον, ' to go the same way '.)

The gen. implies *during a part of*—e.g. του αὐτου ἐτους, ' in the same year ', i.e. ' at some time *within* the year '.   Compare the colloquial Eng. ' of a morning '.

The dat. implies *a point of time*—e.g. τῃ δευτερᾳ ἡμερᾳ, ' on the second day '.

So νυκτα = ' all night long '; νυκτος, ' during part of the night '.

These three basic ideas are at the root of the preps., and apply to most of them.   But there are also—unfortunately for the learner !—many derived and less obvious meanings, some of which are commoner than the original meanings. You are therefore recommended to study very carefully the following table. Preps. are frequently compounded with verbs. In some cases Eng. derivs. are a help to learning their meaning. The numbers in brackets refer to chapters of this book (e.g. 18, 4 = ch. 18, extract 4).

Before proceeding to the prepositions with three cases, you may like to test your memory. How many of these can you get right?

## EXERCISE. PREPOSITIONS (I)

Translate :—

1. δι᾽ ἐρωτα.
2. μετα του γεροντος.
3. ἀνα το ὀρος.
4. ὑπερ των πολιτων.
5. κατα την ἀληθειαν.
6. ὑδωρ ἀντι πυρος.
7. δι᾽ ἀσπιδος.
8. μετα τον θηρα.
9. προ του φυλακος.
10. ὑπερ το τερμα ἰεναι.
11. κατα της μητρος λεγειν.
12. ἀπο της Ἑλλαδος ἡκω.
13. θελομεν ἐχειν εἰρηνην ἀντι πολεμου.

14. οἱ μεν ἀμφι τον στρατηγον ἐμενον συν αὐτῳ ἀνευ σιτου μεχρι νυκτος, οἱ δε ἀλλοι ἐφευγον ἐφ᾽ ἱππου κερδους ἑνεκα προς την πολιν.

15. προς δε τουτοις οἱ κακοι παιδες ἀνα κλιμακα ἀναβαντες λιθους ἐφ᾽ ἡμας κατεβαλλον παρα νομον.

(Contd. p. 226.)

# THE PREPOSITIONS

## A. Governing One Case Only

| | Meaning. | Examples (basic). | Idiomatic Uses. | Eng. Deriv. | Compounds. |
|---|---|---|---|---|---|
| (1) *With the Accusative* | | | | | |
| 1. εἰς or ἐς | 'into', 'to' | εἰς τὸ στόμα (10, 3) εἰς τὸ φῶς (13, 4) εἰς τὸν ποταμόν (22, 1) | εἰς μαρτύριαν (22, 5), 'for a witness' εἰς τριακοσίους, 'up to 300', εἰς τὸ λοιπόν, 'for the future' | None Stamboul is derived from εἰς τὴν πόλιν | εἰσάγειν, 'to bring into' |
| 2. ἀνά | 'up' (opp. of κατά) 'back again' | ἀνὰ τὸν ποταμόν, 'up stream' | ἀνὰ ἑκατόν, 'by hundreds' | anabasis (going up) anathema anachronism (time-back) | ἀναβαίνειν, 'to go up' |
| (2) *With the Genitive* | | | | | |
| 3. ἀντί | (original meaning, 'against'), 'opposite to', 'instead of' | πόλεμος ἀντὶ εἰρήνης, 'war instead of peace' | — | antitoxin antidote antipathy antiseptic antipodes | In compounds often means 'in return'. ἀντίδοσις, 'a giving in return', exchange |
| 4. ἀπό | 'away from', 'from' | ἀπὸ ἐχθρῶν (18, 4), 'from foes', ἀπὸ θεοῦ, 'from god' | — | apostasy apostle apostrophe | ἀποστατεῖν, 'to stand away from', 'revolt', ἀποστέλλειν, 'to send away' |

away'
In compounds often means 'back'; ἀποδιδωμι, 'give back'

| | | | | | |
|---|---|---|---|---|---|
| 5.<br>ἐκ or<br>ἐξ | 'out of' | ἐκ του ὑδατος (10, 3), 'out of the water' ἐκ της πολεως ('from the city') | ἐκ παιδος, 'from boyhood' ἐκ Διος ὀναρ, 'a dream from Zeus' (Homer) | ecstasy exodus | ἐξιστημι, 'I make to stand out of'—i.e. 'drive out of'; e.g. φρενων, 'wits' So ἐκστασις, 'standing outside oneself' |
| 6.<br>προ | 'before' (either of place or of time) | προ της θυρας, 'before the door' προ της μαχης, 'before the battle' | — | prognostic prologue | προδιδωμι, 'betray' προλεγειν, 'foretell' |
| (3) With the Dative<br>7.<br>ἐν | 'in' | ἐν τῳ Νειλῳ (10, 3) ἐν τῃ γῃ (10, 3) ἐν τῳ ποταμῳ (10, 3) | ἐν τῳ παροντι, 'at present', οἱ ἐν τελει, 'those in power', the authorities | endemic energy | ἐνδημος, 'dwelling in', 'native' ἐνεργεια, lit. 'in work', so 'activity' |
| 8.<br>συν | 'with' | In prose 'with' is usually expressed by μετα with gen. (v. sup.) | συν θεος, 'with the help of the gods' | synchronise synonym synopsis syntax synthetic syllabus symmetry sympathy symposium | συλλαμβανω, 'collect' συμποσιον, a drinking party συντιθημι, 'put together' |

## B. Governing Two Cases (Acc. and Gen.).

| | Meaning. | Examples (basic). | Idiomatic Uses. | Eng. Deriv. | Compounds. |
|---|---|---|---|---|---|
| 9. δια | *(1) With the Accusative* 'on account of', 'owing to' | διὰ την φυσιν (22, 3) 'on account of nature' διὰ την ἀρετην (22, 3) | διὰ ταυτα, 'therefore' | diaphanous diameter | Meaning 'right through' διαφαινω, 'show through', δια μετρον, 'transverse measurement' |
| | *(2) With the Genitive* (of place) 'by means of', 'through' | διὰ της πολεως, 'through the city' (of time) διὰ νυκτος, 'through the night' | δι' αὐτου (22. 5), 'by means of him' δι' ὀλιγου, 'after a short interval' | | Meaning 'thoroughly', usual meaning in Gk. compounds—e.g. διαφθειρω, 'destroy utterly' Meaning 'separation, division'—e.g. διαγιγνωσκω, 'distinguish', διαιρεω, 'divide' (diaeresis) |
| 10. κατα | 'down' | — | καθ' ἡμεραν, 'day by day' | catastrophe | καταστρεφω, 'I turn upside down' |
| | *(1) With the Accusative* (a) 'down along' | κατα ποταμον, 'down-stream' | κατα γην και θαλασσαν, 'by land and sea' | cataract | — |
| | (b) 'according to' | κατα τον 'Ομηρον, 'according to Homer' (14, n. 20) κατα νομον, 'according to law' | κατα λογον (10, 3), 'in proportion to' | catalogue cataclysm | καταλογος, 'list' κατακλυζω, 'wash down' |
| | | | καθ' ὁλου, 'wholly' | catalepsy | καταλαμβανω, 'seize' |

**(2) With the Genitive (vertically)**

κατά 'down'

| Preposition / Meaning | Example (local) | | Example (metaphorical) | | Compounds | Compounds (Greek) |
|---|---|---|---|---|---|---|
| (a) 'down from' | κατὰ τοῦ τείχους, 'down from the wall' | — | — | — | — | — |
| (b) 'against' | κατὰ σοῦ λέγω, 'I speak against you' | — | — | — | — | — |
| **11. μετά** (1) *With the Accusative* 'after' (either of time or of place) | μετὰ τοῦτο (22, 5), 'after this', μετὰ τὸν πόλεμον, 'after the war', μεθ᾿ ἡμᾶς, 'in search of us' | — | — | — | metaphysics / metabolic / In compounds frequently denotes 'change'—e.g. μετανοία, 'changing one's mind', and so 'repentance'. Sometimes 'search'—e.g. μεταπέμπω, 'send for' | τὰ μεταφυσικά, 'things after physics'; μεταβάλλω, 'throw together', so 'change' |
| (2) *With the Genitive* 'with' | μετὰ σοῦ, 'with you' (14, n. 17); μετὰ τῶν φίλων, 'with his friends' (23, 1) | — | — | — | | |
| **12. ὑπέρ** (1) *With the Accusative* 'over', 'beyond' | ὑπὲρ τὴν θάλασσαν, 'beyond the sea'; ὑπὲρ Βορέαν, 'beyond the North Wind' | — | ὑπὲρ δύναμιν, 'beyond one's power' | — | hyperbole / hypercritical / hyperborean / hypermetrical / N.B.—In compounds it has the idea of 'excess' | ὑπερβάλλω, 'surpass' |
| (2) *With the Genitive* 'above', 'on behalf of' | ὑπὲρ τῆς γῆς, 'above the earth' | — | ὑπὲρ τῆς πατρίδος, 'on behalf of one's country' | — | | |

## KEY

1. On account of love.
2. With the old man.
3. Up the mountain.
4. On behalf of the citizens.
5. According to the truth.
6. Water instead of fire.
7. Through a shield.
8. After the beast.
9. In front of the guard.
10. To go beyond the boundary.
11. To speak against mother.
12. I have come from Greece.
13. We wish to have peace instead of war.
14. Those around the general remained with him, without food, until night, but the others fled on horseback, for the sake of reward, to the city.
15. But in addition to these things, the naughty boys, having climbed up a ladder, threw down stones on us, against the law.

## C. 'Improper Prepositions'

*With gen.* (1) The following words take a *genitive* case, but cannot be compounded with verbs. Therefore grammarians call them ' improper '.

ἀνευ, ' without ' (ἀνευ φωνης, 22, 2).

ἐνεκα, ' for the sake of ' (generally follows its case : μισθου ἐνεκα, ' for the sake of reward ').

μεχρι, ' as far as ', ' until ' (μεχρι της πολεως).

χαριν, ' for the sake of ' (μνημης χαριν, ' for memory's sake ').

πλην, ' except ' (πλην ἐμου, ' except me ').

*With acc.* (2) ὡς, ' to ', takes the *accusative*, but is used only with persons.

ὡς τον βασιλεα ἡλθον, ' I came to the king '.

*With dat.* (3) ἅμα, ' at the same time as ', takes a
     *dative* : ἅμα τῃ ἡμερᾳ, ' at dawn '.
     ὁμου, ' together with ', takes a *dative*.


## D. Adverbs used as Prepositions

Some adverbs are used as prepositions, and take
a *genitive*.  They include :—

μεταξυ, ' between '.

ἐμπροσθεν, ' in front of '
     (μου, 22, 5).

περαν or περα, ' beyond '
     (του 'Ιορδανου, 22, 5).

ἐντος, ' within ' (της ψυχης,
     22, 2).

ἐγγυς ⎫
πλησιον⎭ ' near '.

εἰσω ⎫
ἐνδον⎭ ' inside '.

ἐξω ⎫
ἐκτος⎭ ' outside '.

ὀπισθεν, ' behind '.

ἐναντιον, ' opposite
     to '.

χωρις, ' apart from '.

# E. Governing Three Cases

[N.B.—Examples of basic meanings given first, then idiomatic usages. Try to discover from which meaning the English derivative (on pages 229, 231) is taken.]

| | Meaning. | With Accusative. | With Genitive. |
|---|---|---|---|
| 13.<br>παρα | 'alongside'<br>[In compounds, 'beside', 'past', 'wrongly', 'amiss'] | παρα την θαλασσαν, 'by the seaside'<br>παρα δυναμιν, 'beyond one's power', (22, 3)<br>παρα τον νομον, 'contrary to the law'<br>παρα δοξαν, 'contrary to expectation' | παρα Θεου, 'at the hands of' or 'from God' (22, 15) |
| 14.<br>ἀμφι | 'on both sides', 'around' | οἱ ἀμφι Σωκρατη, 'those around Socrates'<br>ἀμφι σεληνην, 'around the moon' (13, 10) | (rare in prose)<br>ἀμφι γυναικος 'about a woman' |
| 15.<br>περι | 'around', 'about';<br>[In compounds, also idea of 'excess', or 'survival'] | περι ἀγκιστρον, 'around the hook' (10, 3)<br>περι την πρωτην ὡραν, 'about the first hour'. | περι του φωτος, 'about the light' (22, 5)<br>περι του πραγματος, 'about the matter'<br>περι πολλου ποιεισθαι, 'to value highly' |

## E. Governing Three Cases—continued

| | Meaning. | With Dative. | Eng. Deriv. | Compounds. |
|---|---|---|---|---|
| 13. παρα | 'alongside' [In compounds 'beside', 'past', 'wrongly', 'amiss'] | παρ' ἐμοι, 'chez moi' παρ' ἀλλήλοις, 'alongside one another' (14, n. 10) | parasite (παρα σιτον) parallel parable paragraph paraclete paradox | παρα-διδωμι, 'betray' παρα-βαλλω, 'compare' παρα-καλεω, 'encourage' παρα-βαινω, 'transgress' |
| 14. ἀμφι | 'on both sides', 'around' | ἀμφι ὡμοις, 'around the shoulders'. (Homer) | amphibrach amphitheatre amphibious amphisbaena, 'an animal that walks two ways' (ἀμφι-βαινω) | ἀμφι-θεατρον, 'a round or oval theatre' ἀμφι-βιος, 'living a double life', i.e. 'on land and sea' |
| 15. περι | 'around', 'about', [In compounds also idea of 'excess', or 'survival'] | (chiefly poetic) | peripatetic perimetre periphrasis periscope | περι-πατεω, 'walk round' περιγυνεσθαι, 'survive', 'excel' περι-σκοπεω, 'look around' |

## E. Governing Three Cases—continued

| | Meaning. | With Accusative. | With Genitive. |
|---|---|---|---|
| 16. ὑπό | 'under' [In compounds also 'secretly', 'slightly', 'gradually'] | ὑπὸ κλίμακα βαίνειν, 'to go under a ladder' ('motion'); ὑπὸ νύκτα, 'about nightfall' | ὑπὸ γῆς, 'underground'; ὑπ' αὐτοῦ θανεῖν, 'to be killed by him'; ὑπὸ δέους πράττειν, 'to act through fear' |
| 17. πρός | 'at' or 'by' | πρὸς τὴν πόλιν, 'towards the city'; πρὸς ἑσπέραν, 'towards evening'; πρὸς τοὺς πολεμίους, 'against the enemy'; πρὸς ταῦτα, 'with reference to this'; πρὸς χάριν, 'with a view to giving pleasure' | πρὸς μητρός, 'at the hands of', also 'in favour of a mother'; πρὸς Θεῶν, 'in Heaven's name!' (in oaths) |
| 18. ἐπί | 'on', 'over' | ἐπὶ πλοῖον, 'on to a boat' (22, 4); ἐφ' ἵππον ἀναβαίνειν, 'mount a horse'; ἐπὶ πᾶσαν γῆν, 'over the whole earth' (13, 10); ἐπὶ τοὺς πολεμίους, 'against the enemy'; ἐφ' ὕδωρ, 'to fetch water'; ἐπὶ τὸ πολύ, 'for the most part' | ἐφ' ἵππου, 'on horseback' (22, 4) (you can only sit on *a part of a horse*); ἐπ' ἐμοῦ, 'in my time', but ἐπ' ἐμοί, 'in my power'; ἐπ' οἴκου, 'homewards'; [N.B.—ἐπί is the bad boy of the prepositions, and breaks all the 'rules' of grammar. The variety of its meanings covers five columns in the lexicon!] |

## E. Governing Three Cases—continued

| | Meaning. | With Dative. | Eng. Deriv. | Compounds. |
|---|---|---|---|---|
| 16. ὑπό | 'under' [In compounds also 'secretly', 'slightly', 'gradually'] | ὑπ' Ἀθηναίοις, 'subject to the Athenians' | hypothesis hypodermic δερμα, 'skin' | ὑπο-τίθημι, 'place under' ὑπο-μειδιάω, 'smile slightly' |
| 17. πρός | 'at' or 'by' | πρὸς τῇ θύρᾳ, 'near the door' πρὸς τούτοις, 'in addition to these things' (a common meaning) | proselyte prosody (ᾠδη) (These appear to be the only Eng. derivs. Don't confuse προ with προς | προς-ελθειν 'to come to' προς-γιγνομαι, 'be added' προσβαλλω, 'attack' |
| 18. ἐπί | 'on', 'over' | ἐπὶ τῇ τραπέζῃ, 'on the table' ἐπὶ γέλωτι, 'to cause a laugh' ἐπὶ τούτοις, 'on these conditions' | epidemic, ἐπι and δημος, 'among the people' epidermis, 'on top of the skin' —i.e. 'outer layer' epilogue, 'on top of a speech', or 'spoken in addition' epigram epidiascope episcopal epitaph, etc. | [Gk. can have two preps. in compound, sometimes three, e.g.— ἐξάγω, 'I lead out' παρεξάγω, 'I lead out in line' ἀντιπαρεξάγω, 'I lead out in line against'] |

## EXERCISE. PREPOSITIONS (2)

Translate :—

### A Famous Saying of Heracleitus—Two Versions

1. (a) οὐκ ἐστι ¹ δις εἰς τον αὐτον ² ποταμον ἐμβηναι.³

(b) τοις εἰς τον αὐτον ποταμον εἰσβαινουσι ⁹ ἑτερα και ἑτερα ὑδατα ἐπιρρει.

Heracleitus, the philosopher, lived about 500 B.C. Only fragments of his writings survive, of which παντα ῥει, ' everything is in a state of flux (lit. flows) ', is the most famous. These are two versions of his discovery that matter itself is continually changing —e.g. the water in a river.

### What is Thought?

2. διανοια ἐστιν ἐντος της ψυχης προς αὐτην διαλογος ἀνευ φωνης.—Plato.

### The Greeks

3. (a) και παρα δυναμιν τολμηται και παρα γνω-μην ⁴ κινδυνευται και ἐν τοις δεινοις ⁵ εὐελπιδες.— Thucydides.

(b) και γαρ τοι ἀγηρατοι μεν αὐτων αἱ μνημαι, ζηλωται δε ὑπο ⁶ παντων ἀνθρωπων αἱ τιμαι· οἱ ⁷ πενθουνται μεν δια την φυσιν ὡς θνητοι, ὑμνουνται δε ὡς ἀθανατοι δια την ἀρετην.—Lysias.

---

1. ἐστι, ' here ' = ἐξεστι, ' it is possible ' (v. c. 15). 2. v. c. 24 under ὁ αὐτος. 3. ἐμβηναι, aor. inf. of ἐμβαινω (' I walk ', or ' step in '). ἐμβαινουσι is not 3rd plur. of the pres. ind. What is it? 4. Here ' judgment '. 5. ἐν τοις δεινοις, ' in extremities '—Latin, in extremis. 6. For ὑπο with gen., see c. 22, § E. 7. οἱ comes from ὁς, the rel. pron. δια with acc. = owing to, v. c. 22, B.

## A Learned Fool

4. σχολαστικος τις, ποταμον περαν [8] βουλομενος, ἐπεβη [9] ἐπι πλοιον ἐφ᾽ ἱππου [10] καθημενος. πυθομενου [11] δε τινος δια τι ἐφ᾽ ἱππου, ἐφη [12] σπουδαζειν.[13]

## From the Fourth Gospel

5. ἐγενετο ἀνθρωπος ἀπεσταλμενος [14] παρα Θεου,[15] ὀνομα αὐτῳ ᾽Ιωαννης. οὑτος ἠλθεν [16] εἰς μαρτυριαν, ἱνα μαρτυρηση [17] περι του φωτος, ἱνα παντες πιστευσωσι [17] δι᾽ αὐτου . . . ᾽Ιωαννης μαρτυρει περι αὐτου, λεγων, ῾Ο ὀπισω μου ἐρχομενος ἐμπροσθεν [18] μου γεγονεν [19] . . . ταυτα ἐν Βηθαβαρᾳ ἐγενετο περαν [18] του ᾽Ιορδανου . . . και τῃ ἡμερᾳ τῃ τριτῃ γαμος ἐγενετο ἐν Κανᾳ της Γαλιλαιας· [20] και ἡν ἡ μητηρ του ᾽Ιησου ἐκει . . . ἠσαν δε ἐκει ὑδριαι λιθιναι ἑξ κειμεναι κατα τον καθαρισμον [21] των ᾽Ιουδαιων, χωρουσαι ἀνα μετρητας [22] δυο ἡ τρεις . . . και μετα τουτο κατεβη εἰς Καπερναουμ,[23] και οἱ μαθηται μετ᾽ αὐτου.—ΤΟ ΚΑΤΑ ΙΩΑΝΝΗΝ ΕΥΑΓΓΕΛΙΟΝ.

---

8. περαν can either be a prep. (v. 22, c. 4) or the pres. inf. of περαω. Which is it here ? 9. ἐπεβη, 3rd sing. of ἐπεβην, aor. ind. of ἐπιβαινω. 10. v. c. 22, E, for meaning of ἐπι with gen. 11. Aor. ptcple. of πυνθανομαι, ‘ enquire ’. 12. Impf. of φημι, ‘ I say ’. 13. Inf. because indirect speech, v. c. 26. 14. Perf. ptcple. pass. from ἀποστελλω (‘ I send away ’), here just ‘ send ’. Why is ‘ apostle ’ so called ? 15. v. c. 22, E 13, for meaning of παρα with gen. 16. ἠλθεν, aor. ind. of ἐρχομαι, v. c. 25. 17. Purpose clause, v. c. 28, ‘ to witness ’; μαρτυρηση, subj. mood., also πιστευσωσι, ‘ that they might believe ’. 18. v. c. 22, D. 19. Irreg. perf. of γιγνομαι, ‘ has become ’—i.e. ‘ is ’. 20. Gk. says, ‘ Cana of Galilee ’ (partitive gen.), we say ‘ C. in G.’ 21. ‘ According to the purification rite ’—i.e. for like purpose of it. 22. ἀνα with acc., ‘ up to ’ (of numbers). 23. Indeclinable—a Hebrew, not a Gk. word.

## VOCABULARY

ἀγηρατος, -ον (adj.), ageless (ἀ- not, γηρας, ' old age ').

διαλογος, -ου, conversation (dialogue).

διανοια, -ας, thought (what goes through the νους).

ἐκει (adv.), there.

ἐπιβαινω, I go on to.

ἐπιρρεω, flow over.

ἐρχομαι, I come.

εὐαγγελιον, gospel (lit., good news).

ζηλωτος, -η, -ον, enviable (ζηλοω, I envy).

Ἰορδανος, Jordan (river).

Ἰουδαιος, a Jew.

Ἰωαννης, -ου, John.

κινδυνευτης, -ου, an adventurer, v. c. 7 (κινδυνευω, I run a risk).

λιθινος, -η, -ον (adj.), made of stone (λιθος).

μαθητης, -ου, learner, disciple.

μαρτυρεω, I witness (martyr).

μαρτυρια, -ας, witness, testimony.

μετρητης, -ου, a measure holding 9 gallons.

μνημη, -ης, memory.

ὀπισω, with gen. after, behind.

οὑτος, this (man), v. c. 24.

πενθεω, I mourn (πενθος, grief).

περαν, prep. with gen. across.

περαω, I cross.

πλοιον, -ου, boat (πλεω, I sail).

σχολαστικος, -ου, a learned man (scholastic).

σπουδαζω, I am in a hurry.

τιμη, -ης (f.), honour (τιμαω, I honour).

τολμητης, -ου, a daring man, v. c. 7 (τολμαω, I dare).

ὑδρια, -ας, a water-pot.

ὑμνεω, I sing of (hymn).

χωρεω, I make room for, and hence, hold (of measure). Usually means I go, advance.

# CHAPTER XXIII

## NUMERALS

MOST of the Gk. numerals are easy to learn through Eng. derivatives or similar forms in Latin. The Cardinals from 5 to 100 are indeclinable. The Ordinals (1st, 2nd, 3rd, etc.) decline like regular adjs. in -ος (*e.g.*, πρωτος, -η, -ον, δευτερος, -α, -ον, etc.). The advs. from ' four times ' (τετρακις) onwards end in -ακις. If you read them carefully through several times, you should have no difficulty in recognising them in a sentence. The Gks. used letters (with accents) instead of numbers (*e.g.*, α′ for 1, β′ for 2, etc.), but you need not know these, as, except in Euclid, you are not likely to meet them in Gk. authors.

Translate :—

1. Ἐν τῳ Αἰγαιῳ πελαγει εἰσι πλειονες ἢ διακοσιαι νησοι, αἱ δε πλεισται οὐ μεγαλαι, μεγιστη δε ἡ Εὐβοια ἐστιν.

2. τουτο το βιβλιον ἐχει ὀκτω και εἰκοσι μερη, τοδε δε μερος ἐστι τριτον και εἰκοστον.

3. αἱ ἐννεα Μουσαι ἠλθον ποτε προς τας τρεις Χαριτας, αἱ ἐφερον καλαθους. ἐν δε τοις καλαθοις μηλα ἠν. τουτων δε τινα ἐδοσαν αἱ Χαριτες ταις Μουσαις.

## KEY TO EXERCISE

1. In the Ægean Sea are more than two hundred islands, and most (are) not big, but the biggest is Euboea.

 (*Cont. p.* 238.)

| | Cardinals. | Derivatives. | Ordinals. | Adverbs. | Derivatives. |
|---|---|---|---|---|---|
| 1 | εἷς, μια, ἓν | — | πρωτος | ἁπαξ (once) | Deuteronomy (νομος) |
| 2 | δυο | dual | δευτερος | δις | |
| 3 | τρεις, τρια | tripod | τριτος | τρις | |
| 4 | τετταρες, τετταρα (or τεσσαρες) | tetrarch, | τεταρτος | τετρακις | |
| 5 | πεντε | tessellated pentagon, pentameter | πεμπτος | πεντακις | |
| 6 | ἑξ | hexagon, hexameter | ἑκτος | ἑξακις | |
| 7 | ἑπτα | heptarchy | ἑβδομος | ἑπτακις | hebdomadal (weekly) |
| 8 | ὀκτω | octopus | ὀγδοος | ὀκτακις | |
| 9 | ἐννεα | — | ἐνατος | ἐνακις | |
| 10 | δεκα | decalogue, decade | δεκατος | δεκακις | |
| 11 | ἑνδεκα | hendeca-syllables | ἑνδεκατος | ἑνδεκακις | |
| 12 | δωδεκα | Dodecanese | δωδεκατος | δωδεκακις | |
| 13 | τρεις και δεκα, etc. | — | τριτος και δεκατος | τρις κια δεκακις | |

| | Cardinal | English | Ordinal | Adverbial |
|---|---|---|---|---|
| 20 | εἴκοσι | — | εἰκοστος | εἰκοσάκις etc. |
| 30 | τριάκοντα | — | τριακοστός | |
| 40 | τεσσαράκοντα | — | τεσσαρακοσ-τος | |
| 50 | πεντηκοντα | Pentecost | πεντηκοστος etc. | |
| 60 | ἑξηκοντα | — | | |
| 70 | ἑβδομηκοντα | — | | |
| 80 | ὀγδοηκοντα | — | | |
| 90 | ἐνενηκοντα | — | | |
| 100 | ἑκατον | hecatomb | | |
| 200 | διακοσιοι, -αι, -α | — | | |
| 300 | τριακοσιοι, -αι, -α, etc. | — | | |
| 1,000 | χίλιοι, -αι, -α | kilo, kilo-metre | | |
| 2,000 | δισχίλιοι | — | | |
| 10,000 | μυριοι | myriad | | μυριακις |
| 100,000 | δεκα μυρι-αδες | — | | |

### Declension of First Four Cardinals.

| | | | | |
|---|---|---|---|---|
| N. | εἷς | μια | ἕν | οὐδεις (no |
| A. | ἕνα | μιαν | ἕν | one) simi- |
| G. | ἑνος | μιας | ἑνος | larly de- |
| D. | ἑνι | μιᾳ | ἑνι | clined, οὐ- |
| | | | | δεμια, οὐδεν |

N.⎫
A.⎬ δυο
G.⎫
D.⎭ δυοιν

| N.⎫ | τρεις | τρια |
|---|---|---|
| A.⎭ | | |
| G. | | τριων |
| D. | | τρισι |

| N. | τετταρες | τετταρα |
|---|---|---|
| A. | τετταρας | τετταρα |
| G. | | τεττάρων |
| D. | | τετταρσι |

2. This book has twenty-eight parts, and this part is the twenty-third.

3. The nine Muses once came to the three Graces, who were carrying baskets. And in the baskets were apples, and the Graces gave some of them to the Muses.

## The Four Best Things in Life

Translate :—

1. ὑγιαινειν μεν ἀριστον ἀνδρι θνητῳ,
   δευτερον δε φυην [1] καλον γενεσθαι,
   το τριτον δε πλουτειν ἀδολως,
   και το τεταρτον ἡβαν μετα των φιλων.

Robert Herrick has translated this as follows :—

' Health is the first good lent to men ;
A gentle disposition then :
Next, to be rich by no by-wayes ;
Lastly, with friends to ' enjoy our dayes '.

## Epigram on an Unhappy Man

2. Ἑξηκοντουτης [2] Διονυσιος ἐνθαδε κειμαι,
   Ταρσευς, μη γημας·[3] εἰθε [4] δε μηδ' ὁ πατηρ.

## An Unpopular Lecturer

3. Χαιρετ' Ἀριστειδου του ῥητορος ἑπτα μαθηται,
   τεσσαρες οἱ τοιχοι και τρια συψελια.[5]

---

1. Acc. of the part concerned. ' As to ' and so ' in ' nature. 2. Contracted for ἐξηκοντο-ετης, adj. = sixty years old. 3. Strictly speaking, μη with the ptcple. should mean ' *if* I had not married ', but after the Classical Age μη is often used for οὐ. γημας, aor. ptcple. from γαμεω. 4. εἰθε with an aor. ind. (sc. here ἐγημε) expresses an unfulfilled wish. *v.* c. 28, § 6, μηδε for οὐδε because in a ' wish ' clause. 5. συψελια is not really a Gk. word at all, but a Gk. transliteration of the Latin word subsellia, ' benches '.

## Proverb

4. μια χελιδων ούκ έαρ ποιει.

## Elementary Mathematics

5. τα δωδεκα έστι δις έξ, τρις τετταρα, έξακις δυο, τετρακις τρια.

## A Riddle [6]

6. αί Χαριτες μηλων καλαθους φερον,[6] έν δε
έκαστῳ
ίσον έην[7] πληθος. Μουσαι σφισιν[8] άντεβολησαν
έννεα, και μηλων[9] σφεας ήτεον· αί δ' άρ'
έδωκαν[10]
ίσον έκαστη πληθος, έχον[6] δ' ίσα έννεα και
τρεις.[11]
είπε,[12] ποσον[13] δωκαν,[6] και όπως[13] δ' ίσα[11]
πασαι έχεσκον.[14]

(a) How many apples did the Graces have at first in each basket ?

(b) How many apples did each give to each Muse ?

(c) How many did each have at the end ?

---

6. This riddle is written in hexameters, the ' six-foot ' metre of Homer, Gk. oracles, etc. φερον is for έφερον. In Homer the augment is frequently dropped. Similarly έχον is for είχον, and δωκαν (l. 5) for έδωκαν. 7. έην, poetic form of ήν, ' was '. 8. σφισιν, poetic for αύτοις, ' them ', dat. after άντεβολησαν, ' met '. 9. μηλων (*partitive gen.*), ' asked them (σφεας) for *some* of their apples '. σφεας = αύτας. ήτεον, impf. from αίτεω, ' I ask . . . for '. 10. Aor. from διδωμι, *v. c. 16.* 11. Notice gender of τρεις. What does it agree with ? έννεα is also the subject. ίσα, ' equal things ', i.e. ' an equal amount '. 12. είπε, ' tell ' (me). Imperat. from είπον, ' I said '. 13. ποσον, *v. c.* 24, correlatives. Also όπως, c. 24. 14. έχεσκον, poet. for είχον. Answer to riddle in key.

7. δια τοδε, Ζηνων ἐφη, δυο μεν ὦτα ἐχομεν, στομα δε ἑν, ἱνα πλειω μεν ἀκουωμεν,[15] ἡσσονα δε λεγωμεν.[15]

## A Happy Mother

8. Εἰκοσι Καλλικρατεια και ἐννεα τεκνα τεκουσα,[16]
   οὐδ' ἑνος οὐδε μιας ἐδρακομην [17] θανατον·
   ἀλλ' ἑκατον και πεντε διηνυσαμην [18] ἐνιαυτους,
   σκιπωνι τρομεραν οὐκ ἐπιθεισα [19] χερα.

## Another Riddle

ἀνθρωπου μερος εἰμι, ὁ και τεμνει με σιδηρος.[20]
γραμματος αἱρομενου δυεται ἡελιος.

'I am a part of a man ; iron sometimes cuts me. When one letter is removed, the sun sets.'

## VOCABULARY

ἀδολως (adv.), not treacherously (ἀ-, not, δολος, guile).
αἰτεω, I ask . . . (for). Impf. ἠτεον.
ἀρα (particle), thereupon, after all.
γαμεω, I marry.
διανυω, I bring to an end, conclude.
ἐνθαδε (adv.), here.
ἐνιαυτος, -ου, a year.
Ζηνων, Zeno, a philosopher.
καλαθος, -ου, basket.
μαθητης, learner, student, disciple (in N.T.).
μηλον, an apple.
Μουσα, as a proper noun ' Muse '.

πληθος, -ους, n. number, quantity, crowd.
πλουτεω, I am rich.
ῥητωρ, -ορος, lecturer, public speaker.
σκιπων, -ωνος, a staff (Lat. Scipio).
Ταρσευς (adj.), of Tarsus.
τοιχος, -ου, wall.
τρομερος, -α, -ον, trembling.
ὑγιαινω, I am in good health (ὑγιεια).
φυη, -ης, nature.
Χαρις, -ιτος, as a proper noun in plur., the Graces.
χελιδων, -ονος, swallow.
ὦτα from οὐς, ὠτος (n.) an ear. (See p. 100.)

15. Subj. in purpose clause, v. c. 28, ' in order that we may . . .' 16. τεκουσα, fem. aor. part. of τικτω, ' bring forth '. 17. ἐδρακομην, aor. of δερκομαι, ' I see ', v. c. 15. 18. Aor. mid. from διανυω. 19. ἐπιθεισα, from. ἐπιτιθημι, v. c. 16. 20. Here is another riddle with translation. The answer is a Gk. word that occurs in c. 9 with a guttural stem.

# CHAPTER XXIV

## PRONOUNS AND CORRELATIVES

Pronouns are very common in Greek. You have had several already : ἐκεινος, ἑαυτου in c. 11; οἷος in c. 12; ποιος, ἀλληλους in c. 14; ἡμεις and σος in c. 15—can you remember their meanings? You must expect irregularities among such well-worn words. But you should not find them difficult to recognise whatever the case-ending may be if you study them carefully as set out below.

1. *Personal Pronouns.*

| | | |
|---|---|---|
| *Sing.* N. ἐγω, ' I ' | | συ, ' thou ' |
| A. ἐμε (or με), ' me ' | | σε |
| G. ἐμου (or μου), ' of me ' | | σου |
| D. ἐμοι (or μοι), ' to me ' | | σοι |
| *Plur.* N. ἡμεις, ' we ' | | ὑμεις, ' you ' |
| A. ἡμας, ' us ' | | ὑμας |
| G. ἡμων, ' of us ' | | ὑμων |
| D. ἡμιν, ' to us ' | | ὑμιν |

(1) The alternative με, μου, μοι forms are less emphatic, and are called ' enclitic ' (ἐν-κλινω, ' bending-in ') forms because they are attached for pronunciation to the word which governs them, and which they must follow and not precede. Cf. ' thee ' in ' prithee '. Also they are not used with prepositions—e.g. δι' ἐμε, ' on account of me '.

241

'Remember me' could be either ἐμου μεμνησο or μεμνησο μου.

(2) There is, properly speaking, no 3rd personal pron. in Attic Gk., its place being taken by αὐτος in all cases except the nom. αὐτος declines like the article (τον, την, το) with the syllable αὐ- in front of it—αὐτος, αὐτη, αὐτο, etc. For the nom. case (sing. and plur.), the Gks. used the Demonstrative pron. οὗτος ('this man') or ἐκεινος ('that man'), though ὁ and οἱ survive in the usuage ὁ μεν . . . ὁ δε ('the one . . . the other') and οἱ μεν . . . οἱ δε ('some . . . others'). Thus (ἐγω) ἐβλαψα αὐτον, 'I hurt him'.   (οὗτος) ἐβλαψε με, 'he hurt me.'

## 2. Possessive Pronouns.

These are adjectives formed from the personal pronouns and declined like regular adjectives.  They have the article preceding them.

| Masc. | Fem. | Neut. |
|---|---|---|
| ὁ ἐμος ('my') | ἡ ἐμη | το ἐμον |
| ὁ σος ('thy') | ἡ ση | το σον |
| ὁ ἡμετερος ('our') | ἡ ἡμετερα | το ἡμετερον |
| ὁ ὑμετερος ('your') | ἡ ὑμετερα | το ὑμετερον. |

So 'my brother' is either ὁ ἐμος ἀδελφος or ὁ ἀδελφος μου. The gen. of αὐτος is used for the possessive of the 3rd person—e.g. :—

'his brother',    ὁ ἀδελφος αὐτου.
'her brother',    ὁ ἀδελφος αὐτης.
'their brother',  ὁ ἀδελφος αὐτων.

3. Reflexive Pronouns.   These are made up of the personal pronouns and αὐτος, thus :—

|  | 1st Person<br>(' myself ''). | 2nd Person<br>(' thyself '). | 3rd Person. |
|---|---|---|---|
| Sing. | A. ἐμαυτον (-ην) | σεαυτον or<br>σαυτον (-ην) | ἑαυτον, -την,<br>-το or αὑτον |
|  | G. ἐμαυτου (-ης) | σεαυτου or<br>σαυτου (-ης) | ἑαυτου, -της,<br>-του, etc., or<br>αὑτου |
|  | D. ἐμαυτῳ (η) | σεαυτῳ or<br>σαυτῳ -(η) |  |
| Plur. | A. ἡμας αὑτους (our-<br>selves) | ὑμας αὑτους,<br>etc. | ἑαυτους, -τας,<br>-τα, etc., or<br>αὑτους |
|  | G. ἡμων αὑτων | ὑμων αὑτων | ἑαυτων or<br>αὑτων |
|  | D. ἡμιν αὑτοις (-αις) | ὑμιν αὑτοις<br>(-αις) | ἑαυτοις, -αις,<br>-οις, or αὑτοις |

Another form of the 3rd person reflexive pronoun
in the plural only, is

> σφας αὑτους (' themselves ')
> σφων αὑτων
> σφισιν αὑτοις

and there is a reflexive or possessive adj. (suus in
Lat.) σφετερος, ' their own. . . .'

There is a reciprocal pronoun, ' each other ', ' one
another ', which is thus declined. You had it in
Ch. 14.

*Plur.*

A. ἀλληλους, -ας, -α
G. ἀλληλων, -ων, -ων
D. ἀλληλοις, -αις, -οις

The word is formed by a reduplication of ἀλλος.

## ’ΑΥΤΟΣ ‘Ο—AND ‘Ο ’ΑΥΤΟΣ

Where in English we use ' —self' to intensify a
noun or pronoun, Greek uses αὑτος. Thus αὑτος ὁ

ἄνθρωπος = 'the man himself' (autobiography).
But ὁ αὐτός (or αὑτός, as it is often contracted to)
ἄνθρωπος = '*the same man*', v. ch. 12, 18. Neuter
would be το αὐτό or ταὐτό (note the breathing)
(Eng. tautology). Acc. τον αὐτόν, etc.

### 4. *Demonstrative Pronouns*.

There are only three main ones—οὗτος and ὅδε
'this', ἐκεῖνος 'that'.

*Sing*.

|   | | | | | | |
|---|---|---|---|---|---|---|
| N. | οὗτος | αὕτη | τουτο | ἐκεινος | ἐκεινη | ἐκεινο |
| A. | τουτον | ταυτην | τουτο | ἐκεινον | ἐκεινην | ἐκεινο |
| G. | τουτου | ταυτης | τουτου | ἐκεινου | ἐκεινης | ἐκεινου |
| D. | τουτῳ | ταυτῃ | τουτῳ | ἐκεινῳ | ἐκεινῃ | ἐκεινῳ |

*Plur*.

|   | | | | | | |
|---|---|---|---|---|---|---|
| N. | οὗτοι | αὗται | ταυτα | ἐκεινοι | ἐκειναι | ἐκεινα |
| A. | τουτους | ταυτας | ταυτα | ἐκεινους | ἐκεινας | ἐκεινα |
| G. | τουτων | τουτων | τουτων | ἐκεινων | ἐκεινων | ἐκεινων |
| D. | τουτοις | ταυταις | τουτοις | ἐκεινοις | ἐκειναις | ἐκεινοις |

### Notes on Demonstratives

1. Like οὗτος are declined τοσουτος, 'so great', and
τοιουτος, 'such'.

2. Another word for 'this' is ὅδε, which is declined
exactly like ὁ, ἡ, το with -δε tacked on. οὗτος and its
compound refer back, ὅδε looks forward, thus :—

Ταυτα μεν ἐλεξε, ἐδρασε δε ταδε
= This is what he said, but he did as follows.

So τοιοσδε ('such as this'). ἐλεξε τοιαυτα, 'he spoke as
above', but ἐλεξε τοιαδε, 'he spoke as follows'.

3. The article always goes in between the demonstrative
and the noun, thus—

οὗτος ὁ ἀνηρ.
or ὅδε ὁ ἀνηρ  } 'this man'.

Originally the demonstrative may have been regarded
as a substantive : 'this one (I mean), the man'.

## Exercise I

Translate :—

1. τουτ' ἐστι το ζην [1] οὐχ ἑαυτῳ ζην μονον.— Menander.

2. γνωθι σεαυτον.

3. ὁ φθονερος αὐτῳ πολεμιος καθισταται.[2]

4. οὐκ ἐστιν ὁστις παντ' [3] ἀνηρ εὐδαιμονει.

5. οὐ σπειρουσιν, οὐδε θεριζουσιν, οὐδε συναγουσιν εἰς ἀποθηκας, και ὁ πατηρ ὑμων ὁ οὐρανιος τρεφει αὐτα· οὐχ ὑμεις μαλλον διαφερετε αὐτων ;

6. βαλλων [4] τις λιθῳ τον κυνα, εἰθ' ἁμαρτων και την μητρυιαν παταξας, οὐδ' οὑτως, ἐφη, κακως.

7. Σοφοκλης ἐφη αὐτος [5] μεν οἱους δει [6] ποιειν, Εὐριπιδην δε οἱοι εἰσιν.—Aristotle, *Poetics*.

### War Profiteers

8. ὁτῳ συνενηνοχασιν [7] οἱ αὐτοι καιροι και τοις [8]

---

1. Pres. inf. of ζαω, 'I live', v. c. 20 on why it is not ζαν.
2. καθισταται, pres. ind. mid. of καθιστημι, 'establishes himself', 'becomes', so 'is'. 3. Adverbial acc. 'in all things'. 4. βαλλων means 'throwing at', as well as 'throwing', and can take an acc. of the thing 'aimed at'. 5. αὐτος, for the significance of the nom. with the inf. after verbs of saying, v. c. 26. 6. οἱους δει is ambiguous. The Gk. says only, 'that he made his characters as it was necessary'. An inf. must be understood after δει. This is usually thought to be εἰναι, and the sense to be 'as they *ought to be*' i.e. idealised characters, as opposed to the realistic ones of Euripides ('as they were'). But the Gk. could also mean 'as he needed to make them' (understanding ποιειν)—i.e. as he needed for dramatic reasons. Which interpretation do you prefer? 7. συνενηνοχασιν 3rd plur. perf. ind. act. of the very irregular verb συμφερω (v. 25), which means to 'be an advantage to (dat.)', 'be useful to'. The order of words in Engl. is οὐκ ἐνεστι (= ἐξεστι, 'it is not possible', v. 26) τουτον ('that this man') εἰναι . . . ('should be') . . ., ὁτῳ ('to whom'). 8. Gk. says 'same . . . and to the . . .', we say, 'same

τῆς πολεως ἐχθροις, οὐκ ἐνεστι τουτον εὐνουν εἶναι τῃ πατριδι.—Demosthenes.

## Epigrams

### On the statue of a dog placed on the grave of Diogenes.

9. α. εἶπε, κυον,[9] τινος ἀνδρος ἐφεστως [10] σημα φυλασσεις ;

β. του κυνος.[11]  α. ἀλλα τις ἦν οὗτος ἀνηρ ὁ κυων ;

β. Διογενης·  α. γενος εἶπε.  β. Σινωπευς·[12] α. ὁς πιθον ᾠκει ;

β. και μαλα,[13] νυν δε θανων ἀστερας οἰκον [14] ἐχει.

### Wheel of Fortune

10. χρυσον ἀνηρ εὑρων [15] ἐλιπε βροχον· αὐταρ ὁ χρυσον,[16]

ὁν λιπεν, οὐχ εὑρων, ἡψεν, ὁν εὑρε, βροχον.[17]
—Plato.

---

*as* to the . . .'. Demosthenes was the greatest of the orators of Athens, and warned his countrymen of the black marketers of his day.  9. κυον, voc. τινος = interrogative pronoun, *v.* following section.  Also τις next line.  10. ἐφεστως, 2nd perf. part. of ἐφιστημι (*v.* 16), 'standing'.  11. του κυνος, of the dog, i.e. the Cynic.  For Diogenes, *v.* 21.  12. Of Sinope, a town on the south shore of the Black Sea.  13. και μαλα, 'yes, certainly '.  14. 'As a home ', οἰκον in apposition to ἀστερας.  15. εὑρων, 2nd aor. part. of εὑρισκω, 'I find '. 16. The order is ὁ χρυσον οὐχ εὑρων, ' the original owner who did not find the gold '.  For ὁν see following paragraph. 17. The point of this anecdote of Thief and Miser is that the latter committed suicide because he did not find the gold which he had left.  Coleridge on one occasion translated the couplet extemporarily thus :—

Jack finding gold left a rope in the ground;
Bill missing his gold used the rope which he found

## VOCABULARY

ἀποθηκη, -ης, storehouse, granary, barn (ἀποτιθημι, I store away).

ἁπτω, I fasten, fasten to (aor. ἡψα).

αὐταρ, but.

βροχος, -ου, noose, halter.

διαφερω, (1) I differ from, (2) I am superior to.

εὐδαιμονεω, I am happy (lit. have a good spirit inside me).

θεριζω, I reap or harvest (θερος, summer).

καιρος, -ου, occasion, opportunity.

μητρυια, -ας, mother-in-law.

οἰκεω, I dwell in, live in, inhabit.

οὐρανιος, -α, -ον (adj.), heavenly, of heaven (ουρανος).

πατασσω, παταξω, ἐπαταξα, strike.

πιθος, -ου, cask, tub, large earthenware jar.

σπειρω, I sow.

συναγω, I bring together.

τρεφω, I nourish.

φθονερος (adj.), jealous.

## RELATIVE PRONOUNS

In this last extract you have had in ' ὁν ' the acc. masc. sing. of the relative ὁς, ' who ' or ' which '. It declines like κακος, except that, like all pronouns, it drops the ν in the nom. and acc. neuter sing. Thus :—

|  | Sing. | | | Plur. | | |
|---|---|---|---|---|---|---|
|  | *Masc.* | *Fem.* | *Neut.* | *Masc.* | *Fem.* | *Neut.* |
| N. | ὁς | ἡ | ὁ | οἱ | αἱ | ἁ |
| A. | ὁν | ἡν | ὁ | οὑς | ἁς | ἁ |
| G. | οὑ | ἡς | οὑ | ὡν | ὡν | ὡν |
| D. | ᾡ | ᾑ | ᾡ | οἱς | αἱς | οἱς |

Note the rough breathing, which enables you to distinguish the relative from οὐ (' not '), ὠν (' being '), ἠ (' than '), etc. The relative agrees in gender with the word to which it refers (called the antecedent), but takes its case from its own clause. Thus ὁ ἀνηρ, ὁν ἐβλεψα; ' the man whom I saw ', but ἡ γυνη, ἡν ἐβλεψα. Sometimes the suffix -περ is added to make the relative more emphatic—e.g., ὁσπερ, ' the very man who ', ἡπερ, ὁπερ.

## INTERROGATIVE PRONOUNS

The direct interrogative is τις (' who? '), τι (' what? '), which is declined thus :—

|  | *Sing.* | | | *Plur.* | | |
|  | *Masc. Fem.* | *Neut.* | | *Masc. Fem.* | *Neut.* | |
| N. | τις | τι | | τινες | τινα | |
| A. | τινα | τι | | τινας | τινα | |
| G. | τινος (or του) | | | τινων | | |
| D. | τινι (or τῳ) | | | τισι | | |

E.g. τις ἐστιν οὑτος; = ' who is this man? '
    τι ἐστι τουτο = ' what is this (thing)? '

The indirect interrogative is ὁστις (*whoever*), made up of ὁς and τις, declined separately but written (except in the neut. nom. and acc. sing.) as one word :—

|  | *Sing.* | | | *Plur.* | | |
|  | *Masc.* | *Fem.* | *Neut.* | *Masc.* | *Fem.* | *Neut.* |
| N. | ὁστις | ἡτις | ὁ, τι | οἱτινες | ἁιτινες | ἁτινα (or ἁττα) |
| A. | ὁντινα | ἡντινα | ὁ, τι | οὑστινες | ἁστινας | ἁτινα (or ἁττα) |
| G. | ὁτου | ἡστινος | ὁτου | ὡντινων (or ὁτων) | | |
| D. | ὁτῳ | ἡτινι | ὁτῳ | οἱστισι (or ὁτοις) | αἱστισι | οἱστισι (or ὁτοις) |

The neut. sing. is written ὁ, τι or ὁ τι, to distinguish it from the conjunction ὁτι (' that ', or ' because '). Λεγε μοι ὁστις ἐστιν οὑτος = tell me who this man is. But you can equally well say, Λεγε μοι τις ἐστιν οὑτος = tell me who this man is. ὁστις is also used as a relative—e.g. ὁστις εἱ, λεγε = ' whoever you are, speak '.

## INDEFINITE PRONOUN

τις is also the *indefinite pronoun* meaning ' anyone '. You may think, " How confusing! ", but you can always tell which it is, because when an indefinite pronoun, it is an enclitic (*v.* note 1 of Section 1 of this chapter), and therefore can never be the first word in a sentence, as it usually is when an interrogative.

E.g. ἔλεγε κακόν τι, ' he was saying something bad.'

But τί κακὸν ἔλεγε; ' what bad (thing) was he saying? '

It is declined in the same way whichever pronoun it is.

*Correlatives.*—The following table will show you at a glance the commonest of the correlative pronouns. They occur so frequently that it is worth studying them carefully. What do you notice about the first letters of the words in each class (reading downwards)? What idea does this denote?

## CORRELATIVE PRONOUNS

| | Interrogative. | | Relative. | Indefinite. | Demon- strative. |
|---|---|---|---|---|---|
| | Direct. | Indirect. | | | |
| 1. | τίς; who ? | ὅστις, who | ὅς, who | τις, any, anyone | ὅδε, οὗτος, this |
| 2. | πόσος; how big ? how many ? | ὁπόσος, how big, how many | ὅσος (as big or many) as | — | τοσοσδε, τοσ- οὗτος, so big, so many |
| 3. | ποῖος; of what kind ? | ὁποῖος, of what kind | οἷος, such as | — | τοιοσδε, τοι- οῦτος, such, of such kind |
| 4. | πότερος; which of two ? | ὁπότερος, which (of two) | — | — | ὁ ἕτερος the one (or other) of two |

Except in the case of 1, the direct interrogatives begin with the letters πο- (Lat. qu-).

Except in the case of 1, the indirect interrogatives begin with the letters ὁπο-.

All the relatives begin with the letter ὁ-.

Except in the case of 1 and 4, the demonstratives begin with the letters το-.

## CORRELATIVE ADVERBS

| Interrogative. | | Relative. | Indefinite. | Demon-strative. |
|---|---|---|---|---|
| Direct. | Indirect. | | | |
| που; where ? | ὁπου, where | οὑ, where | που, somewhere anywhere | ἐνταυθα, ἐκει, there |
| ποθεν; whence ? | ὁποθεν, whence | ὁθεν, whence | ποθεν, from somewhere | ἐντευθεν ἐκειθεν } thence |
| ποι; whither ? | ὁποι, whither | οἱ, whither | ποι, to some place | ἐκεισε, thither |
| ποτε; when ? | ὁποτε, when | ὁτε, when | ποτε, at some time or other, once | τοτε, then |
| πως; how ? | ὁπως, how | ὡς, as | πως, some-how | ὡδε οὑτως } thus |
| πῃ; which way ? | ὁπῃ, where | ᾗ, where | πῃ, some-way | τῃδε, ταυτῃ } by this way, thus |

*Examples* :—

που εἰ ; = ' where are you ? '

οὑκ οἰδα ὁπου εἰμι = ' I don't know where I am.'

ποτε τουτο ἐποιησας; = ' when did you do this ? '

τουτο ἐποιησα ποτε = ' I did this once.'

## Exercise 2

(Μαθημα τεταρτον και εἰκοστον)

Translate :—

1. A. τινος ἐστιν ὁδε ὁ ταφος ;
   B. ταφος ἐστι ναυηγου, ὡ φιλε.
   A. τι ἠν το ὀνομα τουτου ;
   B. οὐκ οἰδα, πειρασομαι δε ἐξευρειν.
   A. ποι ἐποντοπορει ἡ ναυς, ὁτε οὑτος ὡλετο ;
   B. οὐκ οἰδα ὁποι, ὁποθεν δε ἠλθεν δυναμαι λεγειν.

2. οὐκ οἰδα, ὡ Ἡρακλειτε, ὁπως ἠ ὁπου ἀπεθανες, ἀλλ’ οὐδ’ Ἀϊδης αὐτος δυνησεται χειρα ἐπιβαλειν ταις σαις ἀηδοσιν.

## KEY (THE 24TH LESSON)

1. A. Whose is this tomb ?
   B. It is the tomb of a shipwrecked (man), oh, friend.
   A. What is his name ?
   B. I don't know, but I will try to find out.
   A. Whither was the ship sea-sailing when he perished ?
   B. I don't know whither, but whence he came I can say.

2. I don't know how or where you died, but not even Hades himself will be able to lay a hand on your nightingales.

## On a Sailor's Grave

Translate :—

1. Ναυηγου [1] ταφος εἰμι· συ δε πλεε·[2] και γαρ
   ὁθ’ [3] ἡμεις
   ὠλομεθ’,[4] αἱ λοιπαι [5] νηες ἐποντοπορουν.[6]

---

1. Ionic form of ναυαγος, ‘a shipwrecked man’.   2. Imperative.   3. The elided letter is ε.   The ι of ὁτι is never elided.   4. ὠλομην is the strong aor. middle of ὁλλυμι, ‘I destroy’.   In the middle it means ‘perish’.   5. ‘Remaining’.   6. ‘Were sailing the sea’, deriv. ποντος, v. c. 11, and πορος, ‘way, passage, ford’.

'A shipwrecked sailor's tomb am I,
But thou sail on; the day
We sank, the convoy's other ships
Kept on their ocean way.'—Michanopoulos.

## A Dead Friend *

2. εἶπε τις, 'Ηρακλειτε,[7] τεον [8] μορον, ἐς δε με δακρυ
ἠγαγεν·[9] ἐμνησθην [10] δ' ὁσσακις ἀμφοτεροι
ἠλιον ἐν λεσχῃ κατεδυσαμεν·[11] ἀλλα συ μεν που,[12]
ξειν'[13] 'Αλικαρνησσευ,[14] τετραπαλαι [15] σποδιη.

---

* This little poignant lyric by Callimachus, who lived about
250 B.C., on the death of a scholar friend is well known from
the translation by Cory, but lovely as his version is it lacks
the simplicity of the Gk., and verges on sentimentality.
Contrast the repetitions in the Eng. with the restraint of
the Gk. H.'s 'nightingales' are probably his poems. One
still survives.

They told me, Heracleitus, they told me you were dead;
They brought me bitter news to hear and bitter tears to shed.
I wept, as I remembered how often you and I
Had tired the sun with talking and sent him down the sky.

And now that thou art lying, my dear old Carian guest,
A handful of grey ashes, long, long ago at rest,
Still are thy pleasant voices, thy nightingales awake,
For Death, he taketh all away, but them he cannot take.
                                                    Cory.

7. Not the philosopher (500 B.C.). 8. τεον, poetic form
of σον, so τεαι for σαι. 9. ἐς governs δακρυ, ' brought me
to a tear '. ἠγαγεν, strong aor. of ἀγω (' I bring '). 10.
ἐμνησθην, aor. of μεμνημαι (' I remember '), which is the
perfect passive of μιμνησκω (' I remind '), ' I have been
reminded ', and so ' remember '. 11. Lit. ' we made the
sun to set ', i.e. talked the sun down. 12. που, an expressive little word at the end of a line, full of pathos. ' I
suppose ' is perhaps the nearest Eng. equivalent. 13. ξεινε,
another form of ξενε. Gk. uses the same word for ' guest '
and ' host '—so sacred did they regard that relationship.
14. ' Of Halicarnassus ', town in Caria. εἱ, ' you are ', is
understood. 15. τετραπαλαι, a rare word meaning literally
' four times long ago ' (παλαι, ' long ago ').

αἱ δε τεαι [8] ζωουσιν[16] ἀηδονες, ἧσιν[17] ὁ παντων[18]
ἁρπακτης Ἀϊδης οὐκ ἐπι χειρα βαλει.[19]

Callimachus.

## VOCABULARY

ἁρπακτης, -ου, stealer, robber
(harpy).
ζαω, I live.
λεσχη, -ης, place where people
talk, so conversation
μορος, -ου, death.
ναυηγος, v. note 1.

ὁσσακις or ὁσακις (in prose),
how often.
πλεω, I sail.
που, somewhere.
σποδια (σποδιη, Ionic), heap
of ashes.

---

16. ζωουσι = ζαουσι. 17. ἧσιν, Ionic for αἷς, 'relative',
dat. gov. by ἐπι . . . βαλϝι, tmesis (i.e. 'cutting off', 'separating') for ἐπιβαλει. Originally the preps. were advs. of
place (v. c. 22). 18. Lit. 'snatcher of all things'. ὁ goes
with Ἀιδης. Ἀϊδης is a poetry form for the more usual
Ἀϊδης. 19. Fut. of βαλλω, here 'will lay a hand'.

# CHAPTER XXV

## IRREGULAR VERBS

A HYPHEN preceding a word indicates that it is only found in compound forms.

\* Conjugated like φιλεω.

| Present. | Future. | Aorist. | Perfect. |
|---|---|---|---|
| ἀγω, lead, bring (mid.), marry | ἀξω | ἠγαγον ἠχθην | -ηχα ἠγμαι |
| αἰνεω, praise, advise | -αινεσομαι | ἠνεσα ἠνεθην | ἠνεκα ἠνημαι |
| αἱρεω, take (mid. choose) (pass) | αἱρησω | εἱλον εἱλομην ἡρεθην | ἡρηκα ἡρημαι |
| αἰσθανομαι, perceive | αἰσθησομαι | ἠσθομην | ἠσθημαι |
| ἀκουω, hear | ἀκουσομαι | ἠκουσα ἠκουσθην | ἀκηκοα |
| ἁλισκομαι, be caught | ἁλωσομαι | ἑαλων | ἑαλωκα or ἡλωκα |
| ἁμαρτανω, miss, sin | ἁμαρτησομαι | ἡμαρτον | ἡμαρτηκα |
| βαινω, come, go | βησομαι | ἐβην | βεβηκα |
| βαλλω, throw, shoot, pelt | βαλω\* | ἐβαλον ἐβληθην | βεβληκα βεβλημαι |
| βλαπτω, harm | βλαψω | ἐβλαψα ἐβλαβην | βεβλαφα βεβλημαι |
| βουλομαι, wish | βουλησομαι | ἐβουληθην | βεβουλημαι |
| γαμεω, marry (governs acc. of woman) | γαμω\* | ἐγημα | γεγαμηκα |
| γαμουμαι (governs dat. of man) | | | |

| Present. | Future. | Aorist. | Perfect. |
|---|---|---|---|
| γιγνομαι, become | γενησομαι | ἐγενομην (ἐγενηθην late) | γεγενημαι γεγονα |
| γιγνωσκω, realise, recognise | γνωσομαι | ἐγνων ἐγνωσθην | ἐγνωκα ἐγνωσμαι |
| γραφω, write | γραψω | ἐγραψα ἐγραφην | γεγραφα γεγραμμαι |
| δακνω, bite | δηξομαι | ἐδακον ἐδηχθην | δεδηγμαι |
| διδασκω, teach | διδαξω | ἐδιδαξα | δεδιδαχα |
| διδωμι, give | δωσω | ἐδωκα | δεδωκα |
| δοκεω, think (Impersonal, it seems good) | δοξω | ἐδοξα | δεδογμαι |
| δυναμαι, be able | δυνησομαι | ἐδυνηθην | δεδυνημαι |
| ἐγειρω, waken (trans.) (mid. intrans.) | ἐγερω* | ἠγειρα | ἐγρηγορα |
| ἐθελω (also θελω), wish, be willing | ἐθελησω | ἠθελησα | ἠθεληκα |
| —know | εἰσομαι | — | οἰδα (pres. meaning) |
| εἰμι, be | ἐσομαι | — | — |
| ἐλαυνω, drive | ἐλω (like τιμαω) | ἠλασα ἠλαθην | ἐληλακα ἐληλαμαι |
| ἐπισταμαι, understand | ἐπιστησομαι | ἠπιστηθην (imperfect ἠπισταμην) | — |
| ἑπομαι, follow | ἑψομαι | ἑσπομην (imperfect εἱπομην) | — |
| ἐρχομαι, come, go | εἰμι | ἠλθον | ἐληλυθα or ἡκω |
| —ask | ἐρησομαι | ἠρομην | — |
| ἐσθιω, eat | ἐδομαι | ἐφαγον | ἐδηδοκα |

| Present. | Future. | Aorist. | Perfect. |
|---|---|---|---|
| εὑρίσκω, find | εὑρήσω | ηὗρον | ηὕρηκα |
| | | ηὑρέθην | ηὕρημαι |
| ἔχω, have (mid. | ἔξω | ἔσχον | ἔσχηκα |
| hold on to) | σχησω | (imperfect | -εσχημαι |
| | | εἶχον) | |
| ϡαω, live | ϡησω, ϡησομαι, | ἐβίων | βεβιωκα |
| | βιωσομαι | | βεβιωται |
| | | | (impers.) |
| θαπτω, bury | θαψω | ἔθαψα | τεθαμμαι |
| | | ἐταφην | — |
| -θνησκω, die, | -θανουμαι* | -εθανον | τεθνηκα |
| be killed | | | |
| ἱημι, let go, | -ησω | -ηκα | -εικα |
| make for | | -ειμην (mid.) | — |
| (mid.) | | -ειθην (pass.) | -ειμαι |
| ἀφ-ικνεομαι, | ἀφ-ιξομαι | ἀφ-ικομην | ἀφ- ιγμαι |
| arrive | | | |
| ἱστημι | στησω | ἔστησα (trans.) | ἔστηκα (in- |
| Trans. set up | | ἔστην (in- | trans.) |
| Intrans. stand | | trans.) | " I stand " |
| | | ἐσταθην (pass.) | |
| καιω, burn | καυσω | ἔκαυσα | -κεκαυκα |
| (trans.) | | | |
| καλεω, call | καλω* | ἐκαλεσα | κεκληκα |
| | | ἐκληθην | κεκλημαι |
| καμνω, labour, | καμουμαι* | ἔκαμον | κεκμηκα |
| be weary | | | |
| κεραννυμι, mix | κερω (like | ἐκερασα | — |
| | τιμαω) | ἐκραθην | κεκραμαι |
| κλαιω, weep | κλαυσομαι | ἔκλαυσα | |
| | | | κεκλαυμαι |
| κλεπτω, steal | κλεψω | ἔκλεψα | κεκλοφα |
| | | ἐκλαπην | κεκλεμμαι |
| κλινω, bend, | -κλινω * | ἔκλινα | |
| incline | | -εκλινην | κεκλιμαι |
| κρινω, distin- | κρινω * | ἔκρινα | κεκρικα |
| guish, judge | | ἐκριθην | κεκριμαι |
| -κτεινω, kill | -κτενω * | -εκτεινα | -εκτονα |
| λαγχανω, get | ληξομαι | ἐλαχον | εἰληχα |
| (by lot) | | ἐληχθην | εἰληγμαι |
| λαμβανω, take | ληψομαι | ἐλαβον | εἰληφα |
| | | ἐληφθην | εἰλημμαι |

| Present. | Future. | Aorist. | Perfect. |
|---|---|---|---|
| λανθανω, elude, escape notice | λησω | ἐλαθον | λεληθα |
| ἐπιλανθανομαι, forget | ἐπιλησομαι | ἐπελαθομην | ἐπιλελησμαι |
| λεγω, say | λεξω ἐρω * (Pass.) | ἐλεξα εἰπον (Pass.) | εἰρηκα |
| ·αγορευω | λεχθησομαι εἰρησομαι ῥηθησομαι | ἐλεχθην ἐρρηθην | εἰρημαι λελεγμαι |
| λειπω, leave | -λειψω | ἐλιπον ἐλειφθην | λελοιπα λελειμμαι |
| μανθανω, learn | μαθησομαι | ἐμαθον | μεμαθηκα |
| μαχομαι, fight | μαχουμαι * | ἐμαχεσαμην | μεμαχημαι |
| μειγνυμι or μιγνυμι, mix | μειξω | ἐμειξα (ἐμιξα) ἐμιγην (ἐμιχθην) | μεμειγμαι |
| μελλω, be about to, intend, delay | μελλησω | ἐμελλησα or ἠμελλησα | — |
| μενω, wait | μενω * | ἐμεινα | μεμενηκα |
| ἀναμιμνησκω, remind | ἀναμνησω | ἀνεμνησα | — |
| μιμνησκομαι, remember | μνησθησομαι (μεμνησομαι) | ἐμνησθην | μεμνημαι (used as present) |
| νεμω, allot, distribute | νεμω * | ἐνειμα ἐνεμηθην | -νενεμηκα νενεμημαι |
| ἀν-οιγνυμι, open | ἀν-οιξω | ἀν-εῳξα (impf. ἀνεῳγον) Pass. ἀνεῳχθην | — ἀνεῳγμαι |
| οἰομαι, think | οἰησομαι | ᾠηθην | — |
| οἰχομαι, be gone | οἰχησομαι | (Imperf. ᾠχομην) | οἰχωκα |
| ἀπ-ολλυμι, destroy | ἀπ-ολω * | ἀπ-ωλεσα ἀπ-ωλομην (intr. perish) | ἀπ-ολωλεκα ἀπ-ολωλα (intr. I am undone !) |
| ὀμνυμι, swear | ὀμουμαι * | ὠμοσα ὠμοθην | ὀμωμοκα ὀμωμομαι |

| Present. | Future. | Aorist. | Perfect. |
|---|---|---|---|
| ὁραω, see | ὀψομαι | εἰδον<br>ὠφθην | ἑορακα  or<br>ἑωρακα<br>ἑωραμαι |
| ὀφειλω, owe | ὀφειλησω | ὠφειλησα<br>ὠφελον | ὠφειληκα |
| ὀφλισκανω, incur a charge of | ὀφλησω | ὠφλον | ὠφληκα<br>ὠφλημαι |
| πασχω, suffer, be treated | πεισομαι | ἐπαθον | πεπονθα |
| πειθω, Act. persuade, Pass. obey | πεισω | ἐπεισα<br>ἐπεισθην | πεπεικα<br>πεπεισμαι |
| πεμπω, send | πεμψω | ἐπεμψα<br>ἐπεμφθην | πεπομφα<br>πεπεμμαι |
| ἐμ-πιμπλημι, fill | ἐμ-πλησω | ἐν-επλησα<br>ἐν-επλησθην | ἐμπεπληκα<br>ἐμπεπλησμαι |
| πινω, drink | πιομαι | ἐπιον<br>ἐποθην | πεπωκα<br>πεπομαι |
| πιπτω, fall | πεσουμαι * | ἐπεσον | πεπτωκα |
| πλεω, sail | πλευσομαι | ἐπλευσα | πεπλευκα |
| πνεω, breathe | -πνευσομαι | ἐπνευσα | -πεπνευκα |
| πυνθανομαι, enquire, learn | πευσομαι | ἐπυθομην | πεπυσμαι |
| πωλεω ἀποδιδομαι, sell | πωλησω<br>ἀποδωσομαι | —<br>ἀπεδομην | πεπρακα |
| πιπρασκομαι, be sold | πεπρασομαι | ἐπραθην | πεπραμαι |
| ῥηγνυμι, break | ῥηξω | ἐρρηξα<br>ἐρραγην | ἐρρωγα<br>(intr.) |
| ῥιπτω, hurl | ῥιψω | ἐρριψα<br>ἐρριφην | ἐρριφα<br>ἐρριμμαι |
| σκοπεω, inspect, examine, consider | σκεψομαι | ἐσκεψαμην | ἐσκεμμαι |
| σπειρω, sow | σπερω * | ἐσπειρα<br>ἐσπαρην | ἐσπαρμαι |
| σπενδω, pour a libation (mid.) make a tune | σπεισω | ἐσπεισα | — |

| Present. | Future. | Aorist. | Perfect. |
|---|---|---|---|
| ἀπο-στελλω, send forth | -στελω * | -εστειλα <br> -εσταλην | -εσταλκα <br> -εσταλμαι |
| στρεφω, turn | -στρεψω | ἐστρεψα <br> ἐστραφην | ἐστραμμαι |
| σφαλλω, trip up, cheat | σφαλω * | ἐσφηλα <br> ἐσφαλην | — <br> ἐσφαλμαι |
| τελεω, complete, finish, pay | τελω * | ἐτελεσα <br> ἐτελεσθην | τετελεκα <br> τετελεσμαι |
| τεμνω, cut | τεμω * | ἐτεμον <br> ἐτμηθην | τετμηκα <br> τετμημαι |
| τιθημι, put | θησω | ἐθηκα <br> ἐθεμην (mid.) <br> ἐτεθην (pass.) | τεθηκα <br> τεθειμαι <br> (mid.) <br> κειμαι (used <br> for pass.) |
| τικτω, beget or bear | τεξομαι | ἐτεκον | τετοκα |
| τινω, pay, require | τεισω or τισω | ἐτεισα (ἐτισα) <br> -ετεισθην | τετεικα <br> τετεισμαι |
| τρεπω, turn | τρεψω <br> τρεψομαι | ἐτρεψα <br> ἐτρεψαμην (I <br> put to flight) <br> ἐτραπομην (I <br> fled) <br> ἐτραπην (I was <br> turned) also <br> ἐτρεφθην | τετροφα <br> τετραμμαι |
| τρεφω, rear, nourish | θρεψω <br> θρεψομαι | ἐθρεψα <br> ἐτραφην | τετροφα <br> τεθραμμαι |
| τρεχω, run | δραμουμαι * | ἐδραμον | δεδραμηκα |
| τυγχανω, happen, light upon, hit | τευξομαι | ἐτυχον | τετυχηκα |
| τυπτω, strike | παταξω | ἐπαταξα <br> ἐπληγην | πεπληγα <br> πεπληγμαι |
| φαινω, show | φανω * | ἐφηνα | πεφηνα <br> (intr.) |
| φαινομαι, appear | φανησομαι | ἐφανην (I appeared) <br> ἐφανθην (I was shown) | πεφασμαι <br> (intr. and <br> pass.) |

| Present. | Future. | Aorist. | Perfect. |
|---|---|---|---|
| φερω, bear (mid.) win | οἰσω | ἠνεγκα or ἠνεγκον | ἐνηνοχα |
| | οἰσομαι | ἠνεχθην | ἐνηνεγμαι |
| φευγω, flee, be exiled, be a defendant | φευξομαι | ἐφυγον | πεφευγα |
| φημι, say (pres. ptcple. φασκων) | φησω | ἐφην | — |
| φθανω, anticipate | φθησομαι | ἐφθασα ἐφθην | — |
| φθειρω, destroy, corrupt. | φθερω * φθερουμαι * -φθαρησομαι | -ἐφθειρα ἐφθαρην | -εφθαρκα -εφθαρμαι |
| φυω, beget (intr.) be | φυσω (tr.) φυσομαι (intr.) | ἐφυσα (tr.) ἐφυν (intr.) | — πεφυκα (intr. " I am ") |
| χαιρω, rejoice, farewell | χαιρησω | ἐχαρην | κεχαρηκα |
| χραομαι, use | χρησομαι | ἐχρησαμην ἐχρησθην (pass.) | κεχρημαι — |
| ὠθεω, push | ὠσω | ἐωσα ἐωσθην | ἐωσμαι — |
| ὠνεομαι, buy | ὠνησομαι | ἐπριαμην ἐωνηθην (pass.) | ἐωνημαι (mid. and pass.) |

## CHAPTER XXVI

## THE INFINITIVE, VERBAL ADJECTIVE, AND IMPERSONAL VERBS

**Syntax.**

So far this book has been mainly devoted to what is called the ' accidence ' of the Greek language—that is, the grammatical forms of the words. In the remaining chapters you will have a few hints on the ' syntax '—that is, the arrangement whereby the words are put together to convey a certain sense. If the accidence of a language represents the building materials, the syntax is the architecture. It is, of course, impossible within the compass of this small book to deal even adequately with the syntax; nevertheless a few remarks will assist you towards the translation of Greek of a slightly more complicated structure than that which you have hitherto met.

**The Infinitive.**

The infinitive, ' to live ', ' to have acted ', ' to be beaten ', etc., is used in a number of ways in Greek that will cause little difficulty in translation, since they closely resemble the English. Thus the Infinitive may be used with an *adjective*—πραγμα χαλεπον ποιειν, a thing difficult to do; or a *noun*—ἀναγκη ἐστιν ἀποθανειν, ' it is necessary (lit. there is necessity) to die '. It may be the object of a *verb of wishing*, βουλεται ἀπιεναι, ' he wishes to go away '; or of *commanding*, ἐκελευσε με πινειν; ' he bade me drink ';

261

of *attempting*, ἐπειρασαμεθα φυγειν, ' we tried to escape ' ; or of *ability*, οὐκ ἐδυνατο τον ἀδελφον εὑρειν, ' he could not find his brother '. The infinitive may be the subject of a verb, as in ἐξεστι δειπνειν, ' it is possible to have dinner '. Such uses as these require little comment, for they are almost self-evident. What is less so, however, is the point that arises when the infinitive as subject of a verb itself has a subject ; this is put into the accusative case. For example, δει σε ἐγειρεσθαι, ' you must wake up ', takes the form in Greek ' you (acc.) to wake up (infin.) is necessary ' (verb). This is called the accusative and infinitive construction, and is of paramount importance in Greek.

**Verbs of Saying, Thinking, Knowing, etc.** This accusative and infinitive construction is used frequently after verbs of saying, thinking, knowing, etc., where we use a subordinate clause beginning with the word ' that '. Greek drops the word for ' that ' (in this construction) and changes the subject into the accusative case, and the verb into the infinitive ; at least, it does so from our point of view —e.g. φασι με πλουτειν, ' they declare me to be rich ' —' they say that I am rich '. If the subject of the main verb is the same as the subject of the infinitive (e.g. ' he said *he* was in a hurry '), Greek omits the subject of the infinitive (ἐφη σπουδαζειν). If it were put in (which happens when there is great need for emphasis) it would be in the nominative—e.g. ἐφη αὐτος ποιησαι, ' he said that he himself did it '. Remember, however, that if the subject of the main verb differs from the subject of the infinitive, the accusative and infinitive construction is used. ἐνομισα αὐτον παρειναι, ' I thought that he was present '. If the verb in the subordinate clause is negatived, the οὐ is usually pushed up forward in front of the verb of saying—e.g. οὐκ ἐφη μαινεσθαι, ' he said that he was not mad '.

Verbs of promising, hoping, expecting, etc., usually refer to the future, even though followed by the present infinitive in English. They are usually followed by the future infinitive in Greek—e.g. ὑπεσχετο τουτο ποιησειν, ' he promised to do this '.

**The Article with the Infinitive.** One important way in which the Greek usage differs from the English is the use of the neuter article with the infinitive, corresponding to our verbal noun ending in -ing. Thus, το ἀποθανειν means ' dying '; καλον ἐστι το ὑπερ της πατριδος ἀποθανειν, ' noble is dying for one's country '. As before, the subject of such an infinitive, where not the same as that of the main verb, will be in the accusative case—οὐδεν θαυμαστον τους κεραμεας των κεραμεων διαφερεσθαι, ' no wonder that potters fall out with potters '.

**Infinitive after Verbs of Preventing.** Where we say, ' I prevented him *from doing* the work ', Greek uses a simple infinitive—ἐκωλυσα αὐτον το ἐργον ἐκτελειν. Sometimes a seemingly unwanted μη is slipped in, because the Greeks looked to the result in their thought. εἰρξουσιν ἡμας μη ἀθροιζεσθαι, ' they will prevent us from assembling '.

**The Infinitive in Clauses of Result.** The infinitive

is also used in clauses indicating the result of something previously asserted, especially when introduced by τοιουτος . . . οἷος or by οὕτως . . . ὥστε,
or even by ὥστε by itself. ὁ λογοποιος τοιουτος τις
ἐστιν οἷος ἐρωτησαι Ποθεν συ; ‘the rumour-monger
is the kind of fellow to ask Where are you from?’
οὐχ οὕτως μωρος εἰμι ὥστε ἀποφευγειν, ‘I am not so
foolish as to run away’. The negative is μη, and
the subject of the infinitive is accusative unless it is
the same as the subject of the main verb.

**Exclamatory Infinitive.** The use of the infinitive
as a kind of shriek is natural enough; το ἐμε τοιαυτα
παθειν, ‘fancy me being treated like that!’ and for
the infinitive as *imperative*, see c. 21.

Translate :—

### Irresistible Right

1. τοις γαρ δικαιοις ἀντεχειν οὐ ῥᾳδιον.

Sophocles.

### ‘A Time to Embrace . . .’

2. ὥρη [1] ἐραν, ὥρη δε γαμειν, ὥρη δε πεπαυσθαι.[2]

Timon (of Athens).

1. Said of one who turned to pleasure in old age. A
dialect form of the more usual ὥρα.  2. πεπαυσθαι, ‘to
have done’, perfect infinitive middle.

### The Gentler Sex

3. οὔτοι [1] συνεχθειν [2] ἀλλα συμφιλειν ἐφυν.[3]

Soph., *Antigone*.

1. οὔτοι (not, mark you). Don't confuse with οὗτοι
(these).  2. Notice the force of the συν, to share in.  3.
ἐφυν, I was born to . . ., intrans. of φυω, see c. 25.

### Riotous Living

4. σωματα πολλα τρεφειν[1] και δωματα πολλ'
   ἀνεγειρειν[2]
   ἀτραπος εἰς πενιην ἐστιν ἑτοιμοτατη.

1. I.e. in entertaining guests.   2. In building ventures.

### ' 'Scruciating Idle '

5. εἰς φυλακην βληθεις ποτε Μαρκος ὁ ἀργος,
   ἑκοντι,[1]
   ὀκνων[2] ἐξελθειν, ὡμολογησε φονον.

1. Adv. ' voluntarily '.   2. Lit. ' hesitating, shrinking '.
He was too idle to walk out, so confessed to murder.

### Black Market

6. τας τριχας, ὠ Νικυλλα, τινες βαπτειν σε λεγουσιν,[1]
   ἀς συ μελαινοτατας[2] ἐξ ἀγορας ἐπριω.[3]

1. Yet λεγω does not often take the acc. and infin.
construction. It is usually followed by ὀτι (that).   2. Acc.
fem. plur.   3. See ὠνεομαι, c. 25.

### Last Scene of All

7. γεροντες οὐδεν ἐσμεν ἀλλο πλην[1] ψοφος
   και σχημ', ὀνειρων δ' ἑρπομεν μιμηματα,[2]
   νους δ' οὐκ ἐνεστιν, οἰομεσθα[3] δ' εὐ φρονειν.
                                        Euripides.

1. Here a conjunction = than.   2. Cf. Tennyson's Tith-
onus, " A white-haired shadow, roaming like a dream."
3. οἰομεσθα, a poetic form of οἰομεθα, whose subject is also
the subject of εὐ φρονειν.

### 'Cold Cascade'

8. τις γλυψας τον Ἐρωτα παρα κρηνησιν [1] ἐθηκεν,
   οἰομενος παυσειν [2] τουτο το πυρ ὑδατι ;

On a statue of Eros near a fountain.   1. Poetic form for
κρηναις.   2. Thinking that he would check—fut. infin.
whose subject is the same as the subject of the main verb.

### Life and Death

9. Τις δ᾽ οἰδεν εἰ το ζην [1] μεν ἐστι κατθανειν,[2]
   το κατθανειν δε ζην κατω [3] νομιζεται ;

                                            Euripides.

1. ζαω is irregular, having η instead of α all through.
This of course is the infin.   2. Short form of καταθανειν, a
verse equivalent of ἀποθανειν.   3. Below—in Hades.

## VERBAL ADJECTIVES

There are two kinds of verbal adjective in Greek :

(1) ending in -τος, -τη, -τον, implying possibility ;

(2) ending in -τεος, -τεα, -τεον, implying necessity.
They are adjectives, derived from verbs, formed by
adding the above suffixes to the stem.   They are
passive in voice.   We are familiar with (1).   All our
words ending in -ible and -able are parallel.

Translate :—

(a) το της Τυχης [1] γαρ ἀφανες οἱ [2] προβησεται
    κἀστ᾽ [3] οὐ διδακτον,[4] οὐδ᾽ ἀλισκεται τεχνη.

                                            Euripides.

1. The quality of Fortune.   2. Not masculine plural.
Then what else ?   3. = και ἐστι.   4. Verbal adj. from διδασκω.

(b) κακοι γαρ εὐ πραττοντες οὐκ ἀνασχετοι.[1]

1. Verbal adjective from ἀνεχω, ' to put up with '.

(i) The adjectives ending in -τεος have no parallel form in English, but you must imagine one, meaning ' must-be- '. The person by whom the thing must be done is put into the dative case.

ὠφελητεα σοι ἡ πολις ἐστιν
The city is to-be-helped by you.

ὁ λεγω ῥητεον ἐστιν
What I say is to-be-spoken = must be spoken.

(ii) If the verb is intransitive, the neuter of the adjective must be used.

οὐχι ὑπεικτεον οὐδε ἀναχωρητεον
There must be no yielding or retreating.

(iii) The neuter of this adjective (either singular or plural) may also be used transitively, governing an object—e.g. οἰστεον ταδε (one) must bear these things.

Translate :—

(a) οὐ δουλευτεον τους νουν ἐχοντας τοις κακως φρονουσιν.

(b) Ὁπῆ ἀν[1] ὁ λογος, ὡσπερ πνευμα, φερῃ[1] ταυτῃ ἰτεον.—Plato.

1. ἀν with the subjunctive makes the sentence unspecific. ' Wheresoever.' For ἀν, see c. 28.

## VOCABULARY

ἀγορα, -ας (f.), market-place.
ἀνασχετος (vb. adj.), from ἀνεχω, to endure.
ἀναχωρεω, retreat.
ἀνεγειρω, raise up.
ἀντεχω, resist.
ἀποφευγω, escape.
ἀργος (ἀ-ἐργον), lazy.

ἀτραπος (f.), path.
ἀφανης, -ες (adj.), obscure.
γλυφω, carve (hieroglyph).
δωμα, -ατος (n.), house.
εἰργω, prevent.
ἑκοντι (adv.), willingly.
ἐκτελεω, do thoroughly, complete.

ἑρπω, creep.
ἑτοιμος, -η, -ον, ready.
ἰτεον (vb. adj. from εἰμι), go.
καταθνησκω, die.
κεραμευς, -εως (m.), potter.
κρηνη, -ης (f.), spring, fountain.
μαινομαι, be mad.
μιμημα, -ατος (n.), imitation.
μωρος, -ον (m.), a fool (moron).
ὀκνεω, hesitate, be unwilling or too lazy.
ὁμολογεω, confess.

ὀνειρος, -ου (m.), dream.
ῥᾳδιος, -α, -ον, easy.
ῥητεος (v adj.), from λεγω (ἐρω), must be spoken.
συνεχθω, join in hating.
συμφιλεω, join in loving.
ὑπεικω, yield
ὑπισχνεομαι, promise.
φονος, -ου (m.), murder.
φρονεω, to be minded. κακα φρονεω, to be ill-disposed.
ψοφος, -ου (m.), sound, noise, opp. to reality.
ὠφελεω, help.

## IMPERSONAL VERBS

If you were to say " It looks like rain ", some wit might enquire, " What looks like rain? " You should then lead your questioner gently but firmly aside and expound to him fully the significance of the grammatical term ' an impersonal verb '. Ignoring his attempt to disengage, you would explain that such verbs are to be found in every language, but more particularly in ancient languages, while in our own they have become for the most part confined to meteorological phenomena, ' it thunders ', ' it is snowing ', and so on. " Even the word ' please '," you would continue, " which you keep anxiously repeating, is an elliptical form of the phrase ' if you please ', or, better still, ' if it please you ', the impersonal nature of which is more clearly seen in the French ' s'il vous plait ' than in our native tongue. What then is an impersonal verb? It is a verb in the third person singular, which may be in any tense, but has no personal subject, for lack of which we are constrained in English to substitute the dummy word ' it ' owing to a feeling in our language that a word in the indicative must have a subject of some sort."

You would then invite your limp auditor to consider with you the Greek impersonal verb. Firstly you would list the weather verbs like ὕει, ' it is raining ', and ἀστραπτει, ' there is lightning '. Secondly, you would remind him of two important words, δει and χρη, which are followed by the accusative of the person and the infinitive thus— δει (imperf. ἐδει) δει με ἀπιεναι, ' it is necessary for me—I must depart.' (ἐ)χρην σε ἀκουειν αὐτου, ' it was right that you—you should have heard him '. You would then proceed to the class of impersonals which are followed by the dative of the person and the genitive or an infinitive. He should then be woken up and the following list placed in his hands.

1. ὕει, ' it rains '; ἀστραπτει, ' it lightens '; βροντει, ' it thunders '.

2. δει, ' it is necessary '; χρη, ' it is right ', accusative and infinitive.

3. δοκει μοι, ' it seems (good) ', ' I am resolved ';
    μελει μοι, ' it concerns me ', dative of person.
    μεταμελει μοι, ' it repents me ', ' I regret '
    μετεστι μοι, ' there is a share to me ', ' I share '  } τουτου, ' this '

    λυσιτελει, ' it is profitable '; συμφερει, ' it is expedient '; πρεπει, ' it is proper '; προσηκει, ' it is fitting '; μοι τουτο ποιειν.

ἐξεστι, ἐνεστι, and παρεστι (all meaning 'it is possible) μοι τουτο ποιειν. ὑπαρχει μοι, 'it belongs to me.'

The noun ἀναγκη and the participle χρεων (from χρη) are followed by the dative and the infinitive and accusative and infinitive, respectively, meaning 'it is necessary' and 'one should'.

## CHAPTER XXVII

### PARTICIPLES

In Chapter XI you were told that participles played a more prominent part in Greek than they do in English. Before you can tackle Greek of much greater complexity, it would be well to study some of the ways in which these participles are used. Remember what a participle is—it is a part of a verb which has all the qualities of an adjective; it says something more about the circumstances in which an action takes place; and it often completes the meaning of a verb in the same way that an Infinitive does.

### I. Participle with the Article.

When the participle has an article in front, it is equivalent to an adjectival clause—he who, or those who—

ὁ μενων ἐν τῃ ἀγαπῃ μενει ἐν τῳ Θεῳ.  (c. 7.)
' He who remains in love remains in God.'

ἡ κεφαλη ἡ τμηθεισα ἀει ᾐδεν.  (c. 15.)
' The head which had been cut off kept constantly singing.'

ἐπει οἱ παιδες συνιασι τα λεγομενα.  (c. 16.)
' As soon as the children understand what is said to them.'

271

**II. Participle Representing Various Clauses.**

(*a*) As an attribute it may qualify a noun—

τι μοι μαχεσθ᾽, ἑταιροι, καὑτῷ θελοντι πινειν;
(c. 8.)
'Why do you quarrel with me, friends, myself too wishing to drink?'

(*b*) It may show a time relation between two events—

σκιρτων ἑλακτισε τον δεσποτην. (c. 11.)
'*While* skipping about he kicked his master.'

καταλιποντες αὑτον ἀπηλθον ἑπι το ὁψον. (c. 11.)
'*After* abandoning him they went for the fish.'

This is perhaps the commonest relation, although the participle may have many and mixed shades of meaning.

(*c*) It may show a relation of Cause, Manner, or Means—

τιμωρουνται τους ἁλισκομενους ὡς κακως κλεπτοντας. (c. 16.)
'They punish those caught *on the ground that* they steal badly.'

νυν δε θανων ἀστερας οἱκον ἑχει (c. 24.)
'But as it is, since he is dead, he has his home among the stars.'

μελλων και διδους χρονον, ἱασατο ἱατρος. (c. 16.)
'*By* delaying and *by* allowing time, the doctor has healed.'

(*d*) The future participle frequently indicates purpose, especially with ὡς—

οἱ κωλυσοντες περαν ἦσαν πολλοι ἱππεις ...
(c. 17.)
'The ones to stop them from crossing were numerous cavalry. . . .'

ἦλθε λυσομενος θυγατερα.
'He came to ransom his daughter.'

(e) The participle is sometimes used where we should use a conditional or 'if' clause —

θεου θελοντος δυνατα παντα γιγνεται. (c. 18.)
'*If* the god wills, everything becomes possible.'

πολλα ὁρω προβατα ἁ ἀποδαρεντα . . . παρεξει
την διαβασιν. (c. 17.)
'I see many beasts which, *if* skinned . . . will facilitate the passage.'

(f) Concession. Often you must translate the participle by 'although'. The word for 'although' is καιπερ, which is only used with a participle. Frequently, however, the participle without καιπερ will have this concessive force.

δασυς ὠν λιαν ᾠον ἁπας γεγονεν. (c. 13.)
'*Though* being excessively hairy, he has become bald as an egg all over.'

## III. Genitive Absolute.

The participle may have any of the above meanings, but if it goes with a noun or pronoun which is not connected grammatically with the rest of the sentence (i.e. not subject, object, or indirect object) it is put into the genitive case, and the whole construction is called the genitive absolute.

εἰπόντος δε αὐτοῦ, Εὐ σοι εἴη, ἐφη . . . (c. 11.)

' He saying (= when he said) that it had, " Good for you ! " said the other.'

πολλων μεν οὐσων την μεν εὑρησεις κακην, την δε λημ᾽ ἐχουσαν εὐγενες . . . (c. 16.)

' There being many women (as there are many women), you will find one bad, and another with noble spirit.'

## IV. Accusative Absolute.

If the verb of the participle is an *impersonal verb* (see c. 26), instead of going into the genitive absolute in the circumstances mentioned above, it is put into the accusative case of the neuter singular—e.g.

δεον ἀποφευγειν ἐκαυσαν την πολιν.

' It being necessary to escape, they burnt the city.'

So similarly παρασχον, an opportunity having offered, εἰρημενον it having been told them, ἀδυνατον ὀν it being impossible, ἐξον, it being possible.

## V. Participle Completing Sense of Verbs.

(*a*) The participle continues the meaning of certain verbs such as ' continue ', ' cease ', ' begin ', ' be ashamed ' and so on.

ἀρ᾽ οὐκ αἰσχυνει τοιαυτα λεγων ; (c. 14.)

' Are you not ashamed *to say* such things ?'

οὐδεποτε παυσει ὀλοφυρομενος. (c. 14.)

' You will never stop wailing.'

(*b*) The participle is used with the object of verbs of finding and perceiving, denoting the state in which the object is found or perceived.

Ἔρως ποτ' ἐν ῥόδοισι
κοιμωμενην μελιτταν
οὐκ εἶδεν . . . (c. 15.)

'Love once failed to see a bee sleeping amid the roses.'

(c) The verbs τυγχανω, λανθανω and φθανω are used in an idiomatic way in Greek, so that the main force of the expression is thrown on to the participle —

λανθανω, 'escape notice of', ἐλαθε τους φυλακας διαβαινων τον ποταμον.

'He crossed the river without being seen by the guards (lit. he escaped the notice of the guards, crossing the river).'

φθανω, 'anticipate', ἐφθασαν τους Περσας ἀφικομενοι.

'They arrived before the Persians (lit. they anticipated the Persians arriving).'

τυγχανω, 'happen', ἐτυχεν ἐγγυς που καθημενος.

'He chanced to be sitting somewhere near.'

## VI. Participle after Verbs of Knowing and Perceiving.

When a verb of saying or thinking takes the nominative and infinitive or accusative and infinitive construction (see c. 26) verbs meaning to see (αἰσθανομαι), know (οἰδα), hear (ἀκουω), learn (γιγνωσκω), remember, forget, show, appear, prove, acknowledge, and announce, take the participle instead of the infinitive. The question of whether the participle is nominative or accusative is decided on the same principles as those laid down in c. 26.

παρακηκοα δε και παρα τουτοις κρυπτομενον τινα. (c. 12.)

' I have heard on the side, moreover, that someone is in hiding in their house.'

χαριν λαβων μεμνησο και δους ἐπιλαθου.   (c. 21.)

' Remember that you have received a favour, and forget that you have granted one.'

(Nominative participles, because the subject of the verb ' remember' is the same as the subject of λαβων, etc.)

φαινεται μαινομενος.

' He is obviously mad.'

---

## Sagacious Elephants
### (from Plutarch)

1. Ἐν Ῥωμῃ οὐ παλαι, πολλων ἐλεφαντων προδι-δασκομενων [1] στασεις τινας ἱστασθαι [2] παραβολους,[3] και κινησεις δυσεξελικτους ἀνακυκλειν,[4] εἱς, ὁ δυσμα-θεστατος, ἀκουων κακως [5] ἑκαστοτε και κολαζομενος πολλακις, ὡφθη [6] νυκτος αὐτος ἐφ' ἑαυτου [7] προς την σεληνην [8] ἀναταττομενος τα μαθηματα και μελετων.

---

1. Genitive absolute; προ-, ' beforehand '—i.e. before the performance.   2. Lit. ' to stand certain standings ', στασεις being what is called a cognate accus. after the verb—i.e. an object suggested by the verb itself. στασις, which means ' an uprising ' in the sense of civil warfare, had a sinister meaning in the fifth century B.C.—that propensity to violent political faction which has dogged the Gks. throughout history.   3. ' Difficult ', even ' dangerous '. The adj. is one of those which has no separate feminine ending.   4. Tr. ' to execute in a circle complicated movements '. ἀνακυκλειν, ' to go through a cycle ', is a word appropriate to a circus. Words beginning δυσ- mean ' hard to ' or ' difficult at '. The prefix implies difficulty or distress; cf. ' dyspepsia ' of indigestion, or ' dysentery ' of bowel trouble. δυσεξελικτος means ' hard to unwind '. Later ' δυσμαθης ', ' slow of study '.   5. κακως ἀκουω is an idiomatic phrase meaning ' I am reproached '. Literally ' to hear badly ', it has the sense of ' to be spoken ill of '.   6. See ὁραω   7. ' Himself of him-self '—i.e. it was his own idea.   8. προς, ' by the light of '.

2. Ἐν δε Συριᾳ προτερον, τρεφομενου κατ᾽ οἰκιαν ἐλεφαντος,[1] ὁ ἐπιστατης λαμβανων κριθων μετρον ὑφαιρει και χρεωκοπει[2] μερος ἡμισυ καθ᾽ ἡμεραν.[3] ἐπει δε, του δεσποτου παροντος[1] ποτε και θεωμενου,[1] παν το μετρον προὔθηκεν,[4] ἐμβλεψας και διαγαγων την προβοσκιδα των κριθων,[5] ἀποδιεστησε, και διεχωρισε το μερος, ὡς ἐνην λογιωτατα[6] κατειπων του ἐπιστατου την ἀδικιαν.

## VOCABULARY

ἀδικια (f.), guilt, wrong-doing.
ἀνακυκλεω, go through an evolution.
ἀναταττομαι, rehearse.
ἀποδιιστημι, separate in half.
διαγω, draw through.
διαχωριζω, separate off.
δυσεξελικτος, hard to unwind, complicated.
δυσμαθης, -ες, dull, stupid.
ἑκαστοτε (adv.), on each occasion.
ἐμβλεπω, look earnestly at.
ἐπιστατης, -ου (m.), keeper.
θεαομαι, look at (cf. theatre).
καταγορευω (aor. κατειπον), condemn.

κινησις, -εως (f.), movement.
κριθη (usu. pl.), barley.
λογιος (adj.), verbal, in words.
μελεταω, practise.
παραβολος (adj.), difficult, dangerous.
προβοσκις, -ιδος (f.), trunk.
προδιδασκω, teach beforehand.
Ῥωμη, -ης (f.), Rome.
στασις, -εως (f.), posture, stance.
ὑφαιρεω, take away surreptitiously.
χρεωκοπεω, defraud (cut down a debt).

1. Gen. abs. 2. Literally, to cut down debts, and so in any way ‘ to defraud ’. 3. Every day. 4. προ before the augment ε becomes πρου-. 5. The gen. is governed by the δια of διαγω, ‘ Drawing his trunk through the barley ’. ἀλφιτα is the ‘ meal ’ of κριθη. 6. Lit. ‘ as verbally as possible ’—i.e. as near in words as he could. ὡς λογιωτατα by itself would do for this meaning, but frequently the impersonal ἐξην or ἐνην was added.

# CHAPTER XXVIII

## THE SUBJUNCTIVE AND OPTATIVE MOODS

1. THE Greek verb has two more ' Moods ', which it uses frequently to express such moods as those of possibility, uncertainty or desirability. In English we use words such as ' would ' or ' might ', but Greek expresses these by terminations of the verb. For instance, ' Let us go ' is expressed by one word in Greek, ἴωμεν, which is the 1st person plur. of the present *subjunctive* (the traditional name in grammar books for this mood, but not an expressive one) of εἶμι, ' I go '. A wish such as ' may you perish ! ' can be expressed by the one word ὄλοιο, which is the 2nd person singular of the aorist *optative* (this is a better name, as it comes from a Latin word meaning ' wishing ') of ὄλλυμαι, ' I perish ' (which, incidentally, is the ' middle ' of ὄλλυμι, ' I destroy '). Although this book has deliberately avoided examples of these moods up to now (it has not been easy, because you will meet them on every page of a Greek author), and although their uses are a little complicated, it will repay you to master them if you want to appreciate the exactness and subtlety with which the Greek verb can express the finest shades of thought. Books have been written on the refinements of Greek syntax, but all we can claim to do in one chapter is to introduce you to the forms of these two moods and their commonest uses.

If you happen to have learnt Latin, you will recognise them as (roughly) the equivalent of one mood in Latin—the *conjunctive* (or, as now called in most grammars, the *subjunctive*), and you will understand when we say that the subj. is *primary* (corresponding to the pres. and perf. subj. in Latin), and the optative *historic* (corresponding to the imperf. and pluperf. in Latin). If this means nothing to you, no matter. But what does matter is that you recognise the forms when you meet them, and something of their significance.

We will therefore deal with the subjunctive first. Look carefully at the following table, and note where the terminations differ from the indic. Learn, at any rate, the λυω forms by heart, and you should have no difficulty with the rest.

### 3. How to Recognise the Subjunctive.

The long vowel of the ending is the key in every case. There is no exception. Every person of the present subjunctive, except the 1st, is different from the indic. As to the 1st person, in practice there is no ambiguity, as you will find in reading. To form the aor. subj. (which, like the imperative, has an instantaneous, and not a past sense) drop the augment of the aor. ind. and change the termination -α into -ω.

e.g. λυωμεν δουλους means 'let us set free slaves' as a general rule.

λυσωμεν δουλους means 'let us set free slaves' on a particular occasion.

## 2. THE SUBJUNCTIVE MOOD

| Verb. | Present Active. | Present Middle and Passive. | Aorist Active. | Aorist Middle. | Aorist Passive. |
|---|---|---|---|---|---|
| λύω 'I loose' | λύω<br>λύῃς<br>λύῃ<br>λύωμεν<br>λύητε<br>λύωσι | λύωμαι<br>λύῃ<br>λύηται<br>λυώμεθα<br>λύησθε<br>λύωνται | λύσω<br>λύσῃς<br>λύσῃ<br>λύσωμεν<br>λύσητε<br>λύσωσι | λύσωμαι<br>λύσῃ<br>λύσηται<br>λυσώμεθα<br>λύσησθε<br>λύσωνται | λυθῶ<br>λυθῇς<br>λυθῇ<br>λυθῶμεν<br>λυθῆτε<br>λυθῶσι |
| τιμάω 'I honour' | (αω) τιμῶ<br>(αῃς) τιμᾷς<br>(αῃ) τιμᾷ<br>(αομεν) τιμῶμεν<br>(αητε) τιμᾶτε<br>(αωσι) τιμῶσι | (αωμαι) τιμῶμαι<br>(αῃ) τιμᾷ<br>(αηται) τιμᾶται<br>(αωμεθα) τιμώμεθα<br>(αησθε) τιμᾶσθε<br>(αωνται) τιμῶνται | τιμήσω, etc. (as λύσω) | τιμήσωμαι, etc. (as λύσωμαι) | τιμηθῶ, etc. (as λυθῶ) |
| φιλέω 'I love' | (εω) φιλῶ<br>(εῃς) φιλῇς<br>(εῃ) φιλῇ<br>(εωμεν) φιλῶμεν<br>(εητε) φιλῆτε<br>(εωσι) φιλῶσι | (εωμαι) φιλῶμαι<br>(εῃ) φιλῇ<br>(εηται) φιλῆται<br>(εωμεθα) φιλώμεθα<br>(εησθε) φιλῆσθε<br>(εωνται) φιλῶνται | φιλήσω, etc. | φιλήσωμαι, etc. | φιληθῶ, etc. |
| δουλόω 'I enslave' | (οω) δουλῶ<br>(οῃς) δουλοῖς<br>(οῃ) δουλοῖ | (οωμαι) δουλῶμαι<br>(οῃ) δουλοῖ<br>(οηται) δουλῶται | δουλώσω, etc. | δουλώσωμαι, etc. | δουλωθῶ, etc. |

| | (οωμεν)(οητε)(οωσι) | δουλωμεν δουλωτε δουλωσι | (οωμεθα)(οησθε)(οωνται) | δουλωμεθα δουλωσθε δουλωνται | | | |
|---|---|---|---|---|---|---|---|
| τίθημι | τιθῶ τιθῇς τιθῇ τιθῶμεν τιθῆτε τιθῶσι | | τιθῶμαι τιθῇ τιθῆται τιθώμεθα τιθῆσθε τιθῶνται | | θῶ θῇς θῇ θῶμεν θῆτε θῶσι | θῶμαι θῇ θῆται θώμεθα θῆσθε θῶνται | τεθῶ, etc. |
| ἵημι | ἱῶ ἱῇς, etc. | | ἱῶμαι ἱῇ, etc. | | ὧ ᾗς, etc. | ὧμαι ᾗ, etc. | ἑθῶ, etc. |
| ἵστημι | ἱστῶ ἱστῇς, etc. | | ἱστῶμαι ἱστῇ, etc. | | στήσω, etc. | στήσωμαι, στήσῃ, etc. | στασθῶ, etc. |
| δίδωμι | διδῶ | | διδῶμαι | | δῶ | δῶμαι | δοθῶ |
| δείκνυμι | δεικνύω | | δεικνύωμαι | | δείξω | δείξωμαι | δειχθῶ |
| εἰμί 'I am' | ὦ ᾖς, etc. | | | | — | — | — |
| εἶμι 'I will go' | ἴω ἴῃς, etc. | | | | — | — | — |
| φημί | φῶ φῇς, etc. | | | | — | — | — |
| οἶδα | εἰδῶ | | | | | | |

*Middle and Passive.*

For the pres. subj. change -ομαι into -ωμαι, but the *aor. passive subj.* needs watching. As with the indic., you can always recognise it by the θ, but it is *conjugated as* if it were an *active* tense, λυθω, λυθης, λυθη, etc.

*Subjunctive of -μι verbs.*

Verbs in -υμι form their subj. like λυω, but the other -μι verbs drop the stem vowel and add -ω— e.g. stem τιθη-, pres. subj. τιθω.

## 4. Three Ways in which the Subjunctive is used in Simple Sentences.

(*a*) *To express exhortation* (1st person only). Negative μη.

> ἰωμεν, ' let us go '.
> μη φιλωμεν, ' let us not love '.

(*b*) *To express particular prohibitions* (2nd pers. of aor. only).

> μη τουτο ποιησης, ' don't do this '.

(*c*) *To express a deliberative question*, i.e. one of doubt or uncertainty.

> τι φω; ' what am I to say? '
> τι μη ποιησω; ' what am I not to do? '

## 5. The Optative.

The optative mood can be recognised, as in every tense and person *it has the letter* ι (in the case of -αω verbs, an iota subscript) *inserted into the ending*, making with another vowel a diphthong. Study carefully the following table, noticing especially the unexpected form in the act. pres. opt. of contracted verbs (termination -οιην instead of -οιμι). Similarly, -ειην, -αιην, or -οιην with the -μι verbs. For the perf. pass. (both subj. and opt.) the perf. ptcple. + subj. (or opt.) of εἰμι is used, e.g. *subj.* λελυμενος ὦ, ἦς, ἦ, etc., and *opt.* λελυμενος εἰην, but this tense is rare, just as in English. The alternative forms in the aor. act. (λυσαις, λυσαι, λυσαιεν) are commoner in poetry than in prose.

## 6. Uses of the Optative.

(*a*) *To express a wish.* Neg. μη. μη γενοιτο, ' may it not happen ', ' God forbid ! ' Wishes are sometimes introduced by εἰθε or εἰ γαρ, with the opt. for a wish in the future, but the aor. ind. for a wish in the past (i.e. an unfulfilled wish).

εἰθε γενοιμην, ' would I were ! ' (9. 11). See Rupert Brooke's poem, ' Granchester ', but εἰθε μη ἠλθον, ' I wish I had not come '.

(*b*) With ἀν to express ' *would* ' or ' might '—a ' possibility ' idea.

ἐλθοιμι ἀν, ' I might come ', or ' I would come, if . . .'

The important little word ἀν has no English equivalent, but is very common in Greek, and has several uses. The best way to understand them is by examples. It is never used with the present, fut. (except in Homer), perf. indic., or imperat., but *with the aor. indic.* it has the sense of ' *would have* ', and it can have a similar force if used with an inf. or participle.

## THE OPTATIVE MOOD

| Verb. | Present Active. | Present Middle and Passive. | Aorist Active. | Aorist Middle. | Aorist Passive. |
|---|---|---|---|---|---|
| λυω | λυοιμι<br>λυοις<br>λυοι<br>λυοιμεν<br>λυοιτε<br>λυοιεν | λυοιμην<br>λυοιο<br>λυοιτο<br>λυοιμεθα<br>λυοισθε<br>λυοιντο | λυσαιμι<br>λυσειας or λυσαις<br>λυσειε or λυσαι<br>λυσαιμεν<br>λυσαιτε<br>λυσειαν or λυσαιεν | λυσαιμην<br>λυσαιο<br>λυσαιτο<br>λυσαιμεθα<br>λυσαισθε<br>λυσαιντο | λυθειην<br>λυθειης<br>λυθειη<br>λυθειημεν or λυθειμεν<br>λυθειητε or λυθειτε<br>λυθειησαν or λυθειεν |
| τιμαω | (αοιην) τιμῳην<br>αοιης τιμῳης<br>αοιη τιμῳη<br>(αοιμεν) τιμῳμεν<br>αοιτε τιμῳτε<br>αοιεν τιμῳεν | (αοιμην) τιμῳμην<br>etc. οῷο<br>αῷτο<br>αῷμεθα<br>αῷσθε<br>τιμῷντο | τιμησαιμι, etc. | τιμησαιμην, etc. | τιμηθειην, etc. |
| φιλεω | (εοιην) φιλοιην<br>φιλοιης<br>φιλοιη<br>φιλοιμεν<br>φιλοιτε<br>φιλοιεν | (εοιμην) φιλοιμην<br>etc. φιλοιο<br>φιλοιτο<br>φιλοιμεθα<br>φιλοισθε<br>φιλοιντο | φιλησαιμι | φιλησαιμην | φιληθειην |
| δουλοω | (οοιην) δουλοιην<br>etc. | (οοιμην) δουλοιμην<br>etc. | δουλωσαιμι<br>etc. | δουλωσαιμην<br>etc. | δουλωθειην |

| | | | | | |
|---|---|---|---|---|---|
| τίθημι | τιθείην<br>τιθείης<br>τιθείη<br>τιθείημεν<br>τιθεῖτε<br>τιθεῖεν | τιθείμην<br>τιθεῖο, etc. | θείην<br>θείης, etc. | θείμην<br>θεῖο, etc. | τεθείην |
| ἵημι | ἱείην<br>ἱείης, etc. | ἱείμην<br>ἱεῖο, etc. | εἵην<br>εἵης, etc. | εἵμην<br>εἷο | ἑθείην |
| ἵστημι | ἱσταίην<br>ἱσταίης, etc. | ἱσταίμην<br>ἵσταιο | σταίην | No strong aor. middle ὀνοσαίμην is trans. (place for myself) | σταθείην |
| δίδωμι | διδοίην, etc. | διδοίμην, etc. | δοίην, etc. | δοίμην, etc. | δοθείην |
| δείκνυμι | δεικνύοιμι (like λύοιμι) | δεικνυοίμην (like λύοιμι) | δείξαιμι | δειξαίμην | δειχθείην |
| εἰμί (' be ') | εἴην<br>εἴης, etc. | — | — | — | — |
| εἶμι, (' I will go ') | ἴοιμι<br>ἴοις, etc. | — | — | — | — |
| φημί | φαίην, etc. | — | — | — | — |
| οἶδα | εἰδείην, etc. | — | — | — | — |

(c) *With* ἄν *in conditions.*

E.g. εἰ τοῦτο ποιήσαιμι, ἁμάρτοιμι ἄν.

> If I should do this, I *should* do wrong.
> (or were to)

But εἰ τοῦτο ἐποίησα, ἥμαρτον ἄν.

> If I had done this, I *should have* done wrong.

When joined to εἰ (i.e. ἐάν) it introduces a future ' if ' clause, and in this case takes the subj.

ἐάν τοῦτο ποιῇς (or ποιήσῃς), ἁμαρτήσει.

If you do this, you will be doing wrong.

Other uses of ἄν will be found in the following section.

## 7. Other Uses of Subjunctive and Optative.

(a) *In purpose clauses.* Introduced by ἵνα or ὅπως (in order that). If the main verb is ' primary ' (i.e. pres., fut. or perf.), the subj. is used in the ' purpose ' clause.

τοῦτο ποιῶ
    ποιήσω     }ἵνα ὦ ἀγαθός.
    πεποίηκα

I     do
      will do    }this, in order that I may be good.
      have done

But if the main verb is ' historic ' (i.e. imperf. or aor.), the opt. is generally used. Sometimes however the subj. is used in historic sequence to obtain more vivid effect.

τουτο ἐποιουν ⎱ ἱνα εἰην ἀγαθος.
ἐποιησα  ⎰ (or ὦ)

I    was doing⎱ this, in order that I might be
     did     ⎰ good.

(b) *After verbs of fearing.* Mood as in ' purpose '
clauses.

    E.g. φοβουμαι μη πεσω, ' I fear that I may fall '
        (μη here is equivalent to ' lest ' in Eng.).

    ἐφοβουμην μη οὐ σε ἰδοιμι, ' I feared that I
    - might not see you '.

(c) *In ' -ever ' clauses.*

*Rule.*—Primary sequence, ἀν with subj.
        Historic sequence, opt. without ἀν.

    E.g. ὁστις ἀν ἐλθῃ, εὐδαιμονει.
      ' Whoever comes, is fortunate '.

    ὁστις ἐλθοι, ηὐδαιμονει.
      ' Whoever came, was fortunate.'

Similarly with ὁτε or ὁποτε (whenever), ὁπου
(wherever), etc. ὁταν is written for ὁτε ἀν.

(d) *Temporal clauses.* When referring to the
future, ἑως (until, or as long as) follows the same
rule. So does πριν (before) when the main verb is
negative. But when it is affirmative, πριν takes
the infinitive.

    μενε ἑως ἀν ἐλθω, ' Wait until I come '.
    νομιζε πριν λεγειν, ' think before speaking '.
    μη ἀπελθῃς πριν ἀν σε ἰδω, ' don't go away
      before I see you '.

(e) *In reported speech and indirect questions.* The opt. can be used, instead of the indic., in historic sequence; but the subj. is never used in primary sequence.

ἐλεξα ὀτι τουτο ἀληθες εἰη, ' I said that this was true ',

but λεγω ὀτι τουτο ἀληθες ἐστι, ' I say that this is true '.

οὐκ ἠδη που εἰην, ' I did not know where I was '.

(f) οὐ μη *followed by the aorist subjunctive* is a strong negation.

οὐ μη φαγω, ' I won't eat '.

### Note on οὐ and μη

Generally speaking, οὐ *denies*, μη *forbids*. Thus οὐ is used in direct statements (τουτ' οὐκ ἐστιν ἀληθες—this is not true) and is the neg. of the indic. mood. μη is used in wishes, prohibitions, hypotheses, etc., and regularly with the infin. except in reported speech—

μη κλεπτε, ' don't steal '.

ἐαν μη τουτο ποιῃς, οὐ σε φιλησω, ' if you don't do this, I will not love you '.

## PASSAGES FOR TRANSLATION, ILLUSTRATING SUBJUNCTIVE AND OPTATIVE MOODS

1. φαγωμεν [1] και πιωμεν·[2] αὐριον γαρ ἀποθνησκομεν.—1 Cor. 15. 32.

---

1. Aor. subj. from ἐσθιω (' I eat '). 2. Aor. subj. from πινω (' I drink ').

2. οἱ μεν κυνες τους ἐχθρους δακνουσιν, ἐγω δε τους
φιλους, ἱνα σωσω.—Diogenes.

3. τον εὐτυχειν δοκουντα μη ζηλου, πριν ἀν
θανοντ' ἰδῃς.—Eur.; *Heracleidæ*, 865.

4. μη κρινετε ἱνα μη κριθητε.

### Father to Son

5. ὡ παι, γενοιο πατρος εὐτυχεστερος,
τα δ' ἀλλ' ὁμοιος· και γενοι' ἀν οὐ κακος.

Soph., *Ajax* 550.

### The Athenians' Reply to Xerxes

6. Ἀπαγγελλε Μαρδονιῳ, ὡς Ἀθηναιοι λεγουσι,
ἑως ἀν ὁ ἡλιος την αὐτην ἰῃ ὁδον και νυν, μηποτε
ὁμολογησειν ἡμας Ξερξῃ.—*Herodotus*.

### A Lover's Wish

7. Ἡ Τανταλου [3] ποτ' ἐστη
λιθος [4] Φρυγων [5] ἐν ὀχθαις,
και παις ποτ' ὀρνις ἐπτη [7]
Πανδιονος [6] χελιδων.
ἐγω δ' ἐσοπτρον εἰην
ὁπως ἀει βλεπῃς με,

---

3. The article with the gen. often means 'the son' of,
so ἡ Τανταλου = the daughter of Tantalus, Niobe, who
boasted of her large family; whereat Apollo and Artemis
killed them with their arrows. Niobe wept for them till
she was turned into stone, from which her tears went
on flowing. 4. λιθος, 'as a stone'. 5. Goes with ἐν
ὀχθαις, 'in the hills of the Phrygians' (in Asia Minor).
6. Pandion's daughter, Procne, was turned into a night-
ingale. For her story (also called Philomela), *v.* a book of
mythology, and countless references in Eng. Literature.
7. ἐπτη, 2nd aor. of irreg. verb πετομαι, 'flew away'.

ἐγω χιτων γενοιμην
ὁπως ἀει φορῃς με.
ὑδωρ θελω γενεσθαι,
ὁπως σε χρωτα [8] λουσω·
μυρον, γυναι, γενοιμην,
ὁπως ἐγω σ᾽ ἀλειψω.—Anacreontea.

Tennyson's poem, ' The Miller's Daughter ' echoes the same idea.

> ' That I would be the jewel
>     That trembles in her ear . . .
> And I would be the girdle
>     About her dainty waist,
> And her heart would beat against me
>     In sorrow and in rest. . . .

### A Bad Boy's Letter to His Father

8. There have recently been discovered in the sands of Egypt a number of letters written on papyrus by Greeks living there in the 3rd or 2nd century B.C., which throw much light on the daily life of that age. They include invitations to dinner and weddings, mothers' letters to a son; and sons' to mothers. One boy ends a letter home with the request ' μνημονευσατε των περιστεριδιων ', ' remember our pigeons '. The following letter from a boy called Theon is full of spelling and grammatical mistakes here corrected (e.g. θελις for θελεις, μετ᾽ ἐσου for μετα σου), but it shows how little bad boys have changed in 2000 years !

---

8. χρωτα acc. of respect, ' as to your flesh '.

Θεων Θεωνι τῳ πατρι χαιρειν [9]

καλως ἐποιησας,[10] οὐκ ἐπενεγκας [11] με μετα σου εἰς
πολιν.  εἰ μη θελεις ἀπενεγκειν μετα σου εἰς Ἀλεξανδρειαν, οὐ μη γραψω [12] σοι ἐπιστολην, οὔτε λαλω σοι,
οὔτε ὑγιαινω [13] σε εἰτα.  ἐαν δε ἐλθῃς εἰς Ἀλεξανδρειαν,
οὐ μη λαβω χειρα παρα σου, οὔτε παλιν χαιρω σε
λοιπον.[14] ἐαν μη θελῃς ἀπενεγκαι με, ταυτα γιγνεται.[15]
και ἡ μητηρ μου εἰπε Ἀρχιλαῳ, ὁτι ἀναστατοι με·
ἀρον αὐτον.  καλως δε ἐποιησας.  δωρα μοι ἐπεμψας
μεγαλα ἀρακια.[16]  πεπλανηκεν ἡμας ἐκει [17] τῃ ἡμερᾳ
ὁτε ἐπλευσας.[18]  λοιπον πεμψον εἰς με,[19] παρακαλω [20]
σε.  ἐαν μη πεμψῃς, οὐ μη φαγω, οὐ μη πινω.  ταυτα.
ἐρρωσθαι [21] σε εὐχομαι.

## The Prayer of Socrates

9. In Plato's dialogue, ' The Phædrus ', Socrates
and Phædrus have been walking on a spring morn-

---

9. χαιρειν, the inf. is frequently used as an imper., ' Greetings ! '  10. Sarcastic.  11. ἐπενεγκας, aor. part of ἐπι-φερω, v.
25.  12. For the force of οὐ μη with the aor. subj. v. § 7 ƒ. of
this chapter.  Instead of continuing with the aor. subj., he
changes to the present ind. (λαλω, ὑγιαινω, and χαιρω, πινω
later).  Colloquial usage often simplifies syntax.  13.
ὑγιαινω, here = I wish you good health.  14. λοιπον,
abbrev. for ἐπι το λοιπον, ' for the future ', ' for the rest '.
15. Surprisingly like our modern idiom, ' that's that ! '
So ταυτα by itself four lines down.  16. ἀρακια, ' beans '.
The significance of a present of big beans to keep the boy
quiet on the day his father went off is not clear.  Anyhow,
they ' diddled ' him (πεπλανηκε).  17. ἐκει, ' there '—i.e.
at home.  18. ἐπλευσα, aor. of πλεω.  19. εἰς με, here ' fo.
me '.  20. παρακαλω σε (lit. ' call to ', so ' invite ', ' invoke '),
' I beg you '.  This is still the mod. Gk. word for ' please ! '
21. ἐρρωσθαι, perf. inf. pass. of ῥωννυμι, ' I make strong '.
The pass., especially the perfect, is used idiomatically like
the Latin ' vale ', ' farewell '.  ἐρρωσο imper. means ' goodbye ').

ing along the banks of the Ilissus, and at midday rest under a plane tree to continue their talk about love and beauty and the purpose of life. Before they part, Socrates offers this prayer to Pan and the other tutelary deities of so beautiful a spot, which gives us a glimpse of Socrates' greatness of soul.

---

Ὦ φιλε Παν τε και ἀλλοι ὁσοι τηδε²² θεοι, δοιητε²³ μοι καλῳ γενεσθαι τἀνδοθεν·²⁴ ἐξωθεν δε ὁσα ἐχω, τοις ἐντος εἰναι μοι φιλια.²⁵ πλουσιον δε νομιζοιμι τον σοφον· το δε χρυσου πληθος εἰη μοι, ὁσον μητε φερειν μητε ἀγειν δυναιτ' ἀλλος ἠ ὁ σωφρων.—Plato, *Phædrus.*

## VOCABULARY

αἰρω, I raise, lift, take away (ἀρον, imperat. of aor. ἠρα).
ἀλειφω, I anoint.
ἀναστατοω, I upset.
ἀπαγγελλω, I announce.
αὐριον (*adv.*), tomorrow.
ἐπιστολη, -ης, letter (epistle —something 'sent to ').

ἐσοπτρον, mirror (something you look into).
εὐχομαι, I pray (εὐχη, a prayer).
μηποτε, never.
φορεω, frequentative of φερω, 'bear constantly,' so 'wear '.

---

**22.** τηδε, sc. εἰσι, ' are here '. **23.** δοιητε, aorist optative (of wishing) 'may you grant'. **24.** τἀνδοθεν = τα ἐνδοθεν, ' as to the things within ' (i.e. the soul). **25** φιλια, ' friendly to ', so ' in harmony with '. He prays that he may regard wisdom as the only riches, and that his wealth may be such as only the temperate can bear.

# VOCABULARY

*The figure after each word indicates the chapter in which it first occurs.*

CHAP.

CHAP.

Γ

CHAP.

CHAP.

CHAP.

προσηλυτης, newcomer
m. . . . . . . 8
προσθεν, before . . . 11
προσκυνεω, prostrate
oneself . . . . 8
προσπαιζω, play with . 11
προστιθημι, put to . . 16
προστρεχω, run to . . 12
προσφερομαι, find . . 20
προσωπον, face, n. . . 4
προτερος, earlier . . 19
προτιθημι, put before . 20
προτρεχω, outrun . . 11
προφητης, prophet, m. . 7
πρωτος, first . . . . 6
πτερυξ, wing, f. . . . 9
πυγμη, boxing, f. . . 20
πυθων, python, m. . . 3
πυλων, gate, m. . . . 10
πυνθανομαι, enquire,
learn . . . . . 22
πυρ, fire, n. . . . . 9
πυρα, funeral pyre, f. . 14
πωλεω, sell . . . . 25
πως, how, somehow . . 12

P

ραδιουργεω, take it easy 16
ραδιος, easy . . . 19
ραδιως, easily . . . 10
ραστος, most easy . . 19
ραων, more easy . . 19
ρευμα, river, n. . . . 10
ρηγνυμι, break . . . 25
ρημα, command, word . 21
ρητεος, must be spoken . 26
ρητορικη, rhetoric, f. . 1

CHAP.

ρητωρ, public speaker, m. 9
ριπτω, hurl . . . 10
ροδον, rose, n. . . . 5
ρυομαι, deliver . . . 21
'Ρωμη, Rome . . . 27
ρωννυμι, strengthen . . 28

Σ

σαββατον, Sabbath, n. . 8
σαρξ, flesh, f. . . . 9
σαφηνιζω, explain . . 16
σαφης, dear, distinct . 16
σεαυτον, thyself (acc.) . 8
Σειρην, Siren . . . . 3
σεληνη, moon, f. . . . 8
σελινον, parsley, n. . . 6
σημα, mark, n. . . . 10
σημειον, point, sign, n. 12, 21
σημερον, today . . . 21
σθενος, strength, n. . . 10
σιγη, silence, f. . . . 7
Σινωπευς, of Sinope . . 24
σιτος, wheat, m. . . . 5
σιωπαω, be silent . . 19
σκαιος, left . . . . 16
σκεδαννυμι, scatter . . 13
σκελετον, skeleton, n. . 3
σκελος, leg, n. . . . 3
σκευος, vessel, tool, n. . 10
σκηνη, tent, f. . . . 3
σκηπτρον, staff, n. . . 5
σκια, shadow, f. . . . 7
σκιπων, staff, m. . . . 23
σκιρταω, spring, leap . 11
σκοπεω, inspect, con-
sider . . . . . 25
σκοτος, darkness, m. . 16

CHAP.

φονευς, murderer, *m.* . 13
φονευω, kill . . . . 8
φονος, murder, *m.* . . 26
φορεω, bear constantly . 28
φρην, heart, *f.* . . . 10
φρονεω, be minded, think 26
φρονιμος, wise . . . 19
φροντις, thought, care *f.* . 19
Φρυξ, Phrygian . . . 28
φυη, nature, *f.* . . . 23
φυλακη, watching, guard,
  *f.* . . . . . . 26
φυλαξ, guard . . . . 9
φυλασσομαι, be on one's
  guard . . . . . 4
φυλασσω, watch . . . 8
φυσαω, blow out . . 17
φυσις, nature, *f.* . . . 10
φυω, beget, *n.* . . . 16
φωνη, voice, *f.* . . . 3
φως, light, *n.* . . . 16
φωσφορος, bringing light 16

## X

χαιρω, rejoice, bid fare-
  well . . . . . 21
χαος, chaos, *n.* . . . 3
χαρακτηρ, mark, charac-
  ter, *m.* . . . . . 3
χαριεις, pleasing . . . 17
χαρις, thanks, delight, *f.* 9
Χαρις, (pl.) Graces . . 23
χασκω, gape . . . . 10
χασμα, chasm, *n.* . . 10
χειλος, lip, *n.* . . . . 10
χειμων, winter, storm, *m.* 10
χειρ, hand, *f.* . . . . 9

CHAP.

χειριστος, worst . . . 19
χειρων, worse . . . 19
χελιδων, swallow, *f.* . . 23
χθων, earth, *f.* . . . 10
χιλιοι, thousands . . . 20
χιτων, tunic, *m.* . . . 10
χιων, snow, *f.* . . . 10
χλευασμος, scorn, *m.* . 20
Χλοη, Chloe . . . . 3
χολερα, cholera, *f.* . . 3
χορευω, dance . . . 8
χορος, dance, *m.* . . . 3
χραομαι, use . . . . 17
χρεωκοπεω, defraud . . 27
χρη, it is necessary . . 26
χρημα, thing, matter, *n.* . 9
χρησμος, oracle, *m.* . . 19
χρηστος, useful . . . 7
Χριστος, Christ . . . 1
χρονικος, concerned with
  time . . . . . 5
χρονος, time, *m.* . . . 5
χρυσος, gold, *m.* . . . 5
χρυσους, golden . . . 18
χρωμα, colour, *n.* . . 10
χρως, skin, *m.* . . . 16
χωρα, place, space, *f.* . 7
χωρεω, go, make room
  for . . . . . . 22
χωριζω, separate . . 15

## Ψ

ψεγω, blame . . . . 16
ψευδης, false . . . . 8
ψευδομαρτυρεω, be false
  witness . . . . . 8
ψευδος, falsehood, *n.* . 10

# KEYS

## KEY TO EXERCISES. CHAPTER I

THE word seen by the rustic was Theseus, the title of the play, written probably with an ancient form of the Theta, not very different from the later form. Note the C form of the sigma:

⊗HCEYC

Eat a bit o' pie !

## CHAPTER III

### Exercise 1. Key to Greek Words

| | | | | |
|---|---|---|---|---|
| Hector | cinema | diagnosis | crisis | character |
| Daphne | drama | analysis | catastrophe | Nemesis |
| metropolis | climax | genesis | ambrosia | scene |
| Criterion | Daphne | psyche | anathema | acme |
| ambrosia | coma | dyspepsia | aphasia | pathos |
| nectar | thorax | zone | nectar | |
| orchestra | Hector | asbestos | stigma | |
| idea | phew phew | nectar | echo | |

### Exercise 2. Key to Greek Words

| | | | | |
|---|---|---|---|---|
| colon | dogma | stole | syncope | Chloe |
| miasma | ethos | pneumonia | delta | Lethe |
| antithesis | hubris | asthma | kudos | Cyclops |
| bathos | cosmos | phthisis | Hellas | Phœnix |
| phalanx | onyx | chaos | Penelope | S(e)iren |
| ibis | hypothesis | apotheosis | Dorothea | Acropolis |
| emphasis | canon | diploma | Zoe | |
| automaton | thermos | phantasia | Agatha | |

### Exercise 3

Early one morning, taking her *atlas*, *Daphne* wandered down to the *basis* of the *crater* to write the *synopsis* of her *thesis* on the *hydra* of the *Parthenon*. The *iris* and *anemone* and *aster* were in bloom, and she thought of all the *heroes* who had trod this *zone* before. With this *idea* in her "*nous*," over the water came a *chorus* as if from the *martyrs*. Suddenly to her great *dilemma* near the *horizon* what should she see but a *python*, a *panther*, a

317

*lynx* and a *bison* making their *exodus* from *Hades*. In her screams she burst her *larynx* and was taken with acute *paralysis* of the *spleen*. Hearing her cries, *Phœbe* hastened to offer her a *telephone*, but found she had succumbed already to the *bacteria* of *cholera*, leaving only an *isosceles·skeleton* behind.

# CHAPTER V

## Key to Piece 1

Stephan was a young doctor who lived alone in an ancient house in the middle of the island. His brother George was a tyrant, and sat on an Olympic throne, but all the best of the people thought Stephan equal to a god, and worthy of a green crown.

He had a secret weapon (in the form of) a drug, hidden, against the law, in a river. When his brother was in a long sleep, Stephan told the pure and beautiful Daphne that he would give her a whole egg if she would be his messenger and run like the wind, and get the treasure which was hidden under a white stone.

Daphne began the work at once, but what should she see but a hostile bull with a face like a misanthropic general! But the image of the wicked animal frightened the good girl so much that she could not utter a word, but held up her evangelical hymn book in mid-air, which the animal swallowed thinking it was a gift of food.

## Key to Piece 2

Hector was a plutocrat and grew prize chrysanthemums. He kept a pet hippopotamus and owned the Hippodrome theatre. As if this wasn't enough for one man, he studied orthodox theology, and what with walking among the rhododendrons brandishing a sceptre, declaiming topical epitaphs before the microphone, and calling upon the hierarchy to exorcise his bacteria, it was all too much for the poor creature, and he became an atheist and interested in polygamy. But after that it became worse, for he used to ride a cycle round the cenotaph, studying arithmetic and biology aloud and declaring that he was a mystical methodist. Then he tried cosmetics and strategy, contracted ophthalmia and chronic hydrophobia and turned a diabolical heliotrope colour.

## Limerick

An author with fancy æsthetic
Once developed ambitions cosmetic
    After agonies chronic
    And results embryonic
His exit was truly pathetic.

## KEY TO SENTENCES. CHAPTER VI

1. A big book (is) a big evil.
2. The unexamined life is no life for a man.
3. Man is a political animal.
4. A friend is a second self.
5. The life of the godless is a wretched one.
6. Time schools the wise.
7. Sleep is the healer of sickness.
8. In the beginning was the Word, and the Word was with God, and the Word was God.
9. I am Alpha and Omega, the beginning and the end, the first and the last.

### Page 55.  Lines from Greek Plays

1. Bad friends bear bad fruit.
2. Time is a cure for all inevitable evils.
3. Among barbarians all are slaves save one.

## KEY TO SENTENCES. CHAPTER VII

1. The tongue is the cause of many evils.
2. Life is short, art long (vita brevis, ars longa).
3. The good friend is the healer of grief.
4. Silence is golden (lit.: has many beautiful things).
5. God is love, and he who remains in love remains in God, and God in him.
6. A bad woman is a treasure-house of ills.
7. Happiness is activity of the soul in accordance with its right functioning in the complete life.
8. The sea and a woman have the same temper (lit.: is an equal thing in anger).

## KEY TO EXERCISE. CHAPTER VII

### The Archbishop

It was the Archbishop's fault.  If he hadn't started running a clinic, the children would never have developed a mania for geometry.  Daphne was listening to a diatribe that Philip the poet was delivering at a late hour on history, in the course of which he said that the Archbishop was more like a machine than an ecclesiastic.

Of course the tyrant George, who was now more of a despot than ever, and becoming something of a kleptomaniac, added his remarks on the tragedy.  He said the Archbishop had cardiac trouble through bringing nautical expressions into his sermons in the cathedral.

There had been an awful scene one Sunday, when, forgetting

his usual pomp of manner, he had produced a lyre and discoursed on it in a very technical way; and even then, he made no apology for his lapse. He then quarrelled with the poet who was somewhat of an athlete, and had written quite a good ode about diet, which really wasn't in his sphere at all.

This comedy was too much for Daphne, who being ephemeral and orthodox had an idea and married a critic of philosophy and finally took to hygiene and telephony.

## KEY TO CHAPTER VIII

(1)        The black earth drinks (i.e. the rain),
The trees drink it (absorb the moisture).
The sea drinks the springs,
The sun drinks the sea.
The moon drinks the sun.
Why do you quarrel with me, messmates,
Myself too wishing to drink?

(2) Exodus, XX.

I am the Lord your God, who led you out of the land of Egypt, out of the house of slavery.

There shall not be for you other gods apart from me.

You shall not make for yourself an idol, nor yet a likeness of anything, (of) all the things that (are) in the heaven above, and that (are) in the earth beneath, and that (are) in the waters underneath the earth.

You shall not make obeisance to them, nor be a servant to them; for I am the Lord your God, a jealous God, referring the sins of fathers upon children, until the third and fourth generation, for those that hate me,

and shewing (lit. making) pity to thousands for those that love me, and those keeping my commandments.

You shall not take the name of the Lord your God for a vain purpose, for the Lord your God will not consider unspotted the one who takes his name for a vain purpose.

Remember the day of the Sabbath, to keep it holy.

For six days you shall work and do all your tasks,

But on the seventh day, (it is) Sabbath to the Lord your God. You shall not do on it any work, you and your son, and your daughter, your servant, and your maidservant, your ox, and your beast of burden, and any animal of yours, and the stranger that lives with you in your house.

For in six days the Lord made the heaven and the earth and the sea and all the things in them, and he rested on the seventh day. Therefore the Lord blessed the seventh day, and he made it holy.

Honour your father and your mother so that it may be well

for you, and that you may become long-lived upon the good earth, which the Lord your God gives you.

You shall not commit adultery.

You shall not steal.

You shall not do murder.

You shall not give false evidence against your neighbour.

You shall not set your heart on your neighbour's wife. You shall not set your heart on your neighbour's house, nor his estate, nor his servant, nor his maidservant, nor his ox, nor his beast of burden, nor any animal of his, nor all the things that are your neighbour's.

## KEY TO CHAPTER IX

1. Not every man can go to Corinth.
2. The Greeks are always children, and no Greek is an old man.
3. Old men are twice children.
4. He makes the elephant out of a fly.
5. Children are a mother's life-anchors.
6. All the earth is a grave of famous men.
7. Hand needs hand and foot foot.
8. Ye children of the Greeks, forward ! Free your fatherland and free your children, wives, the temples of your paternal gods and the tombs of your ancestors. Now everything is at stake (lit.: the contest is on behalf of all).
9. Ye Greeks that have devised barbarous evils.
10. Philip, a father, laid here his twelve-year-old boy, his great hope, Nicoteles.
11. You are gazing at stars, my Star; would I were Heaven that I might look at you with many eyes !
12. Formerly you shone as the Eastern star among the living, but now having died you shine as Hesperus among the dead.

## KEY TO CHAPTER X

1. Man is the measure of all things.
2. The sphinx had a woman's face, a lion's breast and tail, and a bird's wings.
3. *How to catch a crocodile.*

In the Nile are many crocodiles, for the Egyptians do not kill them, thinking them sacred. The nature of the crocodile is as follows :—

During the months of winter he eats nothing; but lays eggs on the ground and hatches them. For most part of the day he lives on land but spends all night in the river; for the water is hotter than the air and the dew.

The crocodile has the eyes of a pig and large teeth in proportion to its body. Alone of beasts it has no tongue, nor does it move the lower jaw. It has also strong claws and a thick hide. In the water it is blind but in the air it sees keenly. The other birds and beasts fly from it, but the sand-piper is at peace with it. When the crocodile is in the water, it has its mouth full of leeches, but when it comes out on to the land from the water, then it opens its mouth. Thereupon the sand-piper entering its mouth swallows the leeches, and the crocodile does not harm it.

There are many and all sorts of ways of catching crocodiles, but I write only of this way. The hunter puts a pig's chine as a bait on a hook and throws it into the middle of the river, while he himself having on the bank of the river a live pig beats it. The crocodile hears the pig's cries and dashes after it, and when it reaches the chine swallows it. Then the hunter drags it ashore. Thereupon he first smears its eyes with mud, and having done this he easily kills it.

# KEY TO CHAPTER XI

Æsop.

## Dog and Master

(1) A certain man once had a Maltese dog and an ass. And he always used to play with the dog. And if ever he had dinner out, he used to bring something (home) for it and throw it before the dog as it approached. And the ass grew jealous, so that he himself ran forward as well. And while skipping about he kicked his master. And the latter became angry and gave orders to beat it (lit.: beating it) and take it to the mill, and tie it up to this.

## Dog and Shadow

(2) A dog who was carrying meat was crossing a river. And when he saw his own shadow on the water he supposed it to be another dog holding meat. Accordingly he threw away his own meat and started forward to grab the other's. So that he lost both. For the one did not exist, and the other was being swept down by the stream.

Strabo.

## " Caller Herring "

Iasos lies on an island, lying close to the mainland. And it has a harbour, and for the inhabitants the greatest part of their livelihood comes from the sea. In fact, they invent stories of the following kind against it. Once upon a time a singer was playing the lyre, giving a recital. And for a while all listened to him, but when the bell rang for the fish-market, they abandoned him and went off for the fish, except one very deaf man. So the singer approaching him said, " Sir, I feel great gratitude towards you for the honour you do me and for your appreciation of music. For the others, as soon as they heard the bell were off and away." "What's that you say?" said he. "Has the bell gone already?" Upon the other saying (that it had), "Good for you!" he said, and he got up and went off himself as well.

## KEY TO CHAPTER XII

Theophrastus.

### Rumour-mongering

Rumour-mongering is the putting together of false stories and events just as the rumour-monger feels inclined. The rumour-monger is the kind of person who upon meeting his friend, immediately dropping the wonted expression on his face, and breaking into a smile, asks " Where are you from? " and " How is it with you? " and " Have you any news to tell me about this? " and not allowing you to reply he says, " What's that you say? Haven't you heard anything? I'm going to give you a feast of the latest stories." And he has either some soldier or the servant of Asteios the bandsman, or Lycon the contractor, who has just come from the battle itself. " I have heard it from him," he says. Now the references for his stories are such that no-one can lay hands on them. He says that these tell him that Polyperchon and the king have won the day and that they have taken Cassander prisoner. And when someone says " Do you believe that? " he replies " The thing has happened. Everybody in the city is shouting it, and they agree. The story is gaining ground. All say the same about the battle. It has been a shocking mess. A sure sign for me is the faces of those in affairs. I observe the faces of them all have changed. I have also heard on the side that with them in hiding in their house is a certain person who has been there now for five days, having come from Macedonia, who knows all of this. But you yourself must be the only one to know." And he has run up to everybody in the city saying that.

I have marvelled at such people, whatever they mean by their rumour-mongering. For not only do they tell falsehoods, but they actually invent things that bring them no profit. Many a time some of them by causing crowds at the baths have lost their cloaks, and others in the Portico, while winning (imaginary) land-battles and sea-engagements, have let lawsuits go against them in default of their appearance. Indeed theirs is an exceedingly hard life.

The Cicada.

### Tettix

What a happy little tettix!
Like a monarch on a treetop

You imbibe a little dewdrop,
And indulge in operatics.
You are lord of all the manor,
Of the things howe'er so many
Seen in field, or grown in spinney;
And we mortals give you honour,
Sweet fore-runner of the reaping,
And the darling of the Muses,
Whom himself Apollo prizes,
Whom he gave a treble piping.
Whom old age will never wither,
Son of Earth, and sage musician,
Body void of blood and passion,
Why, you're all but God's own brother !

                                T. W. M.

# KEY TO CHAPTER XIII

1. A city consists of men, not walls or ships empty of men.
2. The ignorant move about in life as it were in the sea and in the night.
3. Parents and teachers are deserving of respect.
4. Revealing time brings everything to light.
5. A man washing his head lost his hair (itself), and though he was (lit.—being) very shaggy he became all of him an egg.
6. Terrible is the might of sea waves and terrible the blasts of rivers and hot fire, and terrible is poverty, and terrible ten thousand other ills, but nothing is such a terrible evil as a woman.
7. Man saves man and city city.
8. Every country is a fatherland to a noble man.
9. Evening, thou bringest everything that bright dawn scattered. Thou bringest the sheep, thou bringest the goat, thou bringest the child back to its mother.
10. The stars around the lovely moon hide away their bright light (lit.—form) when the moon at her fullest shines over the whole earth.

# KEY TO CHAPTER XIV

## The Wrath of Achilles.—I

For ten years the Achæans fought around Troy. And already in the tenth year they had neither forced their way into the city, nor subdued the Trojans. For others and Hector always kept them off. And in other respects too the affairs of the Achæans were going badly. For Agamemnon and Achilles, being leaders of the Achæans, nevertheless had a difference with each other about a certain maiden. And how this happened you will hear at once.

Chryses, the priest of Apollo, whose daughter Agamemnon had won as spoil, when he wishes to retrieve his maiden, plans thus. " I myself shall go to the Achæans, bearing many beautiful gifts. If they (shall) receive my gifts I shall assuredly ransom the girl. But if again they do not free her, thou, O Apollo, for thus he besought the god, wilt punish them."

O stubborn Achæans ! Why did you not receive the old man amicably ? For you shamefully thrust him forth. Most of all, you, O Agamemnon, with what words did you make reply to the old man ? For you appeared scowling in countenance, and said as follows—" Are you not ashamed, old man, to say such things ? For we Achæans do not fight fruitlessly. If we win any girl in fight, we never send her away from us."

" But neither did I wish," answered the old man, " to get her without ransom. And for this reason I prepared these presents." " See that we don't catch you again near the ships," said Agamemnon. " For now you wail, but then you will never stop wailing. Such evil things will you suffer."

When, Apollo, thou heardest this, thou wert assuredly enraged and didst promise to punish the Achæans.


# KEY TO CHAPTER XIV

## The Wrath of Achilles.—II

Apollo was so angry with the Achæans that coming out by night he slew many. And many were the pyres of those being burnt from time to time. And at last Achilles said, " We shall never escape from death unless we ask the god by means of some seer why he reproaches us. Then Calchas (for he was a seer) prophesied thus—

" You indeed, O Agamemnon, neither received the gifts nor freed the daughter of the priest. Therefore you will not ward off the plague. But if you (shall) send her away from you, all will be well immediately."

Agamemnon was accordingly vexed and answered, " Since you all beseech me, I will dismiss the daughter of the old man, but the daughter of Brises, the maiden of Achilles, I will take instead of her. For otherwise I alone of the Achæans will not have the prize which I won in battle." In answer to this Achilles, showing equal wrath, said, " Will you take away from me my maiden ? But I tell you this. We did not accompany you to Troy because of your enemies but because of booty, so that if you take away this girl I no longer wish to fight on your behalf. And you will suffer many afflictions, but I shall refrain from the war."

And in this way, according to Homer, began the wrath of Achilles.

## KEY TO CHAPTER XV

### Orpheus and Eurydice.—I

And there was once a certain minstrel, by name Orpheus, who played so well on the lyre, that all the animals and the trees and in fact the mountains followed him marvelling. And the wife of this man, while she wanders in the garden, is bitten by a snake. And when the wound is not healed, at last she dies. And she is led by Hermes, the escort of souls, to the house of Hades. And Orpheus bewailed her in such words—

" Ah, me ! Why, Eurydice, were you bitten thus by a snake ? Why were you snatched from me ? Would that I too had been wounded with you, if in fact it is possible for snakes to bite twice. But as it is, I am made exceedingly heavy by grief for you. And I have such grief as I shall never be rid of."

And at last he planned himself to go down to the house of Hades. " For Eurydice," he says, " will be freed by my lyre. And the other gods below and Pluto will be charmed by my lays." Which in fact actually happened. For in a short while the dead were forced to listen, and the dog Cerberus refrained from howling.

### Orpheus and Eurydice.—II

And at last Pluto said this: " We too are melted by your grief. Therefore you will take your wife. But if you (shall) look at your wife on the way up, she will be taken away again from you." And Orpheus was pleased at these words, and they went out, he in front playing the lyre, and she following behind.

Ah, foolish men ! Will you always be conquered by Love ? So too Orpheus at the very exit did not restrain himself, but in yearning for his wife looked round. And she was immediately spirited away.

And in this way Orpheus was again separated from his wife. And hearing it the young men of the Thracians said, " Not indeed shall you alone be parted from your wife. For we wish to share your grief with you. And our wives shall be left at home."

With regard to this the women grew angry saying—" Is it not scandalous if because of some minstrel we are to be deprived for ever of our husbands ? " Accordingly they rushed at Orpheus and tore his limbs asunder. And his head was thrown into the river. And lo ! as it was being borne down the river the severed head kept singing with a voice that was very beautiful.

### Love Among the Roses.

Love once upon a time failed to see a bee sleeping among the roses, but was stung. And being bitten in the finger of his hand cried aloud. And running and spreading wide his wings to lovely Cythera, he said, " Mother, I am ruined. I am ruined and am dying. A tiny winged serpent has smitten me, whom the farmers call a bee. And she said, " If the sting of the bee hurts, how much do you think they suffer, Love, whom you hit (with your arrows)."

## KEY TO CHAPTER XVI
### The Good Shepherd.

I am the good shepherd. The good shepherd lays down his life for his sheep.

The hireling and he who is not a shepherd, whose own sheep they are not, sees the wolf coming, and lets go his sheep and flees.

And the wolf seizes them and scatters the sheep. And the hireling flees, because he is a hireling, and he has no concern for the sheep.

I am the good shepherd. And I know my (sheep), and am known by my (sheep), just as the father knows me and I know the father, and I lay down my life for the sheep.

And other sheep I have which are not from this fold. And those I must lead, and they will hear my voice, and there shall be one flock, one shepherd. Therefore my father loves me, because I lay down my life in order that I may receive it again.

No-one takes away my life from me, but of myself I lay it down. I have power to lay it down, and I have power again to receive it. This commandment I received from my father.

### Literary Fragments

1. He understood many works, but he understood them all badly.

2. They say that Justice is the daughter of Time, and reveals which of us is base or not.

3. Noble birth offers a large hope that they will rule the earth.

4. The Cyprian (Venus) is a friend of the dark, but the light brings the necessity to be sober.

5. This swiftness and nimbleness of mind full oft brings mortals to disaster.

6. By delaying and allowing time to a malady rather than by cutting the flesh, the doctor has wrought a cure ere now.

7. Fame reveals the good man even in earth's darkest place.

8. Not even the War god resists Necessity.

9. Whoever lumping all women together in a class reproaches them in his words is a fool and no wise man. For there being many women, one you will find wicked, and another like this one, possessed of a noble spirit.

## Spartan Education

However, I want to explain the Education of others and of the Spartans. For others, as soon as the children understand what is said to them, immediately they set servants over them as tutors, and immediately send them to schoolmasters' houses, to learn their letters, and literature, and exercises in the gymnasium. And in addition to this they soften their children's feet with sandals, and pamper their bodies with changes of clothing. And again they consider their belly the index of their food requirements. But Lycurgus, instead of each man privately appointing slaves as tutors, appointed a man to rule those from whom the highest appointments are made, who in fact is called a boy-trainer. And this man was appointed with power to assemble the boys, and if anyone slacks to punish him vigorously. And further Lycurgus provided for him out of the youths' class whippers to punish the boys. Again, instead of softening their feet with sandals, he always made it his aim to strengthen them by (their) going barefoot. And instead of being pampered with clothes, he thought to accustom them to one garment throughout the year, as thus better preparing them against cold and heat. Again, he gave orders to provide just so much food that they were never made heavy with satiety, but that they should not be without experience of going short. But in order that they might not be too pinched by hunger, he did not give them leave to partake of delicacies without trouble to themselves, but told them to steal some things, thus helping out their hunger. Now someone will say, " Why indeed, if he thought stealing good, did he inflict many blows on him who was caught ? " Because, I say, in respect of other things also that men teach, they punish one who does not serve efficiently. They too, then, punish those who are caught, as stealing inefficiently. And though he reckoned it a fine achievement to steal as many cheeses as possible from Artemis Orthia, thereupon he ordered others to whip those (who did). For it is better, as they say, enduring pain for a short time, to enjoy being honoured for a long time.

# KEY TO CHAPTER XVII

## A Bright Idea

And when they departed to their quarters, the others busied themselves about the food, but the generals and captains met together. And then there was great perplexity. For on one side were mountains, exceedingly high, and on the other side the river so great in depth that not even the spears of those who were testing the depth protruded (from the water).

And while they were in this perplexity a certain man of Rhodes coming up said, " I am willing, gentlemen, to convey you across by companies of four thousand hoplites. But first you must provide me with what I require, and must pay me a talent as reward." And when he was asked what he required he said, " I shall require two thousand skins. And I observe many sheep and goats and oxen and asses which if they were skinned and blown up would easily afford a transit. And I shall further require the ropes which you use round your pack-mules. With these ropes tying the skins to one another, mooring each skin, by attaching stones thereto and letting them go like anchors into the water, taking the skins across and attaching them from both banks, I shall put wood on top and cover with earth. That you will not sink you will be well assured straight away. For every skin will keep two men from sinking. And the wood and the earth will keep them from slipping. When they heard this the generals thought the idea a pleasing one but its performance impossible. For there were those there to stop them from crossing (in the shape of) numerous cavalry who were likely immediately to stop those at the head from doing this.

## KEY TO CHAPTER XVIII

1. All men are relations of the fortunate.
2. Short is the delight of wicked pleasure.
3. He who is ignorant of letters has eyes but sees not (lit.: seeing does not see).
4. The wise learn many things from their enemies.
5. " Evil communications corrupt good manners."
6. If the gods do anything base, they are not gods.
7. When God wills, all things are possible.
8. This disease is somehow in tyranny, not to trust one's friends.
9. The great city is a great desolation.
10. The body is mortal but the soul immortal.
11. Friendship dances round the world proclaiming to all of us to awake to the praises of a happy life.
12. We are all by nature made in the same way in everything, both foreigners and Greeks.
13. NEW HOPES. We have now in our hands the full text of the agreement between the representatives of the Greek Government and the delegation of E.A.M. and E.L.A.S.

## KEY TO CHAPTER XIX

1. It is better to be silent than to talk in vain.
2. Nothing is more disgraceful than to tell lies.
3. No law has greater power than necessity.

4. Second thoughts are somehow wiser.

5. The man (lit. : he of mortals) who does most things makes the most mistakes.

6. Œdipus was at first a happy man; then he became the most miserable of men.

7. Every uneducated man is wisest when he keeps quiet, and concealing his words as if they were a most shameful disaster.

8. One man is worse, another better at each work; but no man himself is wise in everything.

9. There was an oracle of Apollo in Delphi—Sophocles is wise and Euripides wiser, but Socrates is wisest of all men.

10. Half is more than the whole, as Hesiod says.

11. Water (is) best, as Pindar says.

12. It is a most terrible thing for the worse to rule the better.

13. The last error shall be worse than the first.

14. If you are a slave with a free spirit, you won't be a slave (lit. : be a slave freely; you won't be a slave).

15. The city which gets the fairest constitution in the quickest and best way will continue most blessed.

# KEY TO CHAPTER XX

## Pot-hunter and Pooh-Bah

Nor again do we approve of the excessive ambition and competitive spirit of Theagenes. For he not only won the whole round but also many contests not only in the Pancratium, but also in boxing and the long-distance race. And at last, when he was eating the "hero-feast" of some funeral games celebration, when a portion had been placed before everybody according to the custom, he leaping up performed a whole Pancratium. And thus he showed that he claimed himself alone to be a winner, and did not allow anybody else to conquer if he were present. By this means he amassed one thousand two hundred garlands, of which we consider the majority to be rubbish. In no way different from these, therefore, are those who strip for every political venture, but they quickly render themselves open to criticism by the many, and they become odious. For if one of such people succeed, he becomes envied, but if again he fail, the object of malicious glee. And that which was considered remarkable at the beginning of their term of office ends up by being abused and ridiculed. Of such a kind is—

" Metiochus is general, and Metiochus looks after roads,
Metiochus inspects the bread, and Metiochus the barley-meal,
Metiochus looks to all things, Metiochus will rue the day."

This man was one of Pericles' friends, who used the power he derived from him unpopularly and excessively. The politician should find the people loving him, and if he is not present he should leave in them a yearning after him.

## KEY TO CHAPTER XXI

1. Hope and Fortune, a long farewell. I have found the haven. There is nothing between you and me. Make a mock of those after me.
2. Give me somewhere to stand and I will move the world.
3. Shift a little away from the sunlight.
4. Remember that you have received a favour, and forget that you have granted one.
5. Be sober, and remember to credit nothing.
6. Let no-one enter without a knowledge of geometry.
7. Know thyself.
8. When I am dead, let earth be confounded with fire. In no way does it concern me, for my estate is well.
9. Put you on the full armour of God.
10. Stranger, tell the Spartans that we lie here in obedience to their ordinances. A familiar translation is—

> Go, tell the Spartans, thou that passest by,
> That here obedient to their laws we lie.

11. " Jesus, have mercy on me ! "
   " Take heart, awaken."
   " Go along; your faith has saved you."

12. Pray, then, in this way. Our father in heaven, may your name be kept holy, may your kingdom come, may your will be brought to pass, as in heaven so also on earth. Give us today our bread for the coming day, and forgive us our debts as we also have forgiven our debtors; and do not bring us into temptation, but deliver us from evil (or " the evil one ").

## Euclid.—Elements I. 15

If two straight lines intersect one another they make the vertically opposite angles equal to one another.

For let two lines $AB$, $CD$ intersect one another at the point $E$. I say that the angle $AEC$ is equal to the angle $DEB$, and the angle $CEB$ to $AED$.

For since the line $AE$ stands on the line $CD$, making the angles $CEA$, $AED$, then the angles $CEA$, $AED$ are equal to two right (angles). Again, since the line $DE$ stands on the line $AB$, making the angles $AED$, $DEB$, then the angles $AED$, $DEB$ are equal to two right (angles). But the angles $CEA$, $AED$ also were shown (to be) equal to two right (angles). Then the angles $CEA$, $AED$ are equal to the angles $AED$, $DEB$. Let the common angle $AED$ be taken away. Then the remaining angle $CEA$ is equal to the remaining angle *BED*. Similarly of course it will be shown that the angles *CEB*, *DEA* are equal.

If then two straight lines intersect one another, they make the vertically opposite angles equal to one another. Which it was necessary to show.

## KEY TO CHAPTER XXII

### Exercise 2

1. (*a*) It is not possible to step into the same river twice.

(*b*) Different waters flow over those who step into the same river.

2. Thought is the converse of the soul with itself without speech.

3. (*a*) (They are) both daring beyond their strength, and adventurous beyond their judgment, and hopeful in dangers.

(*b*) (For I tell you) their memory never grows old, their honour is envied by all men; they (lit.: who) are mourned as mortal on account of their nature, but they are sung of as immortal on account of their bravery.

4. A certain learned man, wishing to cross a river, got on to a boat sitting on a horse. When someone asked him for what purpose he was on a horse, he said that he was in a hurry.

5. There was a man sent from God (his name John). This man came for a witness in order that he might witness about the Light, that all men might believe through Him. . . . John witnesses about Him saying, "He who comes behind me is in front of me." . . . These things happened in Bethabara beyond the Jordan. . . . And on the third day there was a marriage in Cana of Galilee and the mother of Jesus was there. . . . And there were six water jars of stone lying there for the purification of the Jews (each) holding (lit.: having room for) two or three 'measures.' . . . After this He went to Capernaum and the disciples with Him.

THE GOSPEL ACCORDING TO ST. JOHN.

## KEY TO CHAPTER XXIII

1. (First) to be healthy is best for a mortal man, and second to be beautiful in nature, and third to be rich without deceit, and fourth to be young with one's friends.

2. Here I lie, Dionysius, of sixty years, a man of Tarsus, unmarried. Would that my father had not (married) either !

3. Hail, seven pupils of the lecturer Aristeides, four walls and three benches !

4. One swallow does not make a spring.

5. Twelve is twice six, three times four, six times two, four times three.

6. A RIDDLE. The Graces were carrying baskets of apples and in each there was an equal number. The nine Muses met them and asked them for some apples. The Graces thereupon gave each an equal number. And then the nine (Muses) and the three (Graces) had equal. Tell me how many they gave, and how all had an equal number.

Answer : (a) 12, (b) 1, (c) 3.
Answer to second riddle : ὄνυξ (νυξ).

7. For this reason, said Zeno, we have two ears and one mouth, that we may hear more and speak less.

8. I, Callicratea, having borne twenty-nine children, did not see the death of either one boy or one girl. But I passed 105 years without supporting my trembling hand on a staff.

# KEY TO CHAPTER XXIV

## Exercise I

1. This is life, not to live only for oneself.
2. Know yourself.
3. The jealous man becomes an enemy to himself.
4. There is not a man who is fortunate in everything.
5. They do not sow nor reap nor gather into barns, and your Father in Heaven looks after them. Are you not much more different from them?
6. A certain man, aiming at a dog with a stone, then missed it and hit his mother-in-law. " Not such a bad shot," said he.
7. Sophocles said that he himself made his characters as they needed to be, but Euripides as they were.
8. It is not possible for a man (lit. : this man) who has made a profit out of the same opportunities as his country's enemies to be patriotic (lit. : loyal to his country).

9. A. Tell me, dog, over the tomb of what man do you stand on guard? (lit. : guard standing).
   B. (Do you mean) the dog's tomb?
   A. Who was this dog man?
   B. Diogenes.
   A. Tell me his family.
   B. From Sinope.
   A. (Do you mean) the one who lived in a tub?
   B. Yes, and now having died he has the stars as his home.

10. A man because he found gold, left behind a halter; but the other man, because he didn't find the gold which he had left, put on the halter which he found.

### Exercise 3
### On a Sailor's Grave

1. I am the tomb of a shipwrecked man. But do you sail on. For when we died the other ships continued their sea journey.

### A Dead Friend

2. Someone mentioned your death, Heracleitus, and brought me to tears and I remembered how often we both had let the sun sink in our conversation; but you, I suppose, my friend from Halicarnassus, are four-times-long-ago dust, but your night-ingales live on, on which Hades who snatches everything will never lay a hand.

## KEY TO CHAPTER XXVI

1. For it is not easy to resist the just.
2. A time to love, a time to wed, a time to have done.
3. I was not born to join in hating but to join in loving.
4. To feed many bodies and rear many houses is the readiest road to poverty.
5. Being cast into prison once lazy Marcus, of his own free will, being too idle to come out, confessed to murder.
6. Some people say, Nicylla, that you dye your hair, which you bought in all its blackness from the market.
7. We old men are nothing else but noise and show, and we creep like imitations of dreams. Intelligence is not in us, but we think we are wise.
8. Who, after carving Love, placed him by the fountains, thinking that he would stop this fire with water?
9. Who knows if life is death, and death is considered life in the world below?

Verbal adjectives.

(a) The quality of Fortune is obscure, whither it will go forward, and it is not capable of being taught, and is not captured by any art.
(b) Evil men when successful are intolerable.
(a) We must not enslave the intelligent to the ill-disposed.
(b) Wherever the argument like a breeze takes us, that way must we go.

## KEY TO CHAPTER XXVII
### Sagacious Elephants

1. In Rome not long ago, when many elephants were being trained beforehand to adopt certain difficult postures, and wheel through complicated movements, one, the dullest, being reproached on each occasion and frequently punished, was seen

by night of his own accord rehearsing his lessons by the light of the moon and practising them.

2. In Syria formerly, when an elephant was being brought up at home, the keeper who brought its measure of grain abstracted and embezzled a half share every day. But when, upon the master once being present and watching, the keeper put the whole measure before the elephant, looking earnestly at it and drawing its trunk through the barley, it divided it in two and separated off its portion, as nearly in words as possible condemning the villainy of the keeper.

## KEY TO CHAPTER XXVIII

1. Let us eat and drink, for tomorrow we die.

2. Dogs bite their enemies, but I my friends, in order to save them.

3. Don't envy the man who seems to be happy until you see that he has died.

4. Don't judge lest you be judged.

5. O son, may you be more lucky than your father but in other things like him; and then you would not be a bad man.

6. Tell Mardonius that the Athenians say that, as long as the sun goes the same way as now, we will never submit to Xerxes.

7. The daughter of Tantalus once stood as a stone in the hills of Phrygia, and the child of Pandion once flew away as a swallow bird. But may I be a mirror that you may always look at me; may I be a garment that you may always wear me; water I should like to be that I may wash your skin; may I be perfume that I may anoint you.

8. Theon to Theon, his father—Greetings,

You did a fine thing when you didn't take me with you to town! If you are not willing to take me with you to Alexandria, I shall never, never write you a letter again, or speak to you, or say " Good morning" to you (lit. : wish you good health). If you go to Alexandria, I shall never, never take your hand or welcome you again for the rest (of my life). If you refuse to take me, that's that !

Even my mother said to Archelaus, " He thoroughly upsets me. Take him away ! "

You did a nice thing when you sent me a present of big beans ' Yes, they took me in all right at home on the day that you sailed.

Well, please send for me, I beg you. If you don't send for me, I won't eat, I won't drink. There !

Goodbye (lit. : I pray for your health).

9. Dear Pan and all the other gods who (dwell) here,

Grant to me to be beautiful (in my soul) within; that all the things that I have outside may be in harmony with the inner man (lit. : things inside). And may I regard the wise man as rich, and may there be to me only the amount of wealth (lit. : gold) which the healthy-minded man can bear or possess.

TEACH YOURSELF BOOKS

## MODERN GREEK

### S. A. Sofroniou

This book provides a complete course in modern or *demotic* Greek, the language spoken in contemporary Greece and Cyprus. Intended for the beginner working whether on his own or in the classroom, it will take the student to a sound working knowledge of modern Greek and to 'O' level standard.

The model used throughout has been the idiom of present-day Athens and the course concentrates on those forms of modern Greek commonly in use. A phonetic introduction by Julian Pring is followed by a series of short grammar sections, each of which includes exercises, translation passages and word lists. At the end of the course are keys to the exercises and extensive Greek–English and English–Greek vocabularies.

| UNITED KINGDOM | 75p |
| AUSTRALIA | $2.45* |
| NEW ZEALAND | $2.40 |

ISBN 0 340 05806 4    *recommended but not obligatory